THE
RESEARCH PAPER
WORKBOOK

Longman English and Humanities Series
Series Editor: Lee Jacobus

THE
RESEARCH PAPER
WORKBOOK

SECOND EDITION

Ellen Strenski
University of California at Los Angeles

Madge Manfred
Mohegan Community College

Longman
New York & London

The Research Paper Workbook (second edition)

Longman Inc., 95 Church Street, White Plains, N.Y. 10601
Associated companies, branches, and representatives
throughout the world.

Developmental Editor: Gordon T. R. Anderson
Editorial and Design Supervisor: Thomas Bacher
Production Supervisor: Ferne Y. Kawahara
Composition: The Composing Room of Michigan
Printing and Binding: The Alpine Press, Inc.

ISBN 0-582-28542-9

Manufactured in the United States of America
Printing: 9 8 7 6 5 4 3   Year: 93 92 91 90 89 88 87

To Robert N. Rue

CONTENTS

Contents   ix

PREFACE

THIS TEXT IS designed primarily for students who have had little or no experience in writing a research paper and who may be working in a variety of libraries. Many parts of the book can also be used profitably by students at more advanced levels.

We began by asking: What do students need to know in order to successfully complete a research paper assignment? After a task analysis, we then searched for materials that would appeal to students of differing abilities, ages, and aspirations; created exercises that would allow students to practice the skills in a purposeful sequence; and provided worksheets which would enable the instructor to monitor the students' progress. The text is comprehensive and clear enough so that students can use this book on their own, spending as little time on each section as their previous training requires. However, there is enough material in the book to allow its use as a text for a semester-long sequence of assignments which culminate in a research paper.

There are a number of changes in this second edition. The new MLA format, which is similar to the APA format used in many disciplines, is explained in detail, along with the footnote system employed by many journals in the humanities and fine arts. We have used the *Chicago Manual of Style* as the guide for the footnote format. There is also a brief explanation of the number system used in many of the sciences. Apart from updating the technical aspects of writing a research paper, we have expanded the section on argumentation, included a sample argumentative paper which demonstrates the technique of running acknowledgement, added an example of how to take notes on one article, how to use a questionnaire, and how to annotate a bibliography.

The *Research Paper Workbook* has been extensively tested in the classroom. We are grateful to our students and colleagues for their cooperation and suggestions, which have made this a much better book than we could have created on our own. In particular we want to thank Theresa Ammirati, John Bassinger, Jim Coleman, John Roche, Gabriella Schlesinger, Mike Sullivan, Louise Walkup, Linda Crootof, David Henry, and Irving Kirsch. Inspiration for parts of the text comes from Shelley Phipps, librarian at the University of

Arizona. Raymond Soto and Marc Gittelsohn, librarians at the University of California at Los Angeles and San Diego, helped us with material in Chapter 2. Two others who deserve special thanks are our editors, Gordon T. Anderson and Lee Jacobus, who encouraged us through the completion of this work.

INTRODUCTION

ANY ALERT HUMAN being is constantly engaged in research; that is, in finding out about a subject that interests him or her. The subject may be how to tune an engine, build a mulch pit, choose the right kind of insurance, or travel on a limited budget. Perhaps you want to know whether nursery school is really helpful for your child or what the best hedge against inflation is today. The sources you consult may include manuals, pamphlets, TV programs, or competent friends. Frequently you have to combine information from a couple of sources or decide on the best authority if you receive conflicting directions or opinions. In the process of gathering information and sorting it out, you transform the material; you make it your own in some special way, and you become a source who can share knowledge with others.

In certain situations, it is important to know how to present your findings in a formal way. For example, suppose you have bought a home in a quiet, rural area. You discover that developers are proposing to build an industrial park very close to you. They claim it will lower taxes and increase jobs in your town. But will it? You engage in a little detective work and conclude that most employees will be hired from outside your town and your taxes are likely to increase because of greater road use and the demand for additional town services. At this point you can mutter and gripe to your friends and neighbors. However, if you want to have an impact, you must reach a larger audience—and this means writing. It means presenting the facts in a persuasive manner and documenting the sources of your information so that people will trust your data.

The academic research paper also presents information formally, and it, too, aims to convince its readers. Professors and researchers at colleges and universities have established certain procedures for conducting their work and for reporting it. Research papers must follow these expectations about method and format in order to persuade readers.

Although there are many instances in which the component skills that go into writing an academic research paper can be helpful, the primary purpose of a formal research paper on the undergraduate level is to give you a chance to learn about some subject in greater detail. At the same time you will be getting practice in thinking in a particular, logical, academic way, and in using an appropriate academic format to present your information. As you write your research paper you will be practicing the ways of thinking and writing that are characteristic of the academic community, and this scholarly practice will help make you an acceptable member of this community.

Primary research, or firsthand investigation, at colleges and universities involves original experiments, observation, or analysis of texts such as historical documents or literary works. Reports on primary research are published in scholarly journals and listed in specialized indexes, such as the ones described on p. 63. However, you, at this stage of your career, are an apprentice scholar and will be concerned mostly with secondary research, which means finding out what the recognized authorities on a particular subject have to say about a topic that has caught your interest.

The research paper, a written document, is only the last step in a process, and it is that process we want to stress in this workbook. We will begin by helping you to identify possible topics and explaining how to locate information. Then we will illustrate how to write a summary, a reaction paper, and an argumentative essay. They are like many papers you may already have written, but we include them because they involve skills that must be mastered before you can prepare a solid research paper. Furthermore, the summary and the reaction paper correspond to the two types of research papers that are usually assigned to undergraduates: the REPORT and the THESIS. In a REPORT you must condense, synthesize, and organize information to present an up-to-date account of a particular subject. For example, you might do a report on the different types of solar heating systems. In a THESIS paper you must go beyond a summary of the important facts and present an analysis of the information. For example, in working with solar heating you would try to draw some conclusions: Is solar heating a practical alternative for the middle-income family? Should the government provide better tax incentives and rebates to encourage solar conversion? In effect, a thesis is an extended argument to support conclusions that you have reached after an open-minded investigation of your topic. The emphasis in this book is on the thesis because it is the more difficult of the two papers to write. But this book will help you to write both types.

The techniques for recording information, organizing it, and documenting it in your paper will all be carefully explained. Much of the anxiety associated with the research paper can be alleviated by breaking the task down into manageable steps and building on the skills that you have already developed. The system presented in this book was developed to help students overcome the common pitfalls. We cannot guarantee a solution to all your problems, but we do think that this workbook will improve your outlook and skills.

The first difficulty that students encounter is getting started. We will show you a variety of methods for developing topics and acquaint you with a spectrum of interesting questions. The second hurdle, finding information on your subject, will seem less difficult because we will be helping you to locate information right from the start. Furthermore, the steps required to complete the research paper will be spread over a long enough period of time so that you will be able to request materials if they are not immediately available at your library. To be honest, the difficulty of locating information can be the most frustrating aspect of writing a paper, but the detective work involved in tracking down sources can be fun.

Sorting and organizing all the notes that you have taken can seem like an overwhelming task, but we have help with this problem also. Again, time and technique are important. The initial investment of time in setting up an organized system of note-taking will save you many hours when it comes to organizing the material. In fact, the system described in this book will foster organizational skills from the very beginning.

Footnotes and technical aspects of form cause some students undue panic. There is no need to memorize all the rules; you will become familiar with the basic models at several steps along the way. When the time comes to write your paper, you will be able to consult the appropriate models in the book. Basically, there are two formats: one which inserts information within the text of your paper by using parentheses; the other which places separate footnotes either at the bottom of the page or at the back of the paper. Both formats also include a list of the sources that were used in your paper. Every academic discipline uses a version of one of these two formats. The best approach for you at this stage of your academic career is to learn the two basic formats. As you go on in your course work, you should consult one of the professional journals in your area of study. You can then model your papers to follow the particular documentation style of that discipline.

A Word of Advice

Throughout this book you will find examples taken from the sample research papers in the last chapter. We have shown how to present one of the papers using the two basic formats: footnotes and parentheses. The sooner you become acquainted with these papers, the easier it will be for you to follow the examples in the book. Make time as soon as possible to look at the sample papers.

If you are one of those students who dreads papers because you hate to write, all we can say is **you are not alone.** Even professionals admit that getting the words down on paper is a difficult chore. Rarely do the words flow from the pen. More often, writing is a matter of discipline, of sitting down and forcing out imperfect ideas that will have to be revised later. What we put down on paper strikes us like a candid photo taken at an unflattering moment. The ideas seem so much more impressive in our heads than they do in black and white. Yet, practice in the process of composition can brin satisfaction. This workbook will give you that practice by breaking the search paper down into steps. At each step you will receive advice from instructor; this will eliminate the feeling that you are floundering. Th be ample time to correct major mistakes *before* you hand in the fi

Much of your dissatisfaction will fade because our approach assumes that your first efforts will be rough and your ideas need time to evolve. This is a research paper that cannot be written the night before it is due. The step-by-step approach will foster a natural evolution of your ideas. The paper will grow by stages into a carefully crafted work that you will be proud to hand in.

Too often students regard the research paper as an academic ritual of patching together a bunch of information and dressing it up with footnotes and a bibliography. And perhaps this attitude is justified by the way research papers are sometimes assigned at the beginning of the term and then barely mentioned again until they are due. Our premise is that research springs from a fundamental human curiosity about the world, a desire to learn the hows and whys of what goes on around us. The formal research paper developed as a means of sharing information with others, which is also a common impulse. We hope that this book will make sense of the form, so that the excitement of learning will not be spoiled by apprehension about technical matters.

To conclude the introduction, here is a feature article that reports on research into a universal human act—yawning. It is a good illustration of the way in which people become involved in research and some of the problems they encounter. Read the article on the following page with these questions in mind:

1. Why did Dr. Lehmann begin to investigate yawning?
2. How did he gather information on the subject?
3. What surprising conclusion did he reach about why we yawn?
4. Why did he have trouble getting his research published?
5. How did he finally get the paper published?
6. Who might benefit from the research that Dr. Lehmann conducted? Are there practical aspects to the research?
7. The newspaper article is a feature story based on Dr. Lehmann's research. How do you think it differs from the article Dr. Lehmann published in the *Bulletin of the Menninger Clinic?*
8. Has Dr. Lehmann solved the mystery of why we yawn?

IT'S (YAWN!) THE NATURAL THING TO DO

Barbara Brotman

This very morning, you probably pandiculated. The back of your jaws began making their intentions clear; your mouth began to gape wide: you took a deep breath; maybe your ears popped; you stretched your whole body; and then you exhaled with a sigh.

You yawned and stretched. Or, from the Latin verb *pandiculari,* to stretch oneself, you pandiculated.

And you weren't alone. Millions of people start their day with a yawn. They often approach the end of their day with a yawn. They liberally sprinkle the times in between with yawns, especially if they happen to attend political rallies or try to read Karl Marx in the original.

Dogs yawn. Cats yawn, a fact which cannot escape you if the cat in question has just quaffed a liver-and-fish-flavored lunch. Crocodiles yawn, and not just to measure the oral fit of a prospective dinner. Turtles and birds yawn. Babies yawn, and they haven't seen nearly enough of the world to be world-weary.

The garden-variety yawn has been described as "halfway between a reflex and an expressive movement." Or as "an indirect vasomotor adjustment furthering the circulation in the lungs and brain."

But the precise reason we yawn is one of life's mysteries, along with the size of the universe and the duration of eternity.

We yawn when we're sleepy; but we stop when we're in bed ready for sleep. We yawn when we're bored or inactive.

We also sometimes yawn when we're sick. Yawning may accompany diabetic coma, kidney disease, asthma, epilepsy, brain tumors, withdrawal from opium dependence, stroke, or large doses of sedatives.

Doctors become alarmed if a patient with a brain hemorrhage starts to yawn; it indicates the patient's brain is dangerously low on oxygen. On the other hand, yawning is a good sign in patients who are convalescing, especially from infectious diseases.

Most people assume yawning is the body's way of taking a good, deep breath to rev up the circulation. They're wrong. In fact, a yawn is followed by a temporary cessation of breathing, called apnea, that undoes any metabolic good the yawn might have done. Besides, if the body wanted to take in lots of oxygen, there's a much more efficient way of doing it—hyperventilation.

No, yawning is a physiological mistake, a vestigial reflex that has outlived its original usefulness, according to Dr. Heinz Lehmann, a professor of psychiatry at McGill University in Montreal. He has traced the evolution of the yawn, and he points out that it was an extremely useful mechanism for prehistoric man.

Australopithecus didn't reach for a gin and tonic when he needed a lift, and other drugs were just a gleam beneath Stone Man's beetle brow, so their bodies did what they could. When pre-historic man needed extra energy, his mouth gaped open and his muscles, from the jaw to the throat to the muscles that move the bones of the inner ear, to the diaphragm, all constricted, pressing into the blood vessels of the neck. He yawned and stretched. He pandiculated.

For just a moment, that pressure on the neck's blood vessels prevents some blood from flowing out of the brain back down to the heart. Instead, Lehmann says, blood accumulates in the brain, giv-ing it just a little more oxygen, a little more energy.

And in the old days, when Paleolithic mommies admonished their children to act their age, not their cubic inch brain measure-ment, that was enough. When the yawn was over, blood coursed even more forcefully through the veins; circulation momentarily im-proved, and cave man perked right up and clubbed his dinner.

Alas, those days are gone. A momentary soaking in blood may be enough even today to jolt a crocodile's energies, but not your modern dog, cat, or human. Bug-eyed from streams of coffee and heaps of sugar, we modern humans need more than a yawn to help us club our dinner.

"But man has done something very interesting," Lehmann ex-plained, warming to the ground where few medical researchers have trod. "He has taken the reflex and made it into a means of expression."

We yawn now to express ourselves, he said, just as we laugh or cry. We yawn to tell somebody he is a bore—"An unconscious ex-pression of hostility," Lehmann calls it, and we yawn to express fatigue.

We do it for all the world as if our bodies thought yawning would help. It doesn't, of course; our bodies, in this case, are wrong, Lehmann says.

Just as we yawn to wake up, we also yawn to reestablish contact with reality. That's why you see people yawn when they leave a movie theater, leaving one reality for another. That's why it's a good sign if a psychotic person yawns: It shows he is trying to maintain contact with the outside world, and probably is in an accessible mood.

For the same reason, Lehmann said, a yawning audience should hardly dismay a speaker. "Those who yawn are at least making some effort to follow him," Lehmann wrote recently in an article published in the *Bulletin of the Menninger Clinic.* "The others may be letting their thoughts wander unchecked or may be asleep with their eyes open."

But a good thing can go too far. A person who yawns too widely may dislocate his jaw. And there have been mysterious cases in which people have yawned continuously for up to two months, a condition known in earlier times as "chasmodia." Lehmann says such paroxysms of yawning are hysterical reactions.

Still, yawning is extremely contagious even for the ordinarily calm; no one really knows why.

And Lehmann says that if someone imitates your yawning, you should take it as a compliment. "We only follow a yawning suggestion by someone who has aroused our interest," even subconsciously and even through such superficial means as eye-catching clothing or an unusual gesture.

"It's a very complex body language," he said. "If I made a motion in a committee, and I know certain people have yawned when I yawned, I know they will be with me."

Lehmann made his own investigation into yawning 35 years ago because he was annoyed when people yawned at him. He also was amused at the descriptions of yawning in physiology textbooks.

As a young doctor working in a psychiatric hospital, he noticed that the hospital patients didn't yawn. He observed people on buses, in restaurants, and at scientific meetings, and decided that something wasn't right.

The next thing he knew, he recalls, he was spending time in medical libraries and administering sedatives to groups of patients to see why some were stimulated to yawn and not others.

"My paper was rejected by two journal editors because it wasn't scientific enough," Lehmann says now. "It was too philosophical."

But a colleague who heard Lehmann speak of it 10 years ago

thought it was an ideal way to prove to his technology-spoiled students that good research could be done with no expensive technology at all.

"I had lost all the references; it was difficult to get it together again," Lehmann said. Still, this time he got the paper published.

1. GETTING STARTED

CHECK THE REQUIREMENTS

BEFORE YOU BEGIN to search for a topic you should make sure you have all the details of the assignment. The requirements in each class will vary slightly; therefore, you must always check on the specifications.

1. Is the paper a report or thesis?
2. When is the paper due?
3. What are the due dates for the preliminary stages of the paper?
4. Is the topic assigned or limited in any way?
5. Is there a suggested number of sources to be consulted?
6. Are certain sources required or prohibited?
7. Is there a minimum or maximum length?
8. Are there any special requirements, such as an interview, survey, or case history?
9. Does the instructor prefer a particular documentation style? *MLA modern Language association*

Browsing in the Library

Some students start off with at least a vague notion of what they want to investigate, for example, the legality of writing their own will, or career opportunities for professional skiers. Other students are not sure where to begin at all and complain that getting started is their biggest problem.

One of the best ways to start developing an interest in a subject and getting some ideas of your own is to respond to other people's ideas. You can talk with friends and family, of course, but another convenient way to start is to browse through some current magazines and journals, sometimes referred to as periodicals. Most college libraries and bookstores have quite an assortment, everything from mass audience news magazines such as *Time* and *Newsweek*, to popular magazines aimed at specialized audiences such as *Field and Stream*, to professional journals like *Journal of Consulting and Clinical Psychology*. Somewhere within that selection are articles that you would enjoy reading and that would trigger ideas of your own.

The first worksheet, which is designed to help you locate possible topics and sources, is not difficult or complicated, but you must be sure to allow yourself enough time in the library to find articles that are truly engaging and substantial. The more interested you are in a topic, the better your paper will be, so at this point try to forget about the assignment and pretend that you are reading for pleasure.

As you locate possible sources for your paper, it is important to keep track of certain bits of information so that if you do use a particular source you will have all the details you need for making footnotes and a bibliography. Listed below is some of the necessary information. Be sure to follow this sequence in listing articles on Worksheet 1.

Required Information

1. Author's name reversed (if available). If you find more than one author, only reverse the first author's name.
2. Title of the article enclosed within quotation marks. Capitalize the first letter of each word, except *a*, *an*, and *the*.
3. Title of the magazine, underlined.
4. Volume number, if there is one.
5. Date of issue.
6. Inclusive pages of the article.
    The correct abbreviations are:
    p.   one page
    pp.   more than one page

EXAMPLE

Moine, Donald J.
"To Trust, Perchance to Buy"
Psychology Today
Volume 16
August 1982
pp. 50-52

SUGGESTIONS FOR IDENTIFYING TOPICS

1. Make up a list of questions that you would like answered. Some of these questions may lead you to a research topic for answers. For example, the research question "Are there enough jobs for everyone who wants to work?" suggests the topic of unemployment. See the following section on "Asking Questions" for tips on how to develop a questioning attitude.
2. Go over Worksheet 1 and examine the titles of articles and books that seemed interesting to you. Some of them are likely to suggest topics. For example, an article entitled "Equal Play, Equal Pay" suggests Women in Sports, Athletic Scholarships, and Women's Rights as possible topics. Another article, "Beware of Greeks Bearing Oil," might suggest subjects such as pollution, oil spills, environmental protection laws, or energy alternatives.
3. Survey the textbooks of subjects you like. Chapter headings or subdivisions may suggest topics such as inflation (economics), family therapy (psychology), immigration laws (history), or search and seizure (law enforcement). Suggestions for further reading are often listed at the end of a chapter.
4. Skim through the subject headings in a periodical index, such as those devoted to special fields like business, health, the sciences, and the humanities. There are other indexes, such as *Reader's Guide* and *Hot Topics,* which list articles published in mass market magazines. The procedure for using an index is explained on pp. 63–64. Examining an index will not only give you ideas for topics but will let you know how many articles have been published on a topic during one year. A related source is an abstract, a compilation of brief summaries of articles and papers that have been presented during the year by researchers in a particular field.

ASKING QUESTIONS

Some people are better at asking questions than others. Some people are shy or just not used to speaking up. But we all ask questions silently ("Who didn't put the cap back on the toothpaste?" or "I wonder what's for supper?"). Paying attention to questions and using them deliberately can aid learning and prevent you from becoming a passive consumer of information. Being able to ask questions will help you with assigned reading as well as with writing, and we will be coming back to this technique several times in this book.

When you make yourself ask a question, the topic begins to appear much more interesting. Since one of the hardest parts of doing a research paper is getting started, anything that helps—like the technique of asking questions to get interested in a subject—is welcome. The next step is to perfect this technique, that is, to practice asking questions deliberately.

Developing Research Questions

How do you get research questions? Where do they come from? One way is to think for a moment about what people discuss when they are just hanging out. Listen to a group of your friends talk. Ninety percent of the time we talk about three things: people, places, and events. We can use this interest, apparently built into all of us, to make up questions.

For instance, take a subject like the 1984 Olympic games. Then make up a question about a *person* (or people) you associate with that topic:

The athletes—Did the smog affect the athletes' performance?
The fans—Did all the fans get a fair chance to buy tickets to events?
The Olympics officials—How were the officials selected?
The sportscasters—etc.
The local Los Angeles businessmen—etc.

Then take the idea of the *place* and make up a question you associate with these Olympic Games.

L.A. Coliseum—How many people fit into that stadium?

And the same thing with an *event*.

The marathon—Why were the route and time of the marathon arranged so that the runners ended up at the finish line downtown at the worst hour for smog and traffic?

EXERCISE

Directions: For each of the following subjects, make up a question you associate with a person (or people), a place, and an event.

1.   Physical fitness

   a.   Person (who) ⎯⎯⎯⎯⎯⎯⎯⎯⎯⎯⎯⎯⎯⎯⎯⎯⎯⎯ ?

   b.   Place (where) ⎯⎯⎯⎯⎯⎯⎯⎯⎯⎯⎯⎯⎯⎯⎯⎯⎯ ?

   c.   Event (which) ⎯⎯⎯⎯⎯⎯⎯⎯⎯⎯⎯⎯⎯⎯⎯⎯ ?

2.   Television news

   a.

   b.

   c.

3. Medicine

    a.

    b.

    c.

4. The environment

    a.

    b.

    c.

5. Music

    a.

    b.

    c.

6. Children

    a.

    b.

    c.

"OK," you may say. "It isn't hard to make up these questions, but they don't look like they have anything to do with research papers."

Well, maybe some do. What makes a question a research question is some problem or puzzle or complication or issue connected with it. Again, we need to distinguish between a REPORT and a THESIS paper. The THESIS paper requires you to interpret and draw conclusions; therefore, your research question must be one that leaves room for analysis. For example, if you were interested in mortgages and wished to prepare a REPORT on that topic, you might ask: What types of mortgages are available? However, if you had to do a THESIS you would want to rephrase the question to give it an argumentative edge: Are middle-class families being squeezed out of the housing market?

Some questions are unsuitable as research questions because they can be easily answered with a factual statement: How many manned flights to the moon have taken place? Who invented polio vaccine? Other questions are unsuitable because they fall at the opposite extreme; they are impossible to answer given the current state of knowledge: Is there life after death? Are UFO's evidence of extraterrestial life? In between these extremes lies a spectrum of suitable questions. You must develop a question that is appropriate for the type of paper that has been assigned and that is neither too specific nor too broad. The extent to which you narrow your question will depend on the required length of the paper and the number of sources you find available. If you begin to research the impact of television on sports, you may decide that there is too much information. What you might then do is narrow the question down to the impact of television on professional football in the United States.

One other criterion for the research question must be mentioned. The question must be open-minded. You cannot ask the equivalent of "When did you stop beating your wife?" The bias in that question is obvious; usually it is less transparent when *we* are asking the questions. We are not always aware of our own predisposition to look at issues from a certain slant. Of course, there is no way that anyone can be completely objective and unbiased. The very choice of a topic implies a set of values that says one topic is more important than another. Nevertheless, it is important to aim for the greatest amount of objectivity that we can muster.

EXERCISE

Directions: Examine the questions below. Which would make good research questions? Would some be better for a report than a thesis? Can you detect bias in any of the questions? If a question is not suitable as a research question, try to rewrite it.

1. What is plea bargaining?
2. What is the highest mountain peak in the continental United States?
3. What causes obesity?
4. How can "goonism" in professional hockey be controlled?
5. Why is modern art such a fake?
6. What can be done about teenage alcoholism?
7. Why is the National Weather Service forecast often wrong?
8. What is the hospice movement?
9. Are zoning laws unfair?
10. What types of toys are suitable for mentally retarded children?

Now look back at the questions you wrote for the exercise on pp. 14–15. Which of those questions would lead to a good thesis or report?

In case our hints and exercises fail to help you discover a topic, we have made a list of questions based on topics that our students have researched in past semesters. Some of them may interest you.

1. What are the moral implications of genetic research?
2. Why has genealogy become so popular?
3. Are Americans overmedicated?
4. Should homosexuals have equal rights?
5. How are children with learning disabilities being helped?
6. Are home births a safe alternative?
7. What is the school's role in dealing with child abuse?
8. Are our national forests being exploited by the lumber companies?
9. Can the spread of nuclear weapons be stopped?
10. What can be done to reduce unemployment among youth?
11. What progress is being made in developing contraceptive devices for men?
12. Why are soap operas so addictive?
13. Does a small, independent business have a future in the American economy?
14. What is normal sexual behavior?
15. Why are people attracted to religious sects?
16. How will the world's expanding population be fed?
17. Have Supreme Court rulings placed unnecessary handicaps on the efforts of police to apprehend criminals?
18. Do people have a right to smoke?
19. How do music and dance reflect cultural values?
20. Should teenagers have the right to medical treatment without their parents' knowledge and consent?
21. Should private schools be tax exempt?
22. Can inflation be controlled?
23. Why have medical costs increased so much?
24. Should compulsory education laws be changed?
25. How have adoption policies changed over the years?
26. What is the future of the private automobile?
27. Can air travel be made safer?
28. Should parents be licensed?
29. Are IQ tests racially slanted?
30. Does diet affect IQ?
31. Should the government subsidize artists?
32. What are the legal rights of the mentally ill or retarded?
33. Should the regulations governing Unemployment Compensation be changed?
34. Have opportunities for minorities improved during the last 10 years?
35. Can alcoholism be cured?
36. Does TV violence cause antisocial behavior?
37. Are the laws regulating nursing homes adequately enforced?
38. Can extrasensory perception be developed?
39. Should juvenile offenders be punished more severely?

40. Do we discriminate against the handicapped?
41. How is the computer affecting the workplace?
42. How is the computer affecting education?
43. Is automation contributing to unemployment?
44. Why have health clubs become so popular?
45. Does bilingual education enhance achievement?
46. Is nuclear power an economical source of energy?
47. Has the U.S. benefited from participating in the International Monetary Fund?
48. How should our legal system deal with the insanity plea?
49. Are Japanese management practices more effective than ours?
50. Can the effects of acid rain be controlled?
51. How should we finance the clean up of hazardous waste sites?
52. Should hypnotists be licensed?
53. Should information obtained under hypnosis be allowed in court testimonies?
54. Should hospitals be required to use heroic measures to save severely handicapped newborns?
55. Should children be financially responsible for their elderly parents?

After completing Worksheet 2 you should have several possible topics for your paper. The next step will be to see how feasible each topic is. This will involve locating sources of information on the topic, a process that we are about to explain. Once you have discovered how much information is available about your possible topics, then you can make a decision about the one that you will continue working on for your research paper.

LIMITING THE SUBJECT

If you compare the entry on hypnosis in the encyclopedia (pp. 27–43) with the sample research paper (p. 307), you will notice an important difference. The research paper describes *one aspect* of the subject *in detail;* whereas, the encyclopedia gives a *general* overview of the *whole* subject. The extent to which you limit your topic will depend on the amount of information available. If you are writing a short research paper of about 1000 words, you should locate 8 to 10 sources, so that you can select a minimum of 5 to work with. You may discover that there are only 3 or 4 sources on the specific aspect of your subject. Another possibility is that some sources will duplicate others. For example, one student read an article describing the effect of birth order among siblings on personality development and decided to follow up on that topic. At first, it looked promising; there were several entries in *Readers' Guide.* However, a reading of the articles revealed that they were all based on one study that had been conducted by a specialist in child development. In effect, the several articles were secondary accounts based on the scholarly report and written in less technical language for mass market magazines.

Let's consider the subject of the other sample research paper on weather. As you can see, there are several ways in which the subject of weather can be limited:

Causes of weather
Weather prediction
Weather control
Environmental implications of weather control
Legal aspects of weather control

What aspect of weather is described in the sample paper? Can you think of other aspects of weather beyond those we listed above?

List as many different aspects as you can think of for each of the following topics:

1. Insurance
2. Sports
3. Education
4. Natural Resources
5. Religion
6. Crime

As you work through the next section on locating information, you will begin to develop a better idea of how you will limit the scope of your paper.

2. LOCATING INFORMATION IN PRINT

Check the Requirements

THE VARIETY OF printed information available in a library is staggering. Where do you begin? That depends partly on the requirements. As indicated on p. 9, you should determine whether your instructor requires or prohibits certain sources. For example, some instructors may not want you to use an encyclopedia because of its general level of information; others may prohibit the use of articles that appear in mass market magazines, such as *Psychology Today*, because they want you to become familiar with scholarly publications such as the *Journal of Consulting and Clinical Psychology*.

REFERENCE WORKS

We suggest that you get an overview of your topic by consulting an encyclopedia or specialized reference book. However, not all subjects can be found in such works. A student interested in the rapid growth of private health clubs and figure salons could not find health clubs in the encyclopedia. Nevertheless, it is often worthwhile to consider the historical perspective and check under a more general heading; in this case, physical education.

How Encyclopedias Can Help You

Even if you have been discussing your subject in class, or reading about it in your textbook, start by looking it up in an encyclopedia and reading the information about it there. Don't worry about taking notes at this point. Your purpose now is to read quickly but attentively in order to get a general orientation. Start with a well-respected general encyclopedia like the *Encyclopedia Americana* or the *Encyclopaedia Britannica*.

There are three reasons for starting with an encyclopedia:

1. The encyclopedia will refresh your memory and give you an overview of the subject by including such information as definitions, history, current statistics, and connections to other subjects. Encyclopedia articles are often divided up under headings or with subtopics in the margins. These subdivisions may

suggest how you might limit your own topic. By identifying specific problems or issues associated with the subject, an encyclopedia may give you a handle on it, again suggesting research questions or approaches you might want to take yourself.

2. Besides giving you a general orientation and background information on your topic, an encyclopedia article will identify key terms related to your topic. Working on unfamiliar vocabulary at this point will pay off particularly well later. These are the terms you will encounter in all your other reading on the subject, and the quicker you learn them, the better. For example, a psychology student with an interest in altered states of consciousness would likely read the following encyclopedia article on hypnosis and might not feel too sure about some of these words in the article:

empirical
placebo
inference
pharmacological

The student's own desk dictionary, such as the *American Heritage Dictionary* or *Webster's New Collegiate Dictionary*, would probably give adequate definitions. But specialized dictionaries also exist to clarify technical terminology applicable to a particular field or audience, and you should be prepared, if necessary, to consult them. Examples include the *American Political Dictionary*, *Dictionary of American Slang*, *Dorland's Illustrated Medical Dictionary*, *Dictionary of Education*, *Mathematics Dictionary*, *McGraw-Hill Dictionary of the Life Sciences*.

3. Encyclopedia articles often include a short bibliography of their own, that is, a list of recommended readings that are considered basic to an understanding of the subject. These readings are often helpful as a short cut if you find yourself swamped with material and are not sure how to select readings to concentrate on or begin with.

Remember, at this point, not to worry about taking notes. Later you may want to return to the encyclopedia to take notes, but right now your job is to read, to get a quick overview of the subject and its scope, and possibly to gain some idea of what books and magazines others have written about it.

A Special Note About Using the *Encyclopaedia Britannica*

Most general encyclopedias are arranged alphabetically and are easy to use. *World Book Encyclopedia* or *Collier's Encyclopedia*, as well as the *Encyclopedia Americana*, will give you a clear, quick overview of your subject. However, college students can usually benefit as well from the more extensive, scholarly approach of the *Encyclopaedia Britannica*—one of the most helpful general resources in the library, but one that is organized rather differently from other encyclopedias.

The 30 volumes of the *Encyclopaedia Britannica* are divided into three parts:

1. A one-volume *Propaedia*, "Outline of Knowledge," and Guide to the *Britannica*.
2. The ten-volume *Micropaedia*, "Ready Reference and Index," which contains many short articles on specific subjects.
3. The 19-volume *Macropaedia*, "Knowledge in Depth," which contains long articles on broad topics.

Steps in Using the *Encyclopaedia Britannica*

Suppose you were interested in possible medical uses of hypnosis.

1. Begin by looking up your subject in the *Micropaedia* or "Ready Reference and Index" volumes:

hypnosis

2. Check to see if there is a major article in the *Macropaedia*. The volume and page number will directly follow the subject heading.

    9:133

hypnosis 9:133, a sleeplike state during which hallucinatory experiences, distortions in memory, and a wide range of behavioral responses may be induced through suggestion. The text article covers the history of hypnosis and modern theoretical interpretations. The article also describes such hypnotic phenomena as muscular and physiological alterations, time distortion, delusions, attitude change, and age regression. An appraisal of the potentials, limitations, and dangers of hypnosis in medicine, dentistry, psychiatry, and criminal interrogation is also included.

3. Read the description of what the major article covers.

REFERENCES in other text articles:
·animal immobility phenomena **2:**542d
·attention, stimulus, and CNV **2:**357g
·Christian Science defensive mental work **4:**563f
·deconditioning concept and usage **15:**148e
·déjà vu induction in normal individuals **11:**890b
·Freud's development of psychoanalysis **7:**739c
·hallucinations and withdrawal **9:**246b
·history of medicine before 1900 **11:**831c
·inflammatory response modification **9:**561g
·Janet's amnesia treatment **11:**886g
·New Thought applications of Quimby **13:**14d
·persuasion of the mentally disturbed **14:**125g
·psychiatry's history **15:**155e
·time perception variation **18:**423h
·treatment of conversion reactions **15:**171g

4. Check "REFERENCES in other text articles" to see if there might be anything useful related to your research question there. If any major articles sound interesting, get them from the *Macropaedia* and read them.

    e.g., *history of medicine before 1900* and *inflammatory response modification* look promising

Reprinted with permission from Encyclopaedia Britannica, *15th edition, Copyright © 1974 by Encyclopaedia Britannica, Inc.*

Here is the major article on hypnosis from the *Macropaedia*. We want you to read it for practice. But before you begin, do this short refresher exercise on the art of asking questions.

EXERCISE

How many questions can you make up based on the following statement? "There can be no separate science of hypnosis."

1.

2.

3.

4.

etc.

The point of this exercise, so far, is to prepare you for the next part—the reading assignment. The technique of asking questions can not only get you interested in a topic, it can also help you read efficiently, that is, focus your attention on important aspects and remember information. We will explain this technique in detail in the next chapter under "Reading for Meaning." But notice, for now, as you read the following *Encyclopaedia Britannica* article, how your preliminary questions help you sort out and understand the information.

Hypnosis

The term hypnosis was coined in the 1840s by James Braid, a Scottish surgeon; it stems from the Greek *hypnos* ("sleep") and refers to a sleeplike state that nevertheless permits a wide range of behavioral responses to stimulation. The hypnotized individual appears to heed only the communications of the hypnotist. He seems to respond in an uncritical, automatic fashion, ignoring all aspects of the environment other than those made relevant by the hypnotist. Apparently with no will of his own, he sees, feels, smells, and tastes in accordance with the suggestions in apparent contradiction to the stimuli that impinge upon him. Even memory and awareness of self may be altered by suggestion, and the effects of the suggestions may be extended (posthypnotically) into subsequent waking activity.

The following descriptive account indicates what typically occurs in a hypnotic encounter. The person to be hypnotized (subject) is invited to relax in comfort and to fix his gaze on some object. The hypnotist continues to suggest, usually in a quiet, low voice, that relaxation will increase and that the subject's eyes will grow tired. Soon the eyes do show the normal signs of fatigue, and it is suggested that they will close. The subject will probably allow his eyes to close and then begin to show signs of profound relaxation such as limpness and regular breathing. The hypnotist now makes suggestions, typically in vivid, concrete terms; thus the subject may be told that his hand is so heavy that he cannot lift it but that he should try. The subject responds, often seeming quite puzzled by his inability to raise the arm. The hypnotist then tells him that it really does not matter, and he need not try any longer, that he is relaxing untroubled except for a mosquito buzzing around and landing on his forehead. The subject probably will grimace and may attempt to brush away or swat the imaginary insect. Relaxation is restored by the suggestion that the mosquito is flying away. It next may be suggested that as the insect departs the subject will totally forget what has happened this year, and last year, and the year before, back to (say) ten years ago. Shortly thereafter, the subject is invited to open his eyes, to walk about, and to engage in conversation. Asked the date, he may give some day a decade past; questioned about the recent news, he probably will describe political or social events of that time.

The session might be concluded by telling the subject that he is returning to the present time and that, on awakening at the count of ten, he will remember nothing of what has just happened until he is asked to relax and to recall everything. It is also suggested that, after the subject wakes, he will remove his wristwatch when he sees the hypnotist signal (*e.g.*, by folding his arms). When he opens his eyes, the subject may act as if he suddenly finds himself in a strange place but seems to feel comfortable. Asked what has just occurred, he may say that he must have just dozed off; he cannot account for the period of hypnosis. If events which occurred during that time are described, he may deny that they did. Yet, when he sees the hypnotist fold his arms, he absent-mindedly takes off his watch. Asked why, he may rationalize by

Induction

Awakening

winding it and return it to his wrist. When the hypnotist later folds his arms, the subject again slips off his watch but may seem embarrassed by his own behaviour; he may begin to suspect that his actions have something to do with the hypnosis. Finally the subject may be asked to relax and, as the hypnotist counts to five, to recall everything that went on since he first was hypnotized. At the count the subject's expression usually will reveal a dawning awareness of the forgotten events. He may now describe his puzzling inability to lift his arm and his annoyance at the mosquito. He may also mention the awakening of memory as if part had been dissociated from awareness and then had suddenly become accessible and, further, his disappointment at knowing where he was and what he was doing.

In general, when a subject is hypnotized, he seems to accept as real the distortions of perception and memory suggested by the hypnotist, even though they surprise him. Activities such as grimacing at an invisible mosquito, quite unremarkable in themselves, strike the observer as strange because they imply the occurrence of perceptual experiences that are not usually brought about by simple assertion. Since, however, subjects characteristically report their experiences to others in much the same way as to the hypnotist, their behaviour cannot be explained as conscious playacting. In addition to responses explicitly suggested, subjects tend to show deep relaxation, regular breathing, passivity, and relative immunity to distractions.

HISTORY

Hypnotic techniques have been used since antiquity; healing practices by priests of ancient Egypt and Greece are striking examples. Trancelike behaviour attributed to "spirit possession" has played a role in Christianity, Judaism, and in many primitive religions. Miraculous powers ascribed to witches and the arts of faith healing throughout the ages are probably related to hypnosis.

The "discovery" of hypnosis in Europe is generally credited to Franz Anton Mesmer (1734–1815), an Austrian physician working in France at the time of the American Revolution. He found that some ailing people were benefitted by passing magnets over their bodies. Participants in his group séances sat around an open tub from which magnetized metal bars protruded; some would develop a "crisis" (a kind of convulsive fit), lapse into apparent sleep, and awaken cured or much improved. Mesmer later found that magnets were not crucial; it often seemed sufficient to touch the person or even to touch (or "magnetize") water before the sufferer drank it. Mesmer concluded that he was gifted with "animal magnetism," a kind of "fluid" that he could store and transfer to others to heal them. A follower of Mesmer, the nobleman Chastenet de Puységur, "magnetized" a tree on his estate, at which his peasants would obtain relief from their ailments. By 1780 he had found that the "mesmeric crisis" was unnecessary and that he could influence a mesmerized person just by talking to him. He, in short, used hypnosis much as it is used today.

The notoriety that followed Mesmer's spectacular therapeutic claims led to the appointment in Paris of an inves-

Mesmer

tigating commission that included the American diplomat Benjamin Franklin and the French chemist Antoine-Laurent Lavoisier. In 1784 it concluded that no magnetic "fluid" exists; striking recoveries from illness were not denied but attributed to "mere imagination." Thus discredited, hypnosis as a topic of objective investigation was neglected and tended to be linked with mysticism and quackery.

About 1840, physicians John Elliotson in London and James Esdaile in Calcutta made extensive use of mesmeric trance to carry out painless major surgery, including leg amputations. Elliotson endorsed belief in Mesmer's invisible "fluid" and held the metal nickel to be particularly useful in trance induction. The editor of the British medical journal *Lancet* surreptitiously exchanged nickel with lead; since the lead seemed to work just as well, he denounced such belief as "mesmeric humbug."

Anesthesia

Braid agreed that no magnetic "fluid" was involved but observed that people being treated with mesmerism seemed profoundly influenced. He introduced the term hypnotism to divorce the phenomenon from theories about animal magnetism and held that concentration on a single focus of attention (monoideism) was a major factor in the situation.

Hypnosis attracted widespread scientific interest in the 1880s as a result of a controversy in France. Ambroise-Auguste Liébeault, an obscure country physician at Nancy who used mesmeric techniques, drew the support of Hippolyte Bernheim, professor of medicine at Strasbourg. Independently they wrote that the phenomenon involved no physical forces and no physiological processes but were psychologically mediated responses to suggestions. In disagreement, Jean-Martin Charcot, professor of neurology at the Sorbonne in Paris, held that hypnosis occurs only in sufferers of hysteria, is therefore pathological, and does involve the influences of magnets and metals. (Charcot had become interested in the possible transfer of symptoms by magnets and in the effects of drugs at a distance.) History has shown that the effects of magnets and similar physical factors are really brought about by implicit psychological suggestions.

Hysteria

At about the same time, the Austrian physician Sigmund Freud visited France and was impressed by the therapeutic potential of hypnosis for neurotic disorders. On his return to Vienna he used hypnosis to help neurotics recall forgotten disturbing events. As he began to develop his system of psychoanalysis, theoretical considerations, as well as the difficulty he encountered in hypnotizing some patients, led Freud to discard hypnosis in favour of free association. Generally psychoanalysts have tended to view hypnosis as a somewhat masked intimate personal relationship.

Despite Freud's influential rejection of hypnosis, some use was made of the technique in treating combat neuroses during World Wars I and II. Pierre Janet in France and Morton Prince in the United States suggested that "dissociation of mental systems" is common both to the neurotic disorder called multiple personality and to the phenomenon of hypnosis. Prince showed that a hypnotized person seems to be able to carry on two or more independent streams of mental activity simultaneously.

Ivan Pavlov, the Russian physiologist, came to view
sleep as reflecting widespread inhibitory processes in the
brain and concluded that hypnosis is a similar inhibitory
state in which there remain a few centres of neural excitation. His views enjoy wide acceptance among Soviet
and eastern European workers who also tend to use prolonged periods of sleep in psychiatric therapy.

In America, experimental psychologist Clark Hull, applying controlled quantitative methods to the laboratory
study of this complex and elusive phenomenon, concluded in 1933 that, as Bernheim had argued, hypnosis is
best understood as a form of hypersuggestibility. Important basic research has continued in Hull's tradition with
normal volunteer subjects. A combined clinical-experi-
mental approach, inspired by Milton Erickson's pioneer-
ing work in the 1940s, has been effective as a research
strategy and has led to novel therapeutic applications
which have helped spark renewed widespread interest in
hypnosis.

**Scientific journals devoted exclusively to hypnosis are
published in England, Japan, South America, the U.S.,
and Sweden. National societies in many countries hold
annual scientific meetings, and international congresses
on hypnosis have been held in France (1965), Japan
(1967), Germany (1970), and Sweden (1973).**

MODERN THEORIES

**Despite active empirical study of hypnotic phenomena,
there is no single generally accepted explanatory theory.
Some theorists influenced by Pavlov think of hypnosis as
a state of altered consciousness or partial sleep in which
a person tends to respond to suggestions automatically
and uncritically. While this view does not ignore increased suggestibility, it still holds that a subject not at
the moment responding to a suggestion may nevertheless
be in a trance state. There may be neurophysiological
components of such a state. Such a position would be
consistent with the notion, not generally accepted, that
some animals can be hypnotized, as when a chick, suddenly placed on its back, tends to remain immobile in
that position (see DORMANCY).**

Other theorists stress the social or interpersonal interactions that hypnotic behaviour involves. They emphasize how an actor willingly and wittingly permits a
director to guide him into living a part; how a patient
may be relieved of a headache if given a pill that is actually pharmacologically inert (a placebo); how an uncommitted person becomes an enthusiastic supporter of
crowd feeling at a demonstration; how a spectator
flinches and jabs along with his favourite fighter; and how
a student changes his views to those of an admired
teacher. Hypnosis is held to consist of nothing more than
events like these, there being no need to assume additional special states such as the inhibition of parts of the
brain. Hypnotic events are results of interpersonal influences in which various abilities, skills, and response
propensities are brought into play.

Evidence can be found to support both major theoretical
approaches. Neural changes indeed do occur in hypnosis,
but a unique physiological basis for the phenomenon remains to be established. Perhaps this reflects incomplete

Hypnosis
as sleep

Social
interaction

understanding of physiological alterations that may produce psychological change. Social-interaction theorists find it difficult to explain why posthypnotic suggestions are carried out even when the hypnotist neither knows nor apparently cares about the subject's behaviour. While most current investigators tend to work within one or the other explanatory framework, most feel free to use propositions from both if they seem consistent with experimental or clinical observations.

INDUCTION OF HYPNOSIS

Techniques to induce hypnosis share common features. Responsiveness is maximized when the subject seems to believe that he can be hypnotized, that the hypnotist is competent and trustworthy, and that the undertaking is safe, appropriate, and congruent with his wishes. Therefore induction is generally preceded by the establishment of suitable rapport between subject and hypnotist. After this the hypnotist proceeds to try to focus attention on the procedure proper.

Establishing rapport

Ordinary inductions begin with simple suggestions that will almost inevitably be accepted by all subjects. At this stage neither subject nor hypnotist can readily tell whether the subject's behaviour constitutes a hypnotic response or mere cooperation. Then, gradually, suggestions are given that demand increasing distortion of perception or memory. In the eye-closure method described above, for example, the suggestions of visual fatigue are consistent with and take advantage of normal strain during fixation and thus serve to heighten expectations of positive response. It is difficult for hypnotist, subject, or outside observer to be sure whether eye closure indicates hypnosis or mere voluntary compliance. But the hypnotist gradually moves on to suggest that it will be difficult or impossible to open the now-shut eyes. Although not all subjects respond positively, those who do seem to have gone beyond the point of simple compliance. By linking any successful responses with ensuing suggestions, the hypnotist often can elicit increasingly marked distortions of perception, belief, memory, and attitude. The success or failure of any suggestion is considerably influenced by how well the hypnotist observes and uses the subject's natural talents.

While induction is usually carried out in a quiet, dimly lit room, it may be done in normal illumination. The subject may be asked to attend to any of a wide variety of stimuli—his own hand, his breathing, an imaginary visual image, or a tone. He need not be seated and relaxed; indeed, in some methods the subject is asked to tense his muscles. Even carefully selected distractions can be used to facilitate progress.

Induction of hypnosis may take considerable time but sometimes requires only a few seconds. Hypnotists in theatres and night clubs capitalize on developing appropriate expectations and selecting individuals ready and willing to enter deep hypnosis. Much of the effort in clinical settings is directed toward establishing appropriate attitudes in the subject. The advertising and publicity given the stage hypnotist before he faces the audience likewise facilitate response; with such preparation, he sometimes can induce hypnosis all but instantaneous-

Expectations

ly, merely by shaking a particularly susceptible subject's hand or by saying in a commanding voice, "Sleep!" Given suitable preparation, tape-recorded induction procedures may be as effective as an experienced hypnotist.

With suitable subjects hypnosis also can be induced by a series of suggestions without any reference to sleep or eye closure. Some waking individuals go directly into the same state produced by telling a deeply hypnotized subject that he will open his eyes while in the trance.

In general, hypnosis cannot be induced against an individual's will. Occasionally experiments have been reported in which individuals were asked to resist but nonetheless were hypnotized. In all such examples the hypnotist solicited the subject's cooperation in an experiment; only then did he ask for resistance. Assuming the subject is capable of hypnosis, his response seems to depend on whether he wishes to help in solving the experimental problem or whether he wants to follow the specific instruction to resist. It is unwarranted to assume that under these circumstances the subject truly does not wish to enter hypnosis; it has not been convincingly shown that hypnosis can be induced in someone independently motivated to resist. This does not mean, however, that a willing person cannot be hypnotized without his formal consent. It is unusual, but in some therapeutic or religious contexts, for example, people have been observed to exhibit trancelike or hypnotic behaviour without evidence of intention on their part or even on the part of a hypnotist.

Resistance to hypnosis

Hypnotic suggestions. A peculiar quality of speech seems helpful in making hypnotic suggestions. Most people can identify the voice quality, traditionally described as monotonous and repetitious but probably more accurately as intense, insistent, and simple. Suggestions seem most effective when the hypnotist paints a vivid word picture of concrete images that are easily imagined.

Suggestions also are best given in indicative rather than imperative form. Instead of saying, "Lift your hand," for example, the hypnotist encourages a passive attitude in which the subject neither strives to help nor to hinder the arm and says, "It is becoming light . . . the fingers are beginning to rise . . . they feel like balloons as they float into the air . . . ."

As the subject begins to respond, the hypnotist often behaves as if he shares the subject's unusual experiences. When, for example, the person seems to be hallucinating a familiar friend in response to suggestion, the hypnotist may ask to be introduced. He will begin to talk to the subject's hallucination as if he too were seeing the imaginary person.

The popular impression of the hypnotist as authoritarian and dominating fits the behaviour of many stage hypnotists and of psychiatrists using hypnosis in the last century. Just as the authoritarian bedside manner of medical practitioners is no longer the norm, however, so has the approach of the medical hypnotist changed with the times. Under most circumstances, therapeutic hypnosis is now carried out in an atmosphere of cooperation, the hypnotist assuming the role of a teacher who can help his student achieve a mutually sought goal.

Technical aids. A wide variety of devices has been employed to facilitate fixation. A rotating picture of a spiral has been popular, its movement tending to focus attention on the centre. Arrangements of mirrors and fixation points also have been used, just as the subject may focus attention on his own breath sounds. Particular theoretical interest has been shown in the use of a flashing light, especially when adjusted to the subject's own electrical brain rhythms (typically nine or ten pulses per second).

Drugs also have been used, especially sedatives (*e.g.*, barbiturates) for relaxation prior to hypnotic induction. (Paradoxically, injections of such stimulants as amphetamines also have been reported to help.) Any procedure that produces momentary clouding of consciousness can be used to activate responses to suggestions. Hypnotic efforts are enhanced when a person is drowsy or about to fall asleep (with or without drugs). Similarly, dulled awareness readily can be achieved by pressure on blood vessels in the neck to deprive the brain of oxygen. This potentially injurious technique most often is employed by medically untrained hypnotists. There also is some indication that people under sensory deprivation (conditions of silence, darkness, and isolation) become unusually suggestible.

Use of drugs

These procedures appear effective primarily in heightening expectations; it has never been shown that persons who are not susceptible to ordinary induction procedures abruptly become hypnotizable with these aids.

HYPNOTIC PHENOMENA

Appropriate suggestions can induce a remarkably wide range of psychological responses among deeply hypnotized persons.

Ideomotor responses. When one vividly imagines moving his body, he has a marked tendency to do what he is thinking. If the responsive subject stands with his back to the hypnotist, for example, and it is suggested that he is falling backward farther and farther, as he concentrates he will begin gradually to sway in that direction. Similarly it may be suggested that his hand will grow lighter and float upward or that it will become heavy and be pulled down. Waking individuals also respond to suggestions of movement, and there is some question whether hypnotic induction increases the probability of such behaviour. Since the tendency of subjects to respond to suggested movement is related to their general suggestibility, such ideomotor phenomena are widely considered to be a kind of hypnotic response.

Challenge suggestions. Challenge suggestions are those in which the subject is told he is unable to implement his own will; for example, "Your eyelids are shutting tight ... tighter ... tighter. You cannot open them even if you try. . . . Try to open them. . . . You cannot. . . . They are stuck together." Similarly, a hypnotized subject may be informed that his eyelids will force themselves open despite his effort to keep them shut. Challenge suggestions are of theoretical interest in that they seem to prevent voluntary action, striking observer and subject as dramatic demonstrations of external control over the individual. Such experiments have little therapeutic application; they also can be carried out with some people without formal hypnotic induction procedure, although response to challenge tends to be augmented during trance states. Response among waking individuals can serve as a test of hypnotic susceptibility; generally, those who respond very positively to challenge subsequently are found to be deeply hypnotizable. Challenge items emphasize the compelling character of hypnotic suggestion.

It has been observed that challenge suggestions may impose a logical "double bind"; *e.g.*, that the instruction to try actually means to attempt and fail to open one's eyes. Some theorists suggest that it is not possible to comply with the instruction to try to open one's eyes and at the same time to cooperate with the generic instruction to be hypnotized. Whatever the validity of this theoretical formulation, many subjects say they feel genuinely unable to overcome such a challenge.

Perceptual distortions. With appropriate suggestion, the hypnotic subject may perceive stimuli not actually present or fail to perceive stimuli that are present. In response, for example, to the suggestion that an absent person is present, the subject may report that he sees, hears, and feels the hallucinated person and even spontaneously carry on a conversation with the hallucinated image.

Other perceptual distortions, such as feeling warm or cold or having a sweet or acid taste, may readily be suggested. It is typically easier to induce illusory experience —for example, that a lemon is a peach of which one can enjoy the delicate flavour—than to produce a positive hallucination in the absence of external objects. The most difficult to elicit are negative hallucinations in which the subject seems unable to perceive objects actually present.

Hypnotic analgesia and anesthesia may involve both the reduction of fear, relatively easily achieved by hypnosis, and the more difficult negative hallucination of pain. Since anticipation of pain tends to heighten discomfort substantially in the dentist's chair, some dentists report that more than 90 percent of their patients show a greatly increased pain threshold and a marked reduction in the need for local anesthesia even under light hypnosis. Such results largely stem from the effect of hypnosis on the reduction of fear; on the other hand, major surgical operations can be performed without anesthetic drugs but require deep hypnosis. This seems feasible with a much smaller number of individuals, and such anesthesia is likely to involve a negative hallucination of the pain experience.

Painless surgery

Negative hallucination also seems to be a major part of hypnotic rapport. Once hypnosis is induced, subjects typically ignore all stimuli but the hypnotist. This appears to be a response to the suggestion to ignore the environment (*e.g.*, "You will pay attention only to my voice."), a kind of negative hallucination for everything outside the hypnotic context. Nevertheless, once hypnotic rapport has been established, it can readily be transferred by suggestion from the hypnotist to someone else.

Alterations of memory. Among the most dramatic experiences of the hypnotized individual are distortions of recall. If it is suggested that fictitious events really have occurred, the subject may not only seem to remember them, he may also elaborate on them. Suggestions may be given to forget what happened yesterday or one's own name. Told to forget the number 6, for example, a subject will count his fingers as . . . 5, 7, 8 . . ., ending with what he seems to perceive as an 11th finger. Encouraged to explore this peculiarity, he may note that he can count five fingers twice with no difficulty and correctly conclude that there must be a problem with his ability to count between five and ten. Yet this inference does not necessarily help him to recall the missing number.

A special case of memory distortion is hypnotic age regression; an adult, for example, appears to relive events that occurred when he was a child—his speech, writing, and general motor behaviour becoming childlike. He appears to recall events and skills long since lost or forgotten, such as playing a musical instrument or speaking a foreign language learned in childhood. Some investigators have taken the phenomenon of age regression as evidence for total storage of all sensory impressions, but carefully controlled studies generally have failed to find support for this assumption. When verifiable details of memory are checked, there seems to be little recall of factual information beyond what was available in the adult waking state.

Age regression

Hypnotic age regression does seem to make the subject less concerned about the accuracy of his memory, and he fills in memory gaps with vivid imagination. This in turn may promote recall of repressed, emotionally charged actual experiences; however, even then it is often difficult to distinguish fact from fiction. The individual may be both convinced and convincing despite a tendency to elaborate, embroider, and distort what actually occurred.

Hypnotic age regression has been advocated and used in legal cases. Great care should be taken in evaluating the accuracy of testimony even if the witness seems to be totally convinced of the honesty of his report. Hypnosis is no guarantee against falsification.

It remains controversial whether hypnotic suggestions can improve memory effectively. The effect, if any, is small for the kinds of information ordinarily employed in laboratory studies of learning and forgetting. The popular opinion that hypnosis facilitates recollection has not been supported by adequately controlled subsequent research. The common belief of the student who has neglected his studies that through hypnosis he may recall enough to pass his examinations, sadly, lacks reliable foundation.

Posthypnotic amnesia. Many subjects seem unable to recall what happened while they were in deep hypnosis. It is unclear whether this posthypnotic amnesia is a spontaneous consequence of deep hypnosis or whether it results entirely from suggestion. While suggestions made during hypnosis do have substantial effects on what the subject subsequently recalls, it remains to be shown that they account for all posthypnotic remembering or forgetting. Posthypnotic amnesia may be successfully removed by appropriate hypnotic suggestions.

Other kinds of hypnotic suggestions. *Delusions.* Appropriate hypnotic suggestions also can prompt the subject to embrace false beliefs (delusions). Told that he is a famous actor on his way to a television interview, the hypnotized person will show through his posture, mannerisms, attitudes, and speech clear alterations that are consistent with the delusion. Deluded behaviour also may be elicited through age progressions, in which it is suggested to a young adult, for example, that he is now an old man. The ease with which subjects respond to suggestions of age progression indicates that age regression, including regression to previous "incarnations," may be equally delusional.

Time distortion. Suggestions may be given that the passing of time will speed up or slow down. In the latter case, for example, a hypnotized subject may seem to experience a full-length motion-picture film in only a few seconds. It is quite unlikely, however, that such hypnotic time distortion can in reality accelerate the learning of new information.

Attitude change. Of special therapeutic potential is the effect of hypnotically suggesting altered attitudes. It may be suggested to someone who feels unattractive, for instance, that he will find that people like him and are drawn to his company. When used judiciously, suggestions such as these may result in enduring therapeutic changes by modifying the person's behaviour toward others. To the degree that his new optimism leads to friendlier, more confident approaches to people, their typically reciprocal responses will reinforce the changes initiated by hypnotic suggestion.

Physiological alterations. A broad variety of bodily changes have been produced by suggestion in hypnotized individuals. These usually are elicited indirectly by mentioning appropriate circumstances; for example, viral cold sores (herpes) have been induced, not by directly suggesting their appearance but rather by suggesting emotional distress of the sort that previously was associated with their eruption. Similarly, suggestions that they feel cold lead some subjects to show such bodily signs as shivering and circulatory alterations. Suggested sudden pain, discomfort, or stress can change the electrical resistance of the subject's skin and alter his respiration and heart rate. On the other hand, successful suggestions of diminished pain do not seem to abolish such bodily responses to the stress.

There is controversy about the hypnotic induction of blisters. Told that a cool coin touching him is red hot, a subject shows intense discomfort; sometimes there may be redness and blistering skin. Generally not reproducible under controlled laboratory conditions with normal volunteer subjects, psychologically induced blisters seem most likely to appear only in those prone to convert emotional disturbances into symptoms of skin disease. Blisters

Although some surgeons and many dentists report hypnotic control of bleeding after such procedures as tooth extraction, this remains to be verified by controlled experiment.

Posthypnotic suggestion. A deeply hypnotized individual can be induced to carry out an action in response to a specific cue some time after trance termination. With adequate amnesia, he will not be aware of the source of his impulse to act and may rationalize his behaviour. Even with awareness, he may still feel compelled to carry out the action and, if he attempts to resist doing so, evidence of conflict can usually be observed.

Posthypnotic suggestion, however, is not a particularly

powerful means of controlling behaviour. Simple requests to a cooperative individual are responded to more consistently and over longer periods than posthypnotic suggestions. A group of subjects in deep hypnosis, for example, given postcards and instructed to mail one every day, sent fewer cards than others merely asked to carry out this action. This holds for trivial tasks, easily carried out, but the situation is reversed when the suggestion concerns behaviours the individual has difficulty in controlling himself.

Thus, posthypnotic suggestions have been quite effective in the treatment of habits such as smoking. In these instances, the posthypnotic suggestion is congruent with the individual's desires and reinforces them. Efforts to use posthypnotic suggestion as a means to force an individual to behave in a manner undesirable to him are usually doomed to failure, though such suggestions may occasionally lead to troublesome mental conflict.

A treatment for smoking

In contrast to a simple request, posthypnotic responses are carried out not simply to please the hypnotist, but rather they may persist even in private when the hypnotist apparently could not know or care about the execution of the action.

All phenomena that can be elicited during hypnosis can, in suitable subjects, be elicited posthypnotically. This raises serious theoretical issues and has led some theorists to argue that the posthypnotic cue reinstates hypnosis.

LIMITATIONS AND POTENTIALITIES OF HYPNOSIS

The objectively observable phenomena of hypnosis are not so different from those of voluntary waking cooperation as once was supposed. It has been shown that during a lecture a student asked by his teacher to take off his shoe, to exchange neckties with a neighbour, or engage in other slightly embarrassing, ludicrous actions will do so. Had hypnosis first been induced, observers might have wrongly concluded that the subject was in the "power" of the hypnotist.

When unhypnotizable subjects are asked to simulate hypnosis, their performance can deceive experienced hypnotists. Simulating subjects convincingly perform extraordinary feats of strength and memory; for example, tolerating a needle through the arm without flinching. Such feats have mistakenly been taken as proof that hypnosis confers abilities that transcend those of waking activity.

Investigators once were inclined to conclude that deeply hypnotized subjects can be compelled against their "will" to carry out self-damaging and antisocial behaviour. They cited independent studies demonstrating that such individuals will attempt to pick up a poisonous snake, to pick up with their bare fingers a coin dissolving in a beaker of fuming nitric acid, and to throw the acid at a research assistant. Asked in the waking state whether they would obey such suggestions, the same subjects were quick to deny the possibility. In subsequent work, however, deeply hypnotized people were mingled with simulating subjects without the experimenter's knowledge, which ensured that he treated all subjects in the same persuasive way. Instructed to carry out these perilous, undesirable acts, five out of six hypnotized subjects did so, but all of six simulators did likewise. The experiment demonstrates that different answers emerge when waking subjects are asked whether they will carry out an action and when they are instructed to do so in a way that clearly communicates expectation of compliance. Under the latter circumstances waking subjects correctly seem to surmise that safety precautions have been taken; indeed, no responsible investigator permits subjects or assistants to be hurt. The further implication is that the genuine hypnotic subjects also may have surmised that the situation was safe; it thus remains undemonstrated that they were under the hypnotist's "power."

This experiment is typical of a number of controlled studies that call many earlier extravagant claims about hypnosis into serious question. It now seems quite unlikely that the hypnotized person can transcend his waking potentials in physical strength, perceptiveness, learning ability, and productivity. Similarly, it seems most improbable that hypnotized people can be compelled to do what they would be most unwilling to do in the waking state. But hypnosis may be used, as various other methods may also be used, to induce a person to alter his usual behaviour.

The inability of the hypnotized subject to transcend his waking potential does not call into question the reality of hypnosis. When a hypnotized person reports a hallucination, all the evidence indicates that it is real to him. The significant aspects of hypnosis are found in the quality or characteristics of the subject's induced experiences. The statements of people after trance indicate that hypnotic experiences are qualitatively distinct from those reported by simulators. Genuinely hypnotized subjects, for example, tolerate the discrepancy of actually seeing a person and of simultaneously hallucinating that person at another location without being especially cued; this does not hold for the simulator. Hypnotized people tend to carry out suggestions during or after trance whether the hypnotist is present or not; simulators cease to respond when they are quite sure they have no audience.

Altogether then, hypnosis should not be considered as a technique for achieving supernormal performance or control. Rather it is a collaborative enterprise in which the inner experience of the subject can be dramatically altered.

Hypnotic responsiveness. Some suggestions, such as those of eye closure and feelings of heaviness, warmth, and relaxation, are effective with most individuals. Other suggestions, including those of analgesia to a pinprick or difficulty in opening one's eyes when challenged, elicit positive responses from a lesser number. Hallucinations, general posthypnotic amnesia, and other memory distortions are achieved only in approximately one-quarter of the population; negative visual hallucinations, profound surgical anesthesia, and response to bizarre posthypnotic suggestions are feasible with only a few people. On this evidence, items of suggestion can be graded roughly in terms of difficulty. Occasionally a subject may respond to a generally difficult item and not to one that is rated easy, but this is not the usually observed pattern.

Such data have led to the development of a number of standardized scales for assessing hypnotic susceptibility.

Designed for research with normal subjects, they avoid highly personal or emotionally upsetting items. *The Stanford Hypnotic Susceptibility Scales* are widely used. Some, consisting of easier items, are used for preliminary screening. Others contain more difficult items, and some are designed to reveal the particular kinds of suggestion to which the subject best responds. Variations of the Stanford scales include the *Children's Hypnotic Susceptibility Scale* and the *Harvard Group Scale*, the latter also employing tape-recorded procedure.

Scales of this sort are fairly reliable in that most subjects' responses are reasonably stable from one time to another and from one form of the scale to another. (If a person chooses to resist the hypnotic procedure, however, he will score low even though he may be quite capable of responding. Susceptibility scales, like intelligence tests, can be misleading unless the individual tries his best.) The Table summarizes typical variations in depth of hypnosis induced among normal college students with a graded series of items from the Stanford scales.

Any individual's overt responses to a standardized scale may be objectively scored and evaluated against such a

Tests of susceptibility

Level of Hypnosis at Initial Induction with Stanford Scale		
level achieved	items passed (max = 12)	percentage of cases
Complete trance	12	4
Very high	11	7
High	8–10	19
Moderate	5–7	28
Low	2–4	32
No response	0–1	10

Source: E.R. Hilgard, *Hypnotic Susceptibility* (1965).

table of norms. The investigator also may ask the individual how strongly he felt affected by the procedure. Results from objective scoring and from the person's subjective report tend to yield similar estimates of depth of hypnosis, but concordance is far from perfect. One subject may give marked overt responses but later say that he merely was trying to be helpful; another more lethargic person may not emphatically respond but subsequently may report profound awareness of hypnotic change. Such verbal reports are of particular interest in clinical, therapeutic settings.

Some subjects manifest very deep hypnosis in responding to even the most difficult items yet later say their experiences differed little from the fantasy of ordinary daydreaming. Others who fail to respond to all of the more difficult suggestions nonetheless seem deeply affected by the discovery that they have responded at all. They may say that having their eyes grow heavy was vastly different from, and more impressive than, any other experience they can recall. In therapeutic contexts this latter evidence of hypnotic depth often seems closely related to the individual's attitude toward his therapist. Probable therapeutic response, however, has not been shown to be adequately predictable from any of these criteria of depth of hypnosis. Sufferers have been deeply

Depth of hypnosis

hypnotized in terms of all such criteria and have failed to be relieved of their psychiatric symptoms; others who seem barely affected during hypnotic efforts nevertheless show substantial improvement under hypnotic treatment.

Effect of repeated hypnosis. Initial anxiety or conflict about entering hypnosis generally interferes with an individual's responsiveness. Subsequent improvement of rapport with the hypnotist and growing familiarity with the procedure help many subjects to produce more profound experiences, but each soon reaches a particular plateau at which the kind of phenomena elicited seems to stabilize. Practice beyond this point, however, does tend to increase the speed of response, which may account for the widely held belief that depth of hypnosis continues to improve with practice.

The posthypnotic suggestion often is given that a subject in future will immediately enter a trance on a specified cue. The ease and rapidity with which this can occur in a trained subject should not be taken to mean that he is becoming more susceptible, nor that he cannot resist if he truly wishes to do so.

Undue dependence on the hypnotist does not ordinarily occur in experimental work but has been reported for some therapeutic relationships. Such a response may complicate all forms of therapy but is most likely to occur with lay hypnotists and other individuals who ineptly attempt psychotherapeutic interventions without appropriate training and experience.

Hypnotizability. The stability of one's hypnotic responsiveness seems as great as that of other abilities such as mechanical or verbal skills, and much research has been devoted to the search for personal attributes related to hypnotizability. Early investigators assumed that women enter hypnosis more readily than men, but this has not been borne out in most studies; similarly, hypnotizability is not especially related to intelligence nor to education. There does appear to be a significant relationship with age, ability to respond reaching a peak before puberty, stabilizing in the early adult years, and declining in very old age. Traits popularly characterized as evidence of gullibility are not related to hypnotizability. There is some indication that a history of parentally approved daydreaming, fantasizing, and imaginative play during childhood is associated with increased ability to respond. The extent to which an individual spontaneously becomes absorbed in a play to the point of feeling the emotions portrayed also has some predictive value. There is evidence that hypnotizability is greater among individuals who seem generally well adjusted. Among those with psychiatric disorders, hysterics respond better than others. Most individuals with obsessive-compulsive or schizophrenic symptoms are unresponsive, but even with these difficulties some can enter deep hypnosis.

EVALUATION OF THE APPLICATIONS OF HYPNOSIS

By the 1970s hypnosis had been officially endorsed as a therapeutic method by medical, psychiatric, dental, and psychological associations throughout the world.

Because of the availability of safe and effective anesthetic drugs, hypnosis is used in major surgery only rarely. On the other hand, it has been found most useful in preparing people for anesthesia, enhancing the drug response, and reducing the required dosage. In childbirth it is particularly helpful, since it is effective in alleviating the mother's discomfort while avoiding drug-induced impairment of the child's physiological function. The technique also has been helpful in painful, relatively minor procedures such as changing dressings over severe burns. Hypnosis is highly regarded in the management of otherwise intractable pain, including that of terminal cancer. It is valuable in reducing the widespread fear of dental procedures; the very people whom dentists find most difficult to treat frequently respond best to suggestions. It has also proven useful in such aspects of dentistry as suppressing undesirable gagging reflexes and in helping people adapt to new dentures.

In the area of psychosomatic medicine hypnosis has been used in a variety of ways. Patients have been trained to relax and to carry out, in the absence of the hypnotist, exercises that have had salutary effects on some forms of high blood pressure, headaches, and functional disorders. Specific suggestions have also been used in some of these contexts but tend to have limited applicability compared with more general procedures designed to reduce the patient's tension. Many fascinating isolated case reports of dramatic therapeutic changes induced by hypnosis, especially in dermatology, are in the literature, but overall effectiveness in dermatology has not yet been adequately evaluated. In many instances, the appropriate treatment for psychosomatic difficulties is psychotherapy, in which hypnosis may or may not be included.

The use of hypnosis in psychotherapy. In psychotherapy, hypnosis has been used in a variety of ways. Specific suggestions to relieve troublesome symptoms have limited utility. Those symptoms that may be suppressed with confidence and safety are the ones least likely to be central problems to the patient, and considerable care should be taken in evaluating the nature of the problem before such treatment is undertaken. The use of hypnotic suggestions to change psychological attitudes has been mentioned. The technique of revivifying traumatic events, leading to a cathartic emotional release, was originally employed by Freud and continues to be a useful treatment in relieving neuroses with traumatic onset (see PSYCHONEUROSES), such as those that develop in combat, among individuals with relatively stable prior adjustments. There are a variety of other, more specialized ways in which hypnosis has been employed to help patients understand their own reactions and to become aware of their own feelings. Hypnosis itself is never the treatment, however; rather, it is a technique used in the context of an overall treatment approach. It has been used in modern behaviour therapy, for example, as well as in psychoanalytically oriented approaches. In countries where the Pavlovian school is particularly important, there has been a tendency to employ prolonged hypnotically induced sleep as a way of bringing about curative rest.

General comments about the use of hypnosis in treatment. The induction of hypnosis requires little training and no particular skill, a tape recording often being sufficient. Though the technique and skill of the hypnotist are not totally irrelevant, the personality and motivation of the subject and his interaction with the situation are of paramount importance. Nevertheless, there is an erroneous though widely held belief that individuals capable of inducing hypnosis have some special power or skill that makes them equipped to treat. Congruent with this belief is the view that there is a science of hypnosis.

While an appropriate topic of scientific inquiry, hypnosis is not a science in its own right. On the contrary, it is the task of psychological science to discover how hypnosis can be accounted for by its general laws. While little skill is required to induce hypnosis, considerable training is needed to evaluate whether it is the appropriate treatment technique and, if so, how it should properly be employed. When used in the treatment context, hypnosis should never be employed by individuals who do not have the competence and skill to treat such problems *without the use of hypnosis*. For this reason hypnosis "schools" or "institutes" cannot provide the needed training for individuals lacking the more general scientific and technical qualifications of the healing professions. In most major cities individuals advertise in the classified sections of telephone books as professional hypnotists, offering to treat a wide range of medical and psychological problems. Since the ethical codes of the professions would prevent any physician, psychologist, or dentist from advertising in such a fashion, individuals who consult someone who holds himself out to be a hypnotist should be aware that such a person is extremely unlikely to have the necessary training or skill to treat medical or psychological problems. Improperly used, hypnosis may add to the patient's psychiatric or medical difficulties. Thus, a sufferer of an undiscovered brain tumor may sacrifice his life in the hands of a practitioner who successfully relieves his headache by hypnotic suggestion, thereby delaying needed surgery. Broad diagnostic training and therapeutic skill are indispensable in avoiding the inappropriate and potentially dangerous use of hypnosis.

Abuse of hypnosis

Interrogation and discovery of truth. Hypnosis has not been found reliable in obtaining truth from a reluctant witness. Even if it were possible to induce hypnosis against one's will, it is well documented that the hypnotized individual still can willfully lie. It is of even greater concern that cooperative hypnotized subjects remember distorted versions of actual events and are themselves deceived. When recalled in hypnosis, such false memories are accompanied by strong subjective conviction and outward signs of conviction that are most compelling to almost any observer. Caution and independent verification are essential in such circumstances.

Augmenting performance. Hypnosis used in attempts to increase athletic prowess usually yields equivocal results. Psychological factors clearly affect performance, and under some circumstances one might expect that hypnosis could be effective; nevertheless, it is seriously questioned whether it ought to be employed in competitive athletics. The widespread belief that hypnosis facilitates total recall is an irresistible idea, especially to students about to be examined. As noted earlier, objective evidence unfortunately fails to support this belief; hypnosis has not been particularly effective as an adjunct to memory or recall. Equal or better performance can be obtained by motivating individuals in other ways.

Antisocial uses of hypnosis. Despite many fictional stories about the use of hypnosis to persuade victims to help in criminal acts, no authenticated instance has come to light where hypnosis was successfully employed to force a person to act criminally to the advantage of the hypnotist, in the absence of an intense personal (but non-hypnotic) relationship with the hypnotist, or a pre-existing willingness to behave criminally. The dangers of antisocial use have been greatly exaggerated.

Future directions in hypnosis. The story of hypnosis illustrates errors not infrequent in the history of science in general. As Mesmer was, other theorists are over-ready to extend a concept beyond the limits of its applicability. Critics, with due regard for evidence, expose the error, but, overdoing skepticism, often fail to discern the real grain of truth in the original material. In the long run, progress is achieved by dint of a succession of nearer approximations. At any time, the way new data are handled depends markedly on the state of science at that time.

Full understanding of hypnosis depends on the state of psychological and psychiatric science. There can be no separate science of hypnosis. More particularly, when there are improved techniques of describing and quantifying mental states and subjective experiences, and greater knowledge of the physiology underlying attention and reality-testing, then a more adequate explanatory account of hypnosis will become possible. However, progress in hypnotic research will not await those achievements, but rather will contribute to them, just as hypnotic studies have already contributed insights about unconscious mental processes, about psychological influences in somatic illnesses, and about the powerful effects of expectations on behaviour.

BIBLIOGRAPHY. A classic of historical interest in its emphasis on the psychological character of hypnosis is H. BERNHEIM, *Hypnosis and Suggestion in Psychotherapy* (Eng. trans. 1888, reprinted 1964). Also of historical interest is C.L. HULL, *Hypnotism and Suggestibility: An Experimental Approach* (1933), the first major systematic effort to study hypnosis in the psychological laboratory. On techniques, a comprehensive treatment of induction and therapeutic application, supported by detailed illustrations, is L.R. WOLBERG, *Medical Hypnosis*, vol. 1, *The Principles of Hypnotherapy*, vol. 2, *The Practice of Hypnotherapy* (1948). A current account of experimental studies of hypnosis, including a substantial amount of original research, is E.R. HILGARD, *Hypnotic Susceptibility* (1965). M.T. ORNE, "Hypnosis, Motivation and the Ecological Validity of the Psychological Experiment," a paper in the *Nebraska Symposium on Motivation* (1970), summarizes empirical work, documenting both the limitations of hypnosis and some of its unique attributes. No single volume adequately covers theorizing about hypnosis. M.M. GILL and M. BRENMAN, *Hypnosis and Related States* (1959), presents a psychoanalytically oriented theory of hypnosis; T.X. BARBER, *Hypnosis: A Scientific Approach* (1969), a skeptical view. Contributions of other theorists, especially those of White, Kubie, Sarbin, and Erickson are included in the collection of basic readings: R.E. SHOR and M.T. ORNE (eds.), *The Nature of Hypnosis* (1965).

(M.T.O./A.G.H.)

1. What would you do if you didn't understand the word "stimuli" or any other terms in the article?

2. This article is subdivided into how many sections? _____

3. How can you identify a subdivision?

4. What are the subdivisions here?

5. Are there any other clues on the page that identify subtopics or issues?

6. Can you find a cross reference, that is, another subject in the encyclopedia that you could consult for additional information? What?

7. Which book was "the first major systematic effort to study hypnosis in the psychological laboratory?"

8. Someone wrote this article. Where would you normally expect to find the author's name? What do you find at the end of this article?

    (M.T.O./A.G.H.) are the authors, and to find out who they are, you have to do some detective work, by consulting the first volume, the *Propaedia*, of the Encyclopedia, which has the "Guide to the Britannica," with information about authors and other features.
      M.T.O. turns out to be M.T. Orne, who has listed one of his own articles in his bibliography.
      It is your responsibility to translate these abbreviations into the author's name if you are actually going to use an article like this in the preparation of your report.

Specialized Encyclopedias and Other Reference Books

Your next step is to consult at least one specialized encyclopedia or reference book.

As a glance through the reference section in a library shows, there are specialized reference books about almost everything. For instance:

The Official Encyclopedia of Football
Encyclopedia of Business Information Sources
Pictorial Encyclopedia of Fishes

How can you tell which you need? There are two shortcuts to help you find the most useful specialized reference book for your project:

1. *Reference Books: A Brief Guide for Students and Other Users of the Library*, published by the Enoch Pratt Free Library, and often referred to as "Enoch Pratt." This is the guide that reference librarians themselves rely on, a trade secret that anyone can use.

   It is an annotated list of specialized reference books (dictionaries, encyclopedias, yearbooks, maps, etc.) that are also organized under subjects. If you are doing a paper on American history, for instance, you can look up that subject in "Enoch Pratt" and find out which standard references are available in this field. The comments are often very helpful, alerting you to special aspects of the text.

2. A librarian, especially reference librarians. They know all about reference books, are usually delighted when anyone else expresses an interest in them, and are eager to help you. Just ask.

Not all specialized reference books are called "Encyclopedias," but they all function the same way: to give you condensed information as efficiently as possible.

Encyclopedias and dictionaries are, of course, arranged alphabetically. So are many other reference books. But if you want to consult one with another arrangement, be prepared to check the index at the back of the volume or the Table of Contents at the front to find the pages that will be useful to you.

These specialized reference books are collected in a special section of the library, and they usually don't circulate, which means they have to be used in the library.

Hint: Often a good investment at this stage is photocopying the few pages on your topic in these encyclopedias so you can have your own copy.

Here is just a sampling of some of the standard specialized reference books:

ART

The Britannica Encyclopaedia of American Art
Encyclopedia of the Arts
Encyclopedia of World Art
McGraw-Hill Dictionary of Art
Oxford Companion to Art
Praeger Encyclopedia of Art

ARCHITECTURE

The Architecture Book: A Companion to the Art and Science of Architecture
Dictionary of Architecture and Construction
Historic Architecture Sourcebook

BIOETHICS

Encyclopedia of Bioethics

BIOGRAPHY

Dictionary of American Biography
Dictionary of National Biography
McGraw-Hill Encyclopedia of World Biography
Who's Who

CURRENT ISSUES AND POPULAR CULTURE

Editorial Research Reports
Handbook of American Popular Culture

DRAMA

McGraw-Hill Encyclopedia of World Drama
The Oxford Companion to the Theatre
The Reader's Encyclopedia of World Drama

ECONOMICS

Encyclopedia of American Economic History

EDUCATION

Encyclopedia of Education
International Encyclopedia of Higher Education

ENVIRONMENT

McGraw-Hill Encyclopedia of Environmental Sciences

FILM

The Film Encyclopedia
The Oxford Companion to Film

FOREIGN RELATIONS

Encyclopedia of American Foreign Policy
Encyclopedia of the Third World

HISTORY

Dictionary of American History
Dictionary of the History of Ideas

LITERATURE

Encyclopedia of World Literature in the 20th Century
A Handbook to Literature
Oxford Companion to American Literature
Oxford Companion to English Literature
The Reader's Encyclopedia

MINORITIES AND ETHNIC GROUPS

Harvard Encyclopedia of American Ethnic Groups
Negro Almanac: The Afro-American

MUSIC

The New Grove Dictionary of Music and Musicians

PAINTING

Encyclopedia of Painting: Painters and Paintings of the World from Prehistoric
   Times to the Present Day

PHILOSOPHY

Dictionary of the History of Ideas
The Encyclopedia of Philosophy
Philosophical Dictionary

PHOTOGRAPHY

Encyclopedia of Photography

PSYCHOLOGY

Encyclopedia of Psychology
International Encyclopedia of Psychiatry, Psychology, Psychoanalysis, and
   Neurology

SCIENCE

Encyclopedia of Chemical Technology
McGraw-Hill Encyclopedia of Science and Technology
Van Nostrand's Scientific Encyclopedia

SOCIAL SCIENCES

International Encyclopedia of Population
International Encyclopedia of the Social Sciences

THEOLOGY AND RELIGION

Encyclopedia of Religion and Ethics

WOMEN

Nature of Women: An Encyclopedia and Guide to the Literature
Women's Action Almanac

ZOOLOGY

Grzimek's Animal Life Encyclopedia

ASSIGNMENT

Before going further with your own research paper, complete the following
worksheet on using encyclopedias. If possible, try to work with a specialized

reference book. For example, if you were planning to write a report on some aspect of weather, as well as consulting L. P. Smith's article in the *Encyclopaedia Britannica,* you might want to look up one of these:

The Weather Almanac
Van Nostrand's Scientific Encyclopedia
The Climate Advisor
McGraw-Hill Dictionary of Scientific and Technical Terms
Traveling Weatherwise in the U.S.A.

MAKING BIBLIOGRAPHY CARDS

You are beginning to prepare a report and, like M.T. Orne when he was preparing his report for the *Encyclopaedia Britannica*, you will need to keep track of your reading and your research.

To do that you will make up two sorts of cards:

1. Bibliography cards—these record publication information about your sources.
2. Note cards—these record ideas and facts that you want to borrow from these sources.

Make them on two different size cards to keep them separate.

Are Cards Really Necessary?

No, but . . .

Let's talk about the bibliography cards first. Every research paper must have a formal bibliography, which is a list of the sources that were consulted in preparing the paper. The list must be arranged alphabetically using the author's *last* name. If you put this information on cards as you go along, then you can simply shuffle the cards into the correct order and write out the bibliography. The alternative is to put the information on a sheet of paper. If you use just one side of the paper, then you can cut it up and shuffle the slips of paper into alphabetical order.

Note cards are more important because they will help improve the organization of your paper and prevent you from writing a paper that is just a series of separate summaries. We will say more about this in the next chapter.

Bibliography Card for an Encyclopedia

List in this order (in a column):

Author's name reversed. Brackets indicate that you are adding something to the original to get a name.
Subject within quotation marks. Quotation marks indicate that you are referring to an excerpt of a larger publication.
Name of encyclopedia underlined. Underlining indicates that it is the title of a publication that stands on its own.
The year of the edition you are using (not the number of the edition). You can find the year in several places, but the handiest is often the back of the title page at the beginning of the particular volume you are using.

Here is a sample bibliography card for an encyclopedia:

```
S[mith], L. P. "Weather Lore"
Encyclopaedia Britannica
1975
```

Notice that the volume number is not necessary. Page reference is only needed occasionally—when you footnote one page of a multipage article.

LOCATING BOOKS

Most students know how the card catalog works in a library, and many have already used the periodical indexes, but not so many can use these resources *efficiently.*

Doing a research paper is a long project, so you don't want to waste any time. This section will explain how to get the most help from these resources in the shortest time; it will also give you practice on some more worksheets and exercises.

Alternatives to Card Catalogs: Microfiches or On-Line Computer Systems

Some libraries no longer catalog their book collections in drawers of cards. Instead, this information is recorded on celluloid microfiches or on computer programs. You need the special equipment of a machine called a "microfiche reader" to magnify a microfiche so you can use it. If your library has an online computerized system, you access that data at a computer terminal. If your library uses either of these alternatives to a traditional card catalogs, a librarian will explain how to use it.

The equipment is different, but the cataloging principles are the same as for a card catalog. Therefore, the information that follows in this book about conventional card catalogs is just as applicable to these different systems. Whether the data about a library's book collection are recorded on paper index cards in drawers, or on celluloid microfiches that need to be projected like film, or on electrical impulses in a computer program, the organizing principles are the same.

How the Card Catalog Can Help You

The card catalog is a guide to the books in a library. Each book on the shelves is arranged in a particular order. Each has its own unique code number (a "call number"), and each is represented in the card catalog by a card. In fact, each book has several cards, which are all arranged in alphabetical order, usually under three headings:

Authors
Titles
Subjects

Note: The author of a book can be a person or an organization. If the author is a person, the author card will be filed alphabetically under the author's last name. The card for a corporate author will be filed alphabetically under the first main word in its name. Here are two author cards, one for a corporate author, the other for a personal author.

1. *A corporate author card:*

```
Ref
Z          University of Chicago Press.
253           The Chicago manual of style : for
.U69       authors, editors, and copywriters. --
1982       13th ed., rev. and expanded. -- Chicago
           : University of Chicago Press, 1982.
              ix, 737 p. : ill. ; 24 cm.
              Rev. ed. of: A manual of style. 12th
           ed., rev. c1969.
              Bibliography: p. 685-694.
              Includes index.
              c.1 127737


              1. Printing, Practical--Style
           manuals.  2. Authorship--Handbooks,
           manuals, etc.  I. Title


      25 JAN 83     8283180  CTWWat        82-2832
```

2. *A personal author card:*

```
LB2369   Turabian, Kate L.
T8          A manual for writers of term papers,
1973     theses, and dissertations / Kate L.
DOCS     Turabian. -- 4th ed. -- Chicago :
         University of Chicago Press, 1973.
            viii, 216 p. ; 22 cm.

            First published in 1937 under title:
         A manual for writers of dissertations.
            Includes index.
            ISBN 0-226-81620-6.   ISBN 0-226-
         81621-4 pbk.


            [1. Dissertations, Academic.   2.
         Report writing.]   I. Title.
AT              800309      CU
L000892         /KNL       C*        14480433
                           73-77792
```

Here are two other card catalog cards for this same book by Kate L. Turabian, which is entitled *A Manual for Writers of Term Papers, Theses, and Dissertations.* How are they different? Why do you think it is necessary to provide so many cards for one book?

3.

```
          DISSERTATIONS, ACADEMIC.

LB2369   Turabian, Kate L.
T8            A manual for writers of term papers,
1973       theses, and dissertations / Kate L.
DOCS       Turabian. -- 4th ed. -- Chicago :
           University of Chicago Press, 1973.
              viii, 216 p. ; 22 cm.

              First published in 1937 under title:
           A manual for writers of dissertations.
           Includes index.
              ISBN 0-226-81620-6.    ISBN 0-226-
           81621-4 pbk.


              [1. Dissertations, Academic.   2.
           Report writing.]    I. Title.
SU                      800309      CU
L001535                 /KNL        C*        14480433
                                    73-77792
```

4.

```
          A manual for writers of term papers,
          theses, and dissertations.

LB2369   Turabian, Kate L.
T8            A manual for writers of term papers,
1973       theses, and dissertations / Kate L.
DOCS       Turabian. -- 4th ed. -- Chicago :
           University of Chicago Press, 1973.
              viii, 216 p. ; 22 cm.

              First published in 1937 under title:
           A manual for writers of dissertations.
           Includes index.
              ISBN 0-226-81620-6.    ISBN 0-226-
           81621-4 pbk.


              [1. Dissertations, Academic.   2.
           Report writing.]    I. Title.
AT                      800309      CU
L001168                 /KNL        C*        14480433
                                    73-77792
```

The information on the catalog card can help you find the book by giving you the book's call number, which is a code symbol for its place on the shelves. Most libraries now use what is called the LC classification (for "Library of Congress"). It starts with letters and arranges books alphabetically in rows. The old system, "Dewey," is a decimal number system, arranging books numerically from 1 to 999.

Here are abbreviated classification schemes for both systems.

Abbreviated Library of Congress Classification Scheme

A	General Works
B	Philosophy, Psychology, Religion
C	History: Auxiliary sciences (Archaeology, Numismatics, Genealogy, etc.)
D	History: General and Old World
E	History: American and U.S., general
F	History: American and U.S., local
G	Geography, Anthropology, Folklore, Dance, Sports
H	Social Sciences: Sociology, Business, and Economics
J	Political Science
K	Law
L	Education
M	Music
N	Fine Arts: Art and Architecture
P	Philology and Literature
Q	Science
R	Medicine
S	Agriculture
T	Technology
U	Military Science
V	Naval Science
Z	Bibliography and Library Science

Abbreviated Dewey Decimal Classification Scheme

000–099	General Works
100–199	Philosophy and Psychology
200–299	Religion
300–399	Social Sciences
400–499	Language
500–599	Pure Sciences
600–699	Technology
700–799	The Arts
800–899	Literature
900–999	History

EXERCISE

1. Is this call number an LC number or a Dewey Decimal number? How can you tell?

   LB
   2369
   .T8
   1973

2. What subject does this Dewey Decimal call number represent?

   917.91
   W939

3. Under what LC classification letter would you expect to find a book entitled *Adventures in the Apache Country: A Tour Through Arizona and Sonora, 1864.*

4. What Dewey Decimal call numbers are the equivalent of the following LC classification letters?

   D _____
   P _____
   N _____
   B _____

EXERCISE

Look at the last card catalog card (Card #4) for Turabian's *Manual* and answer these questions:

1. Was this card filed under author, title, or subject?

2. When was this edition published?

3. How many other editions have been published previously?

4. When was the first edition published?

5. How long is this book?

6. Where was it published?

7. Who is the publisher?

Using Your Imagination

Often you have to guess what subjects to look under in the catalog, another reason why starting with an encyclopedia is helpful.

For instance, if you looked under "Weather" and didn't find anything that looked useful, you might have to look under something else, like "Climate" or "Rain" or "Meteorology."

EXERCISE

Suggest another subject under which you might find books listed for each of the following:

Example: Weather   *Climate, Meteorology, Rain*

1.   Transportation

2.   Musicians

3.   Social conflict

4.   Solar system

5.   Water supply

6.   Bread

7.   Automobiles

8.   Hypnotism

9.   Law

10.   Public Health

11.   Saints

12.   Songs

13.   Travel

14.   Labor unions

15.   Flower gardening

Hint: If you cannot think of alternative subject headings, you can consult a specialized reference book: *Library of Congress Subject Headings.*

Using the Library of Congress Subject Headings

If the term you have in mind *is* a subject heading, it will be printed in boldface type, for example, **Hypnotism; Hypnotism and crime.**

In the example, below, notice that related subject headings are suggested.

"sa" means " see also."
"xx" means "related but more general subject headings."
"See" means "look somewhere else for the right subject heading for this topic."

Hypnotism *(BF1111-1156; Hypnotism and crime, HV6110; Psychiatry, RC490-499)*
  sa Animal magnetism
    Crystal-gazing
    Forensic hypnotism
    Hypnotic susceptibility
    Hypnotism and crime
    Magnetic healing
    Mental suggestion
    Mesmerism
    Mind and body
    Personality, Disorders of
    Psychoanalysis
    Reincarnation therapy
    Rigidity (Psychology)
    Stanford hypnotic susceptibility scale
    Subconsciousness
    Therapeutics, Suggestive
  x Autosuggestion
    Braidism
    Hypnosis
  xx Animal magnetism
    Clairvoyance
    Medicine
    Mental suggestion
    Mesmerism
    Mind and body
    Mind-reading
    Personality, Disorders of
    Psychical research
    Psychoanalysis
    Psychology, Physiological
    Second sight
    Somnambulism
    Subconsciousness
    Thought-transference
    Trance

— Jurisprudence   *(Indirect)*
      Here are entered works on the legal
      aspects of hypnotism. Works on
      hypnosis as an investigative tech-
      nique are entered under the heading
      Forensic hypnotism.
  sa Hypnotism and crime
   x Hypnotism and law
     Law and hypnotism
  xx Hypnotism and crime
     Psychology, Forensic
  Note under Forensic hypnotism
— Sounds
  xx Sounds
— Therapeutic use
  xx Therapeutics, Suggestive
Hypnotism and crime
  sa Hypnotism—Jurisprudence
   x Crime and hypnotism
  xx Crime and criminals
     Criminal psychology
     Hypnotism
     Hypnotism—Jurisprudence
Hypnotism and law
  See Hypnotism—Jurisprudence
Hypnotism in dentistry
  xx Anesthesia in dentistry
     Dentistry
Hypnotism in obstetrics
  xx Anesthesia in obstetrics
     Obstetrics
Hypnotism in surgery   *(RD85.H9)*
  xx Anesthesia
     Surgery
Hypoacoustic children
  See Children, Deaf
Hypoactivity
  See Hypokinesia
Hypocalcemia
  xx Calcium metabolism disorders
Hypochlorinators
  xx Water—Purification
Hypocholesteremic agents
  See Anticholesteremic agents
Hypochondria   *(RC552.H8)*
   x Hypochondriasis
  xx Insanity
     Psychology, Pathological
     Early works to 1900   *(BC552.H8)*
Hypochondria in literature
  xx Anxiety in literature
     Fear in literature

BIBLIOGRAPHY CARD FOR A BOOK

Six items of information are contained in this order (in a column):

Author's name reversed (omit if none).
Title of book underlined. Capitalize first letters of major words, except *a, an, the.*
Place of publication.
Publisher.
Date of publication.
Add the call number for your own convenience.

Example

```
REF
LB
2369      Turabian, Kate L.
.T8       A Manual for Writers of Term Papers,
1973            Theses, and Dissertations
          Chicago
          University of Chicago Press
          1973
```

EXERCISE

Make proper bibliography cards for each of these two books:

1. A book entitled *Weather* by Philip D. Thompson, Robert O'Brien, and the editors of *Life.* It was published in 1965 by Time, Inc. in New York.
2. A book entitled *Weather Proverbs and Paradoxes* by W. J. Humphreys published by Williams and Wilkins Co. in Baltimore in 1923.

PERIODICAL INDEXES

The periodical indexes keep track of which magazine articles have been published on what subjects, when, by whom, and where. Periodical indexes do *not* print the articles themselves. But they do give you all the information you need to find them.

Some indexes cover articles in general magazines, the kind you find on newsstands, for example, *The Readers' Guide to Periodical Literature*. Other indexes, like the *Social Sciences Index*, the *Humanities Index*, or the *Education Index*, are more specialized and cover articles in academic journals. We will demonstrate how to use these indexes with examples from *Readers' Guide* because it can be found in public, as well as college, libraries.

Each index consists of several volumes, with one volume added each year. Supplements keep the present year's listings up to date.

The indexes are arranged alphabetically with cross references, like card catalogs, under subject and author (but not titles). Their information is abbreviated.

Here are two entries from *Readers' Guide*, the first a subject entry and the second an author entry.

```
WEATHER
     Cloud seeding:  one success in 35 years.  A. S. Kerr
        il Science 217:  519-21 Ag 6'82

WEEMS, David
     Build a bike from junk.  il Mother Earth News 76:
        88-91  Jl/Ag '82
```

Readers' Guide to Periodical Literature *Copyright © 1982 by the H. W. Wilson Company. Material reproduced by permission of the publisher.*

The entries are easy to understand once you are familiar with the way information is listed.

1. The first item in an entry is always the title. This is true for subject and author entries.
2. The second item is usually the author's name. There are two exceptions. The author's name will not be repeated if the article is listed under his name. If the author's name did not appear in the magazine, it will not be given in the entry.
3. Abbreviations, such as "il" (to indicate that the article is illustrated), sometimes appear. Every volume of an index will have a page at the beginning that translates these abbreviations for you.
4. The name of the periodical in which the article appeared is frequently abbreviated. The beginning of every volume has a page that lists all the periodicals that are indexed and shows the abbreviation. You must give the full title in your bibliography, so be sure to translate the abbreviation.
5. Immediately after the name of the magazine is a series of numbers. The number before the colon is the volume number, which is important because all the issues of a particular year are bound together and given a volume number. Following the colon are the pages on which the article will be found.
6. The final item is the date of the issue in which the article appeared. Again, you will find abbreviations that you must translate for your bibliography.

Hypertension—Nutritional aspects—*Continued*
Hypotensive effect of fasting: possible involvement of the sympathetic nervous system and endogenous opiates [hypertensive rats] D. Einhorn and others. bibl f il Science 217:727-9 Ag 20 '82
Hyphomycetes, Aquatic. See Aquatic fungi
Hypnotics
See also
Flurazepam

Why pills are becoming passé. Bus Week p 134 O 11 '82
Hypnotism
Research through deception [P. Zimbardo's study of hearing loss and paranoia causes ethical stir] M. M. Hunt. il por N Y Times Mag p66-7+ S 12 '82
To trust, perchance to buy [successful sales techniques are form of hypnotism] D. J. Moine. il Psychol Today 16:50-2+ Ag '82
Hypoglycemia
So you think you have low blood sugar. . . W. A. Nolen. il McCalls 109:44+ S '82
Hypothalamic hormones
Central regulation of intestinal motility by somatostatin and cholecystokinin octapeptide. L. Bueno and J.-P. Ferre. bibl f il Science 216:1427-9 Je 25 '82
Hypothalamic neurons. See Nerve cells
Hypothalamus
Transplantation
See Brain—Transplantation
Hypoxanthine guanine phosphoribosyltransferase gene. See Genes
Hysteria
An epidemic in the works [epidemic or mass hysteria] W. Herbert. il Sci News 122:188-90 S 18 '82

I love you [film] See Motion picture reviews—Single works
I. M. Cookie Company
The fleet-footed monster cookie. M. Tuthill. il por Nations Bus 70:66-7 Ag '82
Iacocca, Lee
How to cut interest rates. por Newsweek 100:6 Ag 16 '82
about
A star is born. il por Forbes 130:79 Ag 16 '82 •
IARC. See International Agency for Research on Cancer
Iatrogenic diseases
Catheter infections: tripled death risk [catheter-caused urinary tract infections; study by Richard Platt and others] J. Arehart-Treichel. Sci News 122:182 S 18 '82
IBH Holding
The bargain hunter nibbling at Harvester. D. B. Tinnin. il pors Fortune 106:174-6+ Ag 23 '82
Ibsen, Henrik
Ghosts. Reviews
N Y il 15:69-70 S 13 '82. J. Simon •
Nation 235:316 O 2 '82. R. Gilman •
New Yorker 58:155 S 13 '82. B. Gill •
Newsweek 100:89 S 13 '82 •
Time il 120:102 S 13 '82. J. Cocks
IC Industries, Inc.
All things in time. L. Gross. il por map Forbes 129:126+ Je 21 '82
ICAO. See International Civil Aviation Organization
Ice
See also
Icebergs
Polar regions
Ancient ice there for the taking? [Allen Hills. Antarctica; work of Ian Whillans and William A. Cassidy] Sci News 122:76 Jl 31 '82
Polynas surrounded by ice and mystery [enclosed area of unfrozen water surrounded by ice] C. Simon. Sci News 122:183 S 18 '82
Ice ages. See Glacial epochs
Ice cream, ices, etc.
About making ice cream. L. Lloyd. South Living 17:178 Jl '82
Easy ice-cream treats. il Good Housekeep 195:176-7 Ag '82
Food [herbal and fruit sorbets] H. Hecht. Vogue 172:166+ Ag '82
Frappes and slushes. M. Gorman. il Org Gard 29:85 Jl '82
Frozen desserts. L. S. Pappas. il Gourmet 42:20-1+ Jl '82
Gelateria at home. il Sunset 169:86-7 S '82
Ice cream delights for young and old. il Ebony 37:96+ Jl '82
Ice cream with coffee bean crunch. il Sunset 169:130 Jl '82
Icy slush. . .Italians call it granita. il Sunset 168:190 Je '82
Italian fruit ices. . .sorbettos. il Sunset 169:176 S '82

The scoop on ice cream. C. E. Trunzo. il Money 11:109-10+ Ag '82
Spumoni elegante. il Good Housekeep 195:98 Ag '82
Tartufo or torte. . .chocolate inside and out. il Sunset 169:122-3 Jl '82
These frozen desserts begin with ice cream. il South Living 17:130-1 Ag '82
What a treat it is: an ice cream social. il Redbook 159:104-5+ Ag '82
Ice cream industry
Pushcart plutocrat [R. LaMotta's Chipwich] il por Money 11:27-8 Jl '82
The scoop on ice cream sales. il Bus Week p73 S 20 '82
Ice cream stores
America's coolest, sweetest, yummiest ice cream parlors. J. Mariani. il Seventeen 41:318-19+ Ag '82
Gelato explosion. . . more than a dozen *gelaterias* in the Bay Area. il Sunset 169:66+ S '82
Chain and franchise operations
The scoop on ice cream sales. il Bus Week p73 S 20 '82
Ice industry
Run a rural ice delivery service. W. L. Stewart. il Mother Earth News 76:54-7 Jl/Ag '82
Ice skaters. See Skaters
Icebergs
Another iceberg try [towing schemes] il Pop Mech 158:173 S '82
Iced tea. See Tea (Beverage)
IDA. See International Development Association
Idaho
See also
Craters of the Moon National Monument
Ideal states. See Utopias
Ideal Toy Corp.
A patent puzzle over Rubik's Cube. il Bus Week p26 Ag 2 '82
Identification
See also
Automobile parts—Identification

He has the right to remain silent, but Seattle's mystery forger takes it to extremes [refusal to reveal identity] B. Shaw. il People Wkly 18:30 Jl 26 '82
Identification cards, certificates, etc.
The heart chart [medical information card containing a copy of an EKG] M. Rosenberg. il McCalls 109:48 Ag '82
Should you carry a medical ID? H. T. Leavy. il Good Housekeep 195:191 Ag '82
Identification tags, bracelets, etc.
In an emergency [medical identification] B. Weinhouse. Ladies Home J 99:45 S '82
IFR landing. See Airplanes—Landing
IIASA. See International Institute for Applied Systems Analysis
Iizuka, Akio
The spirit of harmonious competition. il Technol Rev 85:53-4 Ag/S '82
Iker, Sam
The promise and peril of pesticides. il Int Wildl 12:14-18 Jl/Ag '82
Iliffe, Thomas M.
Argonaut: octopus in a parchment shell [with biographical sketch] il Sea Front 28:224-8, 252 Jl/Ag '82
Illinois
See also
Colleges and universities—Illinois
Historic houses, sites, etc.—Illinois
Music festivals—Illinois
Opera—Illinois
Police—Illinois
Traffic regulations—Illinois
Unemployment—Illinois
Politics and government
Adlai III, part 2. il Time 120:11 S 20 '82
The 'wimp factor' [A. E. Stevenson race against Gov. J. R. Thompson] M. Reese. il pors Newsweek 100:42 O 4 '82
Religious institutions and affairs
Ministering to the unemployed [program of First Baptist Church in Evanston] R. V. Thompson. Christ Century 99:888-90 S 1-8 '82
Illinois Central Gulf RR. Co.
All things in time. L. Gross. il por map Forbes 129:126+ Je 21 '82
Illiteracy
Statistics
Illiteracy in the United States. W. V. Grant. il Am Educ 18:inside back cover Ag/S '82
Underdeveloped areas
See Underdeveloped areas—Illiteracy
Illustration
The art of James McMullan: a psychological imperative. R. DeNeve. il por Am Artist 46:58-63+ Jl '82

A typical page from the *Readers' Guide* to *Periodical Literature* appears on the preceding page. Study it and then do the exercise that follows.

EXERCISE

1. Does this page list any magazine articles about iced tea?

    a. Where would you look for articles about iced tea?

    b. Why do you think the heading "Tea" has the subheading (Beverage) after it?

    c. What other subheadings for "Tea" might there possibly be?

2. Iker, Sam. This is an author entry. What subject heading would give you exactly the same information about Iker's article in *International Wildlife*?

3. What is the title of the article about chain and franchise operations of ice cream stores?

    a. Is the author of this article identified?

    b. On what page or pages of *Business Week* did the article appear?

    c. Is a volume identified for this issue?

    d. What is its date of issue?

    e. Does this article have any pictures or illustrations?

4. What is the title of the article about Lee Iacocca? Does this article have a picture of him?

5. What is the title of the article written by Lee Iacocca?

6. What subject headings could you look under for articles about Illinois?

    a. Where would you look if you wanted to find an article about North-western University in Evanston, Illinois?

    b. What are the two subheadings under Illinois?

7. What is the title of the article about a program operated by the First Baptist Church in Evanston, Illinois?

    a. Who wrote this article?

    b. In what volume of *Christian Century* did this article appear?

    c. What was its date of issue?

    d. On what page or pages did it appear?

8. If you were looking for a recipe for making ice cream at home, which of these articles would you consult?

    "The Scoop on Ice Cream"
    "Frozen Desserts"
    "Easy Ice-Cream Treats"

    Explain your choice.

9. Can you find an article which might be even better if you wanted a recipe for making ice cream at home? Explain your choice.

SAMPLE BIBLIOGRAPHY CARD FOR AN ARTICLE

Six items are listed in this order:

Author's name reversed.
Title of article within quotation marks, capitalizing first letter of each word except
  a, and, the, and *prepositions.*
Complete title of magazine itself, underlined.
Volume number.
Date of issue.
Inclusive pages of the article.

Remember to capitalize first letters of major words in the title (ignore *the, and, a,* and *prepositions*).

Example:

Hypnotism
See also
  Forensic hypnotism

Hypnosis: put your mind power to work. S. D.
  Bryant. Essence 12:52+ Ap '82
Research through deception [P. Zimbardo's study
  of hearing loss and paranoia causes ethical
  stir] M. M. Hunt. il por N Y Times Mag p66-
  7+ S 12 '82
To trust, perchance to buy [successful sales
  techniques are form of hypnotism] D. J.
  Moine. il Psychol Today 16:50-2+ Ag '82

Police use
Hypnosis: guilty of fraud? [unreliable memory
  of witnesses; study by Martin T. Orne] Sci
  News 121:42 Ja 16 '82

Therapeutic use
Hypnosis can increase antibodies [increase in
  lymphocyte count; research by Howard R.
  Hall] USA Today 110:8 Je '82
Sci-fi images aid hypnosis [therapy for chil-
  dren; work of Bryan Carter and Gary El-
  kins] Sci Dig 90:91 N '82
Spellbinders [teaching tales of M. Erickson] por
  Psychol Today 16:39-42+ F '82

Moine, D.J.

"To Trust, Perchance to Buy"

Psychology Today

volume 16

August 1982

pp. 50-52

EXERCISE

Make proper bibliography cards for each of the following items from *Readers' Guide to Periodical Literature:*

1. Weather forecasts: fair, gradual clearing, rising accuracy. Changing T 32: 45-7 F 78
2. Tired of the weather bureau? Try the Old Farmer's Almanac. M. Grosswirth Sci Digest 80: 69 S 76
3. If a horse yawns, rain is coming. D. Anderson Natur Hist 84: 104-10 N 75
4. Forecast for forecasting: cloudy. A. Anderson NY Times Mag 10: 11+ D 29 74
5. How to forecast your own weather. I. Ross Mech Ill 70: 16+ May 74
6. Build your own weather monitor. J. Dillon Motor B & S 134: 70 D 74

Other One-Step Indexes

Readers' Guide is called a one-step index because using it involves only one step: looking up a subject heading or author entry. Any relevant articles are identified immediately.

College students also depend on other, specialized one-step periodical indexes. Here are some of the most widely used ones:

Social Science Index
Humanities Index
Education Index
Applied Science and Technology Index
Business Periodicals Index
Public Affairs Information Service Bulletin

These specialized indexes work exactly the same way as *Readers' Guide.*

ABSTRACTS

Using these indexes involves two steps to get from the author or subject heading to information about specific articles. This procedure is more complicated, but there is an additional benefit. Along the way you also get not only a bibliographical citation identifying the article and source, but also a short description or brief summary of its contents. Consequently, you can often weed out unsuitable articles and save time. An example of a two-step index is *Psychological Abstracts*, but college students rely on many others, including, for example:

Women's Studies Abstracts
Sociological Abstracts
Food Science and Technology Abstracts
Computer and Control Abstracts

The Two-Step Procedure

Step One.   Look up your topic under an appropriate subject heading in an *index* volume. Find the number for the abstract of a suitable article. This number is *not* a page number. Each abstract has its own number. Here is an example from *Psychological Abstracts*:

Hypnosis [See Also Autohypnosis]

suggestive nature of trance experience & future of hypnosis as "shared delusion", 9693

Step Two.   Look up the abstract number in a separate volume. The abstract will give you a summary of the article. It will also refer you to the original source of the article, which you can then consult if it looks promising.

9693. **Gibbons, Don E.** (Allentown Coll of St Francis De Sales) **Hypnosis as a trance state: The future of a shared delusion.** *Bulletin of the British Society of Experimental & Clinical Hypnosis,* 1982(Apr), No 5, 1–4. —Argues that unless the subjective nature of trance experience is fully appreciated, the relationship between suggestor and S may itself take on some of the aspects of a shared delusional system, with both believing in the objective reality of the hypnotic trance and of its supposed "properties." If the true potentials of the human imagination are to be fully realized, it is necessary that trance experience be recognized for what it is: an experience rather than an objectively identified "state" with a fixed set of physiological and mental correlates. If the experience of hypnosis implies to a sufficiently hypnotic S that he/she either will or will not be amnesic, these expectations tend to function as self-fulfilling prophecies unless such expectations are countered by explicit suggestions to the contrary. (9 ref) —*C. P. Landry.*

Summary

The following are steps in the process of identifying and finding an article on a particular subject in a periodical in the library.

1. Is there a specialized periodical index, besides *Reader's Guide,* that I could consult? Which periodical index is most appropriate for my subject?

    Example: Subject—legal aspects of hypnotism
    Periodical index—*Public Affairs Information Service Bulletin (PAIS)*

2. What subject heading should I use to look for articles on this subject?

    Example: legal aspects of hypnotism? In *PAIS: HYPNOTISM, FORENSIC*

3. What articles on my research subject look as though they will contain useful information:

    HYPNOTISM

    Legal aspects

    The admissibility of testimony influenced by hypnosis. Va Law R 67:1203-33 S '81

    HYPNOTISM, FORENSIC

    Alderman, Eric M. and Joseph A. Barrette. Hypnosis on trial: a practical perspective on the application of forensic hypnosis in criminal cases. *Criminal Law Bul* 18:5-37 Ja/F '82

    Copyright © 1982 by PAIS Bulletin *and reprinted by their permission.*

4. What is the complete bibliographical citation for the article I want to read?
5. In what periodical will I find this article? or What is the full unabbreviated title of the periodical in which I will find this article? (Use the list of abbreviations at the front of the index volume.)

    Example: *Va Law R = Virginia Law Review*

6. How is this abbreviated information translated to a bibliography card?

    > "The Admissibility of Testimony
    >   Influenced by Hypnosis"
    >
    > Virginia Law Review
    >
    > volume 67
    >
    > September 1981
    >
    > pp. 1203-33

NEWSPAPERS AND OTHER SOURCES

The *New York Times*

For current or very recent information, you may need to consult a newspaper. The *New York Times* is one of the most important and useful newspaper sources because it covers national and international news, as well as local city and state news. It also gives complete transcripts and texts of important speeches and documents.

To find a useful newspaper article on your topic, consult subject headings in the *New York Times Index,* which arranges references to specific articles chronologically as they appear during a particular year and provides a brief description of them.

Here is an example from the 1982 volume:

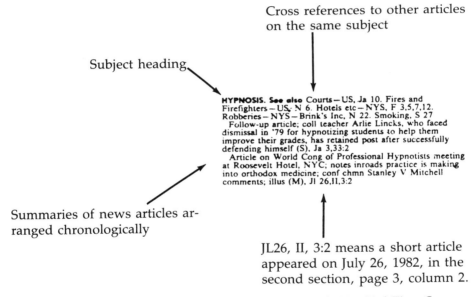

From the New York Times Index *1982 Copyright © 1982 by The New York Times Company. Reprinted by permission.*

Facts on File

This reference is just what it says—a looseleaf arrangement of important up-to-date facts.

Gallup Poll Reports

Results and interpretations of this well-known survey are available in report form.

Summary of Information Sources in the Library

1. Books—card catalog
2. Magazine articles—indexes and abstracts
3. Newspaper articles—indexes
4. Pamphlets—file cabinets
5. Librarians
6. Interlibrary loan—just that. If your library doesn't have a book, your librarian will arrange to get it for you from another library.
7. *Facts on File*
8. Gallup poll reports

There are many other sources of information in the library. Everybody has favorites and they vary slightly from library to library, but the ones listed above are the old reliables for college students.

Here is a flow chart diagram which outlines steps in a research strategy for locating library information:

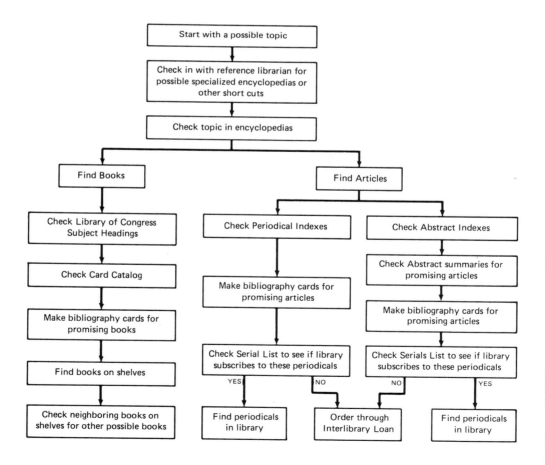

EXERCISE

A student who was working on the subject of "Health Insurance" could find these references to printed material. How could this student decide which sources looked most promising and worth reading?

For each item, assess the kind of information likely to be covered in the source, the kind of audience who might be interested in that information, and the kind of appropriate student research question that this information might help answer.

1. A catalog card for a book:

INSURANCE, HEALTH — UNITED STATES.

```
HD7102      Davis, Karen.
U4D281          National health insurance :
SOCIAL      benefits, costs, and consequences /
SCIENCE     Karen Davis. -- Washington : Brookings
            Institution, [1975]
                xiii, 182 p. : ill. ; 24 cm. --
            (Studies in social economics)

                Includes bibliographical references
            and index.
                ISBN 0-8157-1760-1 : $8.95.
                ISBN 0-8157-1759-8 pbk. : $2.95

                1. Insurance, Health — United
            States.  2. Medical care — United
            States. I. Title.  II. Series.

SU          770111                CU L
1167006                           75-5154
                                  PPW
HD7102.U4.D28
```

2. *Reader's Guide to Periodical Literature:*

INSURANCE, Health
    Health insurance: how much do you need. Gla-
    mour 77:53 Ap '79

3. *Humanities Index:*

Subsidized abortion: moral rights and moral
    compromise. G. Sher. Philos & Pub Affairs
    10:361-72 Fall '81

4. *Social Science Index:*

Live now, pay later. Economist 286:21 F 12-18 '83

5.   *PAIS Bulletin*

> Demkovich, Linda E. "PPO": three letters that may form
> one answer to runaway health costs; fast-growing
> preferred provider organizations guarantee prompt
> payment to doctors who offer discounts. il *Nat J*
> *15:1176-7 Je 4 '83*

6.   *Psychological Abstracts:*

> **Health Insurance** [See Also Employee Health Insurance, Workmens
>   Compensation Insurance]
> inclusion of psychology & psychiatry in national health insurance,
>   rebuttal to G. F. Derner's argument, 14490

7.   *New York Times Index*

> NY Times/CBS News Poll indicates little public
> support for all-out Govt effort on natl health ins (S).
> Ja 31,1:1

8.   *Facts on File*

> **Insurance—See also 'Malpractice' and
> 'Medicaid' below**
> Carter budget omits funds 1-22, 44G2

3. COLLECTING FIRSTHAND INFORMATION

AT THIS STAGE in your research paper project, you will be shaping some ideas of your own on your topic. Some aspects will intrigue you more than others. Now is the time for you to actively follow up these ideas firsthand. Some elaborate, complicated research projects—for instance, the ones undertaken by graduate students—often depend on gathering firsthand statistical data through questionnaires and experiments. Designing them requires special training. You, of course, are not expected to gather data this way now. However, there are several straightforward ways whereby anyone can obtain useful firsthand information. In addition to reading about your topic in the library, you can telephone, write a letter, observe a public meeting or event, conduct an interview, or use a questionnaire to survey opinion. Any information you obtain this way will be recorded later on appropriate note cards, just as you do for printed sources. But first you have to get the information.

TELEPHONING

This resource is not suitable for all topics, but it is very valuable for some, and is often overlooked by students. For example, one student interested in single-parent adoption called a local adoption agency that was very helpful in sending copies of state regulations and the agency's application forms. You can also use your telephone call as an opportunity to ask for an interview.

EXERCISE

1. Where in a local telephone book might a student look for local numbers related to the following topics?

   Zoning restrictions
   Solar energy
   Hedges against inflation
   Starting a small business
   Teenage alcoholism

2. Look back at the research questions on pp. 17–18. Which questions lend themselves to a telephone inquiry? Where would a student look in a telephone book for a local number related to each of these questions you consider appropriate?

What to Say

Begin by briefly identifying yourself and explaining why you are calling (because you are working on a college research paper project). Then ask if you have called the appropriate number to request information. If not, call the correct source. Go ahead and ask for information related to your topic, emphasizing that it would probably be most helpful to you if the authority would send you printed data, pamphlets, and so on in the mail.

WRITING A LETTER

A local telephone call will do the same thing, but for out-of-town sources, write a letter. Besides making sure that you follow standard business letter format, there are three other points to consider: *who* to write, *where* to send your letter, and *what* to include in it.

You will probably be writing to one of the following sources. In addition to the *National Directory of Addresses and Telephone Numbers,* a reference book that gives "50,000 most wanted addresses and telephone numbers in the U.S.," there are specialized library reference books that will give you addresses. Here is a sampling:

1. A business: *Million Dollar Directory,* produced by Dun and Bradstreet. A student who was researching fast-food restaurants found the correct address for McDonald's Corporation in this directory.
2. An organization: *Encyclopedia of Associations.* One student was researching legal rights of the mentally ill. By checking "Mental Health" in the index of this book, he found out about the existence of a Center for the Study of Legal Authority and Mental Patient Status and its address.
3. A person: *Who's Who* and other specialized directories. One nursing student was intrigued by the historical figure of Dr. Samuel Mudd, the physician who treated the broken leg of Lincoln's assassin and was subsequently convicted of treason. She found from her preliminary reading in an encyclopedia that Samuel Mudd's grandson has been trying to clear his grandfather's reputation. The encyclopedia also indicated that Mudd's grandson is a physician, so the student looked him up in the *American Medical Association Directory,* found his address, and wrote a letter. The present Dr. Mudd was very interested and helpful, and sent copies of such things as his letter to the President presenting reasons for exonerating Samuel Mudd.

OBSERVING A PUBLIC MEETING OR EVENT

Again, not all topics lend themselves to this source of information, but some do—for example, any issues about local government. The student researching zoning and land use policy attended a zoning commission meeting. Most local government committee meetings are open to the public, and are held at regularly posted times. Call your town hall or government center for dates and places.

Sometimes out-of-town experts give local talks or presentations to which the public is invited. Another student, who was researching the influence of different kinds of toys on preschool children, attended a public meeting that was part of a regional social services seminar. A nationally known authority on child development spoke, and the student was able not only to take notes on what she said, but was also able to ask a question. Calendars in newspapers, both campus and town or city, are good places to find out about this possibility.

A more unusual but sometimes quite possible source of information is firsthand observation. This requires tact, careful planning (a telephone call or letter beforehand), and sometimes a letter of introduction from your instructor. Nonetheless, it is often worth pursuing. One student researching judicial reform observed a court in session; another student obtained an invitation to ride in a police patrol car.

CONDUCTING AN INTERVIEW

The advantages of a personal interview are, first, that you can follow up an answer with more questions, testing ideas of your own against an expert's experience. Second, the authority you are interviewing can often give you practical suggestions about further reading, or comments on your thesis and approach to the topic. In other words, you will be gathering more facts about the subject as well as expert opinion.

Arranging the Interview

Begin with a telephone call to request an interview. Explain who you are and your reasons for calling (your research project). Set a specific date that is mutually convenient. Before you arrive, prepare a short list of questions based on your reading so far and your ideas about it. Write your questions on a notepad, leaving enough room for answers. Be on time, even a few minutes early. Take a tape recorder if you wish, but ask permission before you use it.

What to Say

If the other person does not take the initiative, begin by asking your first question. Jot down answers in abbreviated form. If you miss something important, ask the person to repeat it. Don't hesitate to say that you don't understand. It is quite normal to ask for clarification of a point or further explanation. On the other hand, don't annoy the person by trying to take down each word. Don't waste time recording the obvious.

Kinds of Questions

You can ask both direct and indirect questions. A direct question is one that begins with *why, when, where, who, what, how*—for example, "What medicine is routinely given to the patients to counteract depression?" An indirect question is an open-ended opportunity to respond: "I wonder if there are any other realistic alternatives to medication for depressed patients?"

Two thoughtful techniques can help you avoid the unpleasant impression of grilling the person at your interview. The first is to use the person's name: "Dr. Brown, why does your agency disapprove of interracial adoption?" The second technique is to introduce your question courteously: "May I ask you what you think of this statement I just read . . ." or "If you wouldn't mind, I would appreciate hearing your perspective on interracial adoption."

After the Interview

Don't stay too long. An hour would be a maximum, but many interviews will not take that long. When you get home, write a short letter thanking the person again. This courtesy is appropriate because the person has willingly given time to help you and, insofar as you automatically represent other students, by showing your genuine appreciation you will make it easier for other students to obtain an interview in the future. Examples of students who have gathered information through interviews include those working on depression among the elderly (interviewing a nurse in a nursing home); religious cults (a priest); wild animals as pets (an animal trainer at an aquarium); hedges against inflation (a stockbroker).

SURVEYING OPINION WITH A QUESTIONNAIRE

There is a whole complicated science of constructing good questionnaires in order to get useful and accurate information. Without feeling overwhelmed by technical difficulties, however, you might consider experimenting with a questionnaire to use on an appropriate sample of people. For instance, one student was concerned about the authorities in her small town who were trying to strictly regulate, if not close down, the only video arcade. She enjoyed playing the games there and thought that the public had somehow got a wrong impression, based on wrong information. She wanted to get some firsthand information besides her own opinion, so she made up a short questionnaire with these questions:

1. How many hours a week do you spend here? _____
2. How many hours a week do you spend on homework? _____
3. How many hours a week do you spend on sports? _____
4. How many hours a week do you spend watching TV? _____
5. Do you come here alone? (yes or no) _____
6. Do you come here with friends? (yes or no) _____
7. How much money a week do you spend here, on average? _____
8. If you were not spending it here, what would you be spending it on? _____
9. A lot of people criticize video arcades. What benefits do you get from coming here?

The important thing on a questionnaire is to create questions so that most of them give comparable answers. That means that they can be counted up and averaged: so many "yes's," so many "no's," so many hours, etc. The first seven questions here are like that; the last two questions are more open-ended.

Once the student had made up a number of copies of this questionnaire, she went to the video arcade and asked players to answer her questions, one questionnaire for each player. She explained her purpose, read the questions out loud, and jotted down the player's answers. She then went home, tallied up the answers, and averaged them into a profile of the typical player. This all provided excellent information for her research paper on video arcades.

EXERCISE

Look back at the research questions on pp. 17–18. For each question suggest the best way, or ways, of getting firsthand information. In each case, what kinds of information would be most helpful, and what kinds of questions would be most likely to get this information?

4. UNDERSTANDING AND CONDENSING INFORMATION

Goals in This Chapter

IN THIS CHAPTER we want to review some basic skills that must be mastered before you begin the more complex task of assembling information from several sources. We will start with a skill that is at the heart of research: understanding what you have read. When the information is complicated, you need to know how to sort it out before you can record what you need to use for your paper. After practicing the steps involved in close reading, we will show you how to write a summary.

Summarizing is a basic skill that we have all developed to some extent, and it is an enormously useful skill to perfect for school and work. A written summary is sometimes referred to as an abstract or a précis. Learning to summarize accurately is essential to writing any good research paper. It is essential, first, because it will enable you to read and understand your source material so that you can take good notes. Second, if you are writing your paper according to the format recommended in many of the sciences, you will have to begin your paper with an abstract which summarizes your own paper (see p. 247 for an example of an abstract).

READING FOR MEANING

Many people think the first step in taking notes is to sit down with a book or magazine article, a nice sharp pencil, and a pile of blank notecards, and start at the top of the first page jotting down interesting points as you read them. Right or wrong? WRONG. This is the common way, and it is a big waste of time. Why? Because until you have read the article or chapter in a book you don't know what is important and therefore what to record as notes.

Start with a self-contained logical unit to read: an article or a chapter in a book, and forget about your notes for the moment. The first, and *essential*, step in taking notes is reading for meaning. This step may look like it is going to use up a lot of valuable time, but it will really pay off and, believe it or not, will actually save you time.

Your first reading should give you a sense of the author's purpose. Try to decide whether the author is giving information about a topic or trying to convince you in some way. Many authors have a thesis, a position, on the topic they are discussing. You should try to decide whether the material you are reading is more like a REPORT or a THESIS (see p. 2).

Tips on Reading for Meaning

1. Survey the article

    a. What does the title tell you? Some titles give only the general subject.

        Examples: "Fly Fishing." "Weather Lore."

        Other titles state or imply the main idea of the article.

        Examples: "The Futility of Terrorism" = Terrorism is futile. "How Banks Spoil the Economy" = Banks spoil the economy. "Weather Forecasts: Fair, Gradual Clearing, Rising Accuracy" = Weather forecasts are becoming more accurate.

    b. Are subdivisions indicated in bold type? The subdivisions usually give you hints about the organization of the article.

    c. Check the length and difficulty of the article. Do you have enough time to read the article now? Will you need a dictionary beside you while you read?

    d. Skim the first few and the last paragraphs. If the article is organized around a thesis, you will often find it stated at the beginning or end of the article. This is not always the case, of course. Sometimes the writer will imply or suggest the thesis without ever stating it directly.

2. Read actively.

    a. Turn the title into a question or a series of questions. In this way you will be reading to find the answers to the questions and this will help you identify the main ideas. For example, "Weather Forecasts: Fair, Gradual Clearing, Rising Accuracy" suggests:

        (1) How accurate are weather forecasts?
        (2) Why are they becoming more accurate?
        (3) Why is accuracy so important?

    b. Underline—or better—jot down main ideas as you read. Write cue words or questions in the margin or on a separate piece of paper.

    c. Relate each section to what has gone before and to the main idea of the article. Keep asking yourself: What does this have to do with the preceding paragraph?

Read the following article on successful sales techniques, using the tips we have just presented.

TO TRUST, PERCHANCE TO BUY

Donald J. Moine

> *Maybe what Willy Loman needed was lessons from*
> *Dr. Mesmer. The best persuaders build trust by mirroring*
> *the thoughts, tone of voice, speech tempo, and mood of*
> *the customer—literally the techniques of*
> *the clinical hypnotist.*

The real-estate agent, who normally speaks quickly and loudly, is responding in a slow, soft, rhythmic voice to her slow-speaking, quiet customer. The agent opened the sales interview with a series of bland and flatly accurate remarks about the cool weather and the lack of rain. Now she is explaining her hesitation in showing her customer a particular house: "I know you want to see that house, but I don't know whether I should show it to you. It is expensive, and"—an imperceptible pause—*"just looking at it will make you want to buy it."* A bit later she repeats something that, she says, a previous customer told her about a house he'd bought: "The house has been worth every penny. My wife and I just enjoy it so much"—another pause—*"we can't understand why we took so long to buy it."*

The agent, an extremely successful saleswoman, is instinctively using weapons from the arsenal of the skilled clinical hypnotist, whose initial aim is to create in a subject a state of intensified attention and receptiveness, leading to increased suggestibility. All successful persuaders produce such an effect, probably without understanding the exact nature of the techniques that accomplish it. Our real-estate woman is lulling her customer into a mood of trust and rapport by taking on his verbal and emotional coloring, and her techniques are almost identical to those that therapists like Herbert Spiegel use with patients who come to them to be hypnotized out of, say, their fear of cats.

The conclusion that a successul sales presentation is an intuitive form of indirect hypnosis is the most provocative finding of a psycholinguistic analysis that I performed in 1981. My initial study focused

Donald J. Moine received his Ph.D. in psychology from the University of Oregon for his study of successful sales people. He lives in Redondo Beach, California.

on eight life-insurance salesmen, four of whom were identified as "top producers" by the presidents of their companies, and four as only average. The two groups were closely matched on such characteristics as age and experience. Taking the role of the customer, I spoke with the eight men, recorded their comments, and analyzed those comments for the 30 techniques of persuasion that Richard Bandler and John Grinder had identified in the work of the master hypnotist Milton Erickson. I next examined the work of 14 top sellers of real estate, luxury automobiles, stocks, commodities, and trust deeds. Since 1981, I have tested my findings with more than 50 other people, who sell, among other products, jets, computers, and oil and gas leases. My basic finding was confirmed: Superior sellers use the techniques of the clinical hypnotist; mediocre ones do not.

GETTING IN SYNC

The best sales people first establish a mood of trust and rapport by means of "hypnotic pacing"—statements and gestures that play back a customer's observations, experience, or behavior. Pacing is a kind of mirror-like matching, a way of suggesting: "I am like you. We are in sync. You can trust me."

The simplest form of pacing is "descriptive pacing," in which the seller formulates accurate, if banal, descriptions of the customer's experience. "It's been awfully hot these last few days, hasn't it?" "You said you were going to graduate in June." These statements serve the purpose of establishing agreement and developing an unconscious affinity between seller and customer. In clinical hypnosis, the hypnotist might make comparable pacing statements: "You are here today to see me for hypnosis." "You told me over the phone about a problem that concerns you." Sales agents with only average success tend to jump immediately into their memorized sales pitches or to hit the customer with a barrage of questions. Neglecting to pace the customer, the mediocre sales agent creates no common ground on which to build trust.

A second type of hypnotic pacing statement is the "objection pacing" comment. A customer objects or resists, and the sales agent agrees, matching his or her remarks to the remarks of the customer. A superior insurance agent might agree that "insurance is not the best investment out there," just as a clinical hypnotist might tell a difficult subject, "You are resisting going into trance. That's good, I encourage that." The customer, pushing against a wall, finds that the wall has disappeared. The agent, having confirmed the customer's objection, then leads the customer to a position that negates or undermines the objection. The insurance salesman who agreed that "insurance is not the best investment out there" went on to tell his customer, "but it does have a few uses." He then described all the benefits of life insurance. Mediocre sales people generally respond to resistance head-on, with arguments that presumably answer the customer's objection. This response often leads the customer to dig in his heels all the harder.

The most powerful forms of pacing have more to do with how something is said than with what is said. The good salesman or -woman has a chameleon-like ability to pace the language and thought of any customer. With hypnotic effect, the agent matches the voice tone, rhythm, volume, and speech rate of the customer. He matches the customer's posture, body language, and mood. He adopts the characteristic verbal language of the customer ("sounds good," "rings a bell," "get a grip on it"). If the customer is slightly depressed, the agent shares that feeling and acknowledges that he has been feeling "a little down" lately. In essence, the top sales producer becomes a sophisticated biofeedback mechanism, sharing and reflecting the customer's reality—even to the point of breathing in and out with the customer.

I have found only one area in which the top sales people do not regularly pace their customers' behavior and attitudes—the area of beliefs and values. For example, if a customer shows up on a car lot and explains that she is a Republican, a moderately successful salesman is likely to say that he is too, even if he isn't. The best sales people, even if they are Republicans, are unlikely to say so, perhaps because they understand that "talk is cheap" and recognize intuitively that there are deeper, more binding ways of "getting in sync" with the customer.

THE SOFT SELL

Only after they have created a bond of trust and rapport do the top sales people begin to add the suggestions and indirect commands that they hope will lead the customer to buy. One such soft-sell technique is using their patently true pacing statements as bridges to introduce influencing statements that lead to a desired response or action. For example: "You are looking at this car and you can remember the joy of owning a new reliable car," or "You are 27 years old, and we figure that your need for life insurance is $50,000." These pacing-and-leading statements resemble the way a hypnotist leads a client into hypnosis. "You are sitting in this chair, and you are listening to my voice"—the unarguable pacing statements—"and your eyelids are getting heavy, and they are beginning to close. . . ."

There does not have to be any logical connection between the pacing statement and the leading statement. They can be totally unrelated, yet when they are connected linguistically, they form a "sales logic" that can be powerfully effective, even with such presumably analytic and thoughtful customers as doctors and college professors.

The power of these leading statements comes from the fact that they capitalize on the affirmative mental state built by the undeniably true pacing statements, with which the customer is now familiar. Customers who have agreed with sales people expect, unconsciously, further agreement, just as customers who have disagreed expect further disagreement. The "traditional" truth of these pacing statements rubs off on the leading statements, and, without knowing it, the customer begins to take more and more of what the sales agent says as both factual and personally significant. Using hypnotic language, the agent activates the customer's desire for the product.

Average sellers combine pacing and leading statements less frequently and with less skill than do their superior colleagues. They also speak in shorter, choppier sentences, and thus fail to create the emotional web of statements in which the truthful and the possible seem to merge.

One of the most subtle soft-sell techniques is to embed a command into a seemingly innocuous statement. "A smart investor knows how to *make a quick decision, Robert.*" "I'm going to show you a product that will help you, *Jim, save money.*"

Sales people insure that their embedded commands come across by changing the tone, rhythm, and volume of their speech. Typically, as they pronounce the commands, they intuitively slow their speech, look the customer directly in the eyes, and say each word forcefully. A clinical hypnotist does the same thing deliberately. "If you will *listen to the sound of my voice,* you will be able to relax."

The placement of an individual's name in a sentence seems like a trivial matter, yet the position of a name can make a significant difference in how strongly the sentence influences the listener. Placed before or after the command portion of a sentence, it gives the command an extra power.

By changing their speech rate, volume, and tone, the best sales agents are able to give certain phrases the effect of commands. "If you can *imagine yourself owning this beautiful car,* and *imagine how happy it will make you,* you will want to, *Mr. Benson, buy this car.*" The two phrases beginning with 'imagine' become commands for the customer to do just that. Owning the car is linked to the leading statement of how happy it will make the customer. Finally, the statement carries the embedded command: "*Mr. Benson, buy this car.*"

THE POWER OF PARABLES

A final soft-sell technique of the best sales people is the ability to tell ancedotes, parables, and stories, and to frame their comments in metaphors. For thousands of years, human beings have been influencing, guiding, and inspiring one another with stories and metaphors, so it should be no surprise that sales people routinely use them to influence customers. What is surprising is the frequency and skill with which they do so.

Some sales agents I have studied do almost nothing but tell stories. They tell them to get the customer's attention, to build trust and rapport, and even to deliver product information. A piece of information that in itself might be boring takes on a human dimension and stays in the customer's memory when placed in the context of a story. "I sold a receiver like this a week ago to a surfer from Torrance and what he liked best about it was its FM sensitivity of 1.7 microvolts."

Metaphors and stories are used to handle customers' resistance and to "close" on them without endangering rapport. A top insurance agent was attempting to close a deal for a policy with a young man who was considering signing with a smaller company. As part of his clinching argument, the salesman wove the following metaphor into his pitch: "It's like taking your family on a long voyage across the Atlantic Ocean, and you want to get from here to England, and you have the choice of either going on this tugboat or on the Queen Mary. Which one would you *feel safe* on?" Had the salesman tried to make his point with a litany of facts and figures, he might never have focused his customer's attention; the discussion could have descended into a dispute about numbers. Instead, his story spoke directly to the customer's concern about his family's safety and implied that it was now in the customer's power to decide between two choices that were clearly unequal.

Note, too, that the salesman used conjunctions to link the metaphor in one unbroken chain and give it a hypnotic cadence. Mediocre sales people who know such a story would probably tell it as several separate sentences. In addition, they probably would give no special emphasis to the phrase "feel safe" even if they had heard better sales people do so. The skill in telling it is more important than the material itself.

The same can be said about all the skills that constitute the intuitively hypnotic arsenal of the best sales agents. But obviously, these skills are not exclusive to sellers. They are common to others— politicians, lawyers, even preachers. No less than sales people, these persuaders try to influence their audiences. No less than sales people, they attempt to implant in their audiences a resolve to do something. And, like sales people, all of them use, to some extent, variations of the techniques of Mesmer, Cagliostro, and Rasputin.

EXERCISE

1. Did the title give you a clue to the main idea (the thesis) of the article?
2. Do you know who Willy Loman and Dr. Mesmer are? If you don't, how could you find out?
3. Read the first three paragraphs again. Can you find a place where the author states the main idea? Is the main idea stated anywhere else?
4. What do the headings tell you about the organization of the article?
5. Does the last paragraph restate the author's thesis?
6. Make up some questions based on your survey of the article.
7. Are there any words you are unfamiliar with?
8. Can you answer your questions after reading the article?

After a careful reading of the article, you should be able to state the author's thesis. Sometimes articles simply report different points of view and do not have a clear thesis. If you are working with such an article, you should try to describe the author's purpose. At this point, you should be able to distinguish between three related terms and use them correctly:

Term	Meaning	Example
Topic	The subject	Police use of hypnosis
Purpose	Author's intention	To show the problems with police use of hypnosis
Thesis	The main idea, position, or opinion	Police use of hypnosis may lead to injustices

OUTLINING

Now you are ready to reconstruct the logical skeleton of the article, that is, to write an outline of the article's main points. An outline is like an x ray. It shows how major points are connected to supporting details, and it shows the order of the major points. Making an outline is a good way to check your understanding of an article. If you cannot tell what one paragraph of an article has to do with the main idea, then your understanding of the article is superficial. You will not have to outline every source that you use for your research paper, but this is an important step in writing a summary and a reaction paper, and an important skill to master.

A Preliminary Exercise

Outlining is not just an academic assignment. The process of outlining is the same process as sorting, which is something we all do all the time in our everyday lives. For instance, if you go to a store to do the weekly shopping, you will probably arrive home with several armloads of paper bags full of purchases. Let's say you walk in the door and dump them all on the kitchen counter. Now what? Do you take the first thing on top, toothpaste maybe, and carry it into the bathroom, come back to the kitchen, find some spare fuses and carry them down to the basement, and so on? No, you unload the bags and sort things out first.

What groups of things would you be likely to accumulate on your kitchen counter? List some groups:

Groups
   I.
   II.
   III.
   IV.

Now take your first group. What items might you find in it? List them below:

   A.
   B.
   C.

Now put them together:

I.
   A.
   B.
   C.

Do the same for other groups. Can you subdivide further?

II.
   A.
      1.
      2.
   B.
      1.
      2.

The Point of This Exercise

What you are doing is outlining, and you have been using symbols from an outline frame. All that is left is to remember to indent subdivisions.

Steps in Getting Ready to Construct an Outline

1. Look over the sentences you have underlined. How can the important generalizations be grouped together? You will have to experiment with different groupings to see which ones make the most sense.
2. Decide on the major subdivisions of the article and label them. In a short article you will generally find two to five subdivisions. If you identify more, perhaps you have not done enough grouping of ideas.
3. List the important generalizations under appropriately labeled subdivisions.
4. Decide on the amount of supporting information to put in the outline. This will depend on the purpose of the outline. Outlines can be used to study material for tests, to prepare information for a written assignment, such as a summary, or as a check on your understanding of the relationship of ideas.
5. Use a standard format for presenting title, author, source.
6. Revise the thesis statement, if necessary, to be sure it accurately reflects the main idea of the article. As indicated earlier, you may not find a complete statement of the thesis anywhere in the article. You may have to piece it together yourself.

Mechanics of Outlining

Some people get all hung up on deciding where to put Roman numerals and when to stick in capital letters or small letters. The important part of outlining is the logical arrangement of boiled-down ideas, not the frame to put them in, or the symbols for this frame.

However, an outline frame does use three techniques to illustrate this logical arrangement.

First, related ideas are grouped under columns and given the same symbol, using the symbols up in this order: Start with Roman numerals, then CAPITAL LETTERS, then Arabic numerals, then small letters.

Second, subordinate ideas are indented in a group under the main idea. Make sure you have at least two ideas in an indented subdivision. If you have only one, you have an example, not a subdivision, and it can go next to its main idea, not below it.

Third, the thesis is always stated at the beginning. It is not a subdivision, so no letters or numbers are used with it.

Sample Outline

"To Trust, Perchance to Buy" by Donald J. Moine
Psychology Today, August 1982, pp. 51–54.

Thesis: The best sales people use hypnotic techniques.
I.   Moine studied successful sales people.
   A.   1981 study focused on eight life insurance salesmen.
   B.   Initial findings were later confirmed with additional subjects.
II. Successful sales people intuitively use hypnotic techniques.
   A.   They create trust by using hypnotic pacing.
      1.   Descriptive pacing establishes a link with the customer.
      2.   Objection pacing acknowledges the customer's concerns.
      3.   Nonverbal pacing is the most effective approach.
      4.   Values and attitudes are not paced.
   B.   Their language is subtly suggestive.
      1.   Leading statements are linked to pacing statements.
      2.   Commands are woven into the sentence structure.
   C.   They rely on parables and metaphors throughout the encounter.
      1.   Stories add a human element.
      2.   Skill in storytelling is necessary.
III. Hypnotic techniques are used by many other people who want to persuade.

Short Topic Outline

Depending on your purpose, you may need only a shorter, topic outline. A topic outline is exactly the same as the sentence outline we have just given you, but it uses words and phrases instead of sentences.

Thesis: Advances in technology have enabled meteorologists to improve their short-range predictions, although they are still experimenting with ways to improve long-range predictions.

I.   Short-range predictions more accurate
   A.   Hurricane alerts
   B.   Other storm warnings
   C.   Improved temperature and precipitation estimates
II. Long-range predictions promising but harder
   A.   Would be almost same as guessing
   B.   Would be more helpful, e.g., to farmers
   C.   Are more likely because of new research

If you use the shorter topic outline (instead of the longer sentence one), you should aim at grammatical parallelism. That means that each item in a group—in other words, each item with the same symbol: I, II, III, or A, B, C, D, or 1, 2, 3—should be in the same grammatical form. If one is a verb, all items in that group should be verbs. If one is a noun, all should be nouns, or adjectives, or whatever you start with in that group.

Example:

    A.   hurricane *alerts*
    B.   other storm *warnings*   *Nouns*
    C.   improved temperature and precipitation *estimates*
                     OR
    A.   *alerting* the public of hurricanes
    B.   *warning* the public of other storms
    C.   *improving* estimates of temperature   *Participles*
         and precipitation

EXERCISE

Parallelism is important, not only because it is grammatically correct, but also because it expresses clear, logical relationships. Being aware of this grammar point will help you clarify your logic.

    Correct the mistake(s) in grammatical parallelism in each of the following sentences. Begin by identifying any comparable, balanced components or series of items; they should be parallel.

1.   The rainbow indicates that rain is falling and also the reflection of sunlight in raindrops.

2.   Workers on land and who fish at sea are very conscious of wind direction and how it changes.

3.   Human beings with chronic ailments such as rheumatism, gout, and aching from arthritic pains are supposed to be able to forecast the weather as well as indicating when it will happen.

OUTLINING EXERCISES

A. The following sentences are in the correct order for an outline. Insert the proper symbols to indicate the relationship between ideas.

Thesis: There is considerable controversy over the Pass/Fail grading system.

_____ The Pass/Fail system differs from the letter grade system.

_____ It has only two options.

_____ It ignores the concept of a curve.

_____ Critics of the Pass/Fail concept claim it has many disadvantages.

_____ It lessens students' incentive.

_____ It removes the reward–punishment system from the teacher.

_____ It denies the competitiveness of life.

_____ Pass/Fail grading shelters students from facing their limitations.

_____ Advocates of Pass/Fail grading stress its advantages.

_____ The academic pressure on students is reduced.

_____ Better learning takes place under stress-free conditions.

_____ Students do not fear to try new areas.

_____ Teachers are forced to make classes more interesting.

B. Arrange the following statements into outline form, using the proper symbols. The statements are *not* in the correct order, but the thesis is provided. We have numbered them for identification purposes only.

Thesis: Buying a car is a major step and should be carefully thought out.

(1)   A used car may be a better deal than a new car.

(2)   There are different ways to finance the purchase.

(3)   Many car dealers provide financing plans.

(4)   First, one must decide whether to buy a new or used car.

(5)   New cars are usually guaranteed for longer periods of time than used cars.

(6)   Used cars are much cheaper.

(7)   There are certain advantages to a new car.

(8)   The best way to finance the purchase of a car is to save the money ahead of time.

(9)   Reputable used car dealers will guarantee the car for at least 30 days.

(10) Personal loans from a bank are another method of financing.

(11) A new car provides personal satisfaction.

(12) The classified ads often contain good buys on used cars.

(13) There is a greater range of choices if you are purchasing a new car.

C. From the statements below, choose one that will best serve as a thesis. Then arrange the remaining statements into an outline that shows the relationship between ideas. The statements are *not* in correct order. Again we have numbered these statements for identification purposes only.

(1) Cars are a drain on our energy resources.

(2) The amount of traffic can be regulated through improved mass transit, car pools, and gasoline taxes.

(3) Steps can be taken to solve many of the problems caused by the use of private cars, thereby ensuring a continuation of their true usefulness.

(4) There are justified complaints against the widespread use of private cars.

(5) Cars contribute to pollution.

(6) Remedies can be found for most of the complaints.

(7) Private cars still have many benefits.

(8) Cars are needed for quick transportation in case of emergencies.

(9) Safety features would help to reduce death and injury.

(10) Cars are needed for vacations when people do not want to follow a schedule.

(11) Cars are largely responsible for traffic congestion.

(12) Pollution control devices are now being perfected.

(13) Cars are a major source of death and injury.

D. Organize the following statements into outline form. There is no thesis statement included in the list. After you have made an outline, write your own thesis statement to fit the information.

   (1) Soap operas provide a substitute family for many lonely people.
   (2) Twenty million viewers watch the soaps.
   (3) The soap operas are technically sophisticated in their production aspects.
   (4) The sets on soap operas tend to be very monotonous.
   (5) The plots are full of suspense, a tried and true device for hooking the audience.
   (6) The viewers come from all walks of life, from homemakers to federal judges.
   (7) Soap operas are a popular pastime.
   (8) The problems with soaps are due to limited budgets and the serial form.
   (9) There are several reasons for the popularity of soap operas.
  (10) Viewers develop a strong allegiance to actors who stay with a role for many years.
  (11) Each segment tends to repeat a good deal of what happened in previous episodes.
  (12) The soaps are thematically relevant to contemporary problems, such as drug abuse.

E. Find at least four mistakes in the following topic outline.

  I. **Thesis:** The problems of overpopulation
    II. Causes of overpopulation
      A. Medical advances
        1. lower infant mortality rate
        2. longer life span
        3. control of fatal diseases
      B. Resistance to birth control
        1. religious reasons
      C. In countries without social services, parents want large families as a guarantee of protection in their old age, and to help them by working and contributing to the family income.
    III. Dealing with overpopulation
      A. Find means of birth control that are acceptable to religious opponents.
      B. Provide incentives for sterilization and limitation of family size.
      C. Governments should not restrict abortions.

PARAPHRASING AND QUOTING

Paraphrasing means putting information into your own words. Instructors prefer to have you paraphrase as much as possible, rather than use lengthy quotations, because it demonstrates that you have understood the material. Of course, it is difficult to paraphrase if you are looking right at the author's words. A better approach is to read a paragraph or two and then close your eyes. Now try to say aloud what you have just read. Unless you have a photographic memory, you will put most of the information into your own words. Another strategy is to invent a question based on the section you have just read and then answer the question without looking back at the text.

Direct quotation should be used sparingly. There are three occasions when it is advisable to quote: when there is no way to accurately reword or condense the information; when the author has stated an idea in a memorable fashion; or when the information is so surprising that a reader might question the accuracy of your paraphrase. If you are going to quote part of a sentence, you must fit it into your own sentence in a grammatically acceptable way. If you read your writing aloud, you can usually tell that something is wrong. Here is a sentence that sounds terrible because the quotation is not properly worked in:

> The states that have passed laws about weather control, "almost all are regarded as inadequate."

Here is the same idea reworked:

> Most of the laws that states have passed on weather control "are regarded as inadequate."

If you are going to quote a whole sentence, you must lead into it so that the reader will be able to follow you. Here is an example that fails to provide an adequate transition:

> Not everyone is happy about the prospect of weather modification. "He asked that environmental consequences be studied before weather modification is accepted as a cure for the West's water problems."

Here is the same material with a better transition:

> Not everyone is happy about the prospect of weather modification. Speaking at a recent conference, one scientist "asked that environmental consequences be studied before weather modification is accepted as a cure for the West's water problems."

Sometimes you may want to leave out some of the words in a quotation. You can do this if the omission will not change the meaning and provided you indicate the omission with three dots (. . .) called an ellipsis. For example, you might write:

> One scientist "asked that environmental consequences be studied before weather modification is accepted as a cure. . . ." (The fourth dot is the period.)

AVOIDING PLAGIARISM

Most students know that it is dishonest to hand in another person's work as their own or to copy paragraphs of information and put them in a paper without using quotation marks. However, students sometimes unintentionally borrow an author's wording so closely that it constitutes plagarism. There are two techniques that you can practice at this point to help you avoid unintentional plagiarism: paraphrase your information in chunks of a paragraph or more without looking directly at the material; then check what you have written against the original material and put quotation marks around any significant portions that follow the original wording closely. (See p. 176 for examples of material that is poorly paraphrased and which would be considered plagiarism).

EXERCISE

A. **Directions:** Summarize each of the paragraphs. Use a partial quotation and weave it skillfully into your own sentence.*

   1. "At this point weather modification is so much in its infancy that the future social and legal issues are just beginning to emerge. Few people have been affected so far. But many responsible persons feel that the time to examine the issues is now, before the capability to cause widespread effects is developed."

*Paragraphs in this section are taken from "Hard Questions About Weather Modification" by Kendrick Frazier, Science News (May 9, 1970), 97, 19, 461–463.

2. "A rain that benefits one farmer may ruin the crops of another. Increased rainfall that profits a hydroelectric company might depress an area's tourist industry. Heavy mountain snow that looks good to reclamation officials and thirsty down-basin residents might not have quite the same appearance to the mountain rancher with a cabin below an avalanche-prone ridge."

3. "If the pilot project is as successful as its proponents hope, the economic pressures for additional winter cloud seeding are sure to mount. Southern California water officials are watching the effort closely in the hope that it will provide a solution to expected water shortages in the lower Colorado River basin in coming decades. Already Dr. Kahan's office has prepared a list, in tentative order of seeding priority, of seven other runoff-producing areas in Colorado, Wyoming, and Utah that look favorable for similar weather modification efforts in future years."

B. **Directions:** Indicate whether the paraphrase is accurate or inaccurate. If it is inaccurate, write a better version:*

1. *original:* "Because recent research suggests that some memories retrieved under hypnosis may be inaccurate, many states are re-evaluating the use of eye witness testimony obtained by hypnosis."

    paraphrase: The state of hypnosis can cause eye witnesses to remember testimony incorrectly.

*Original *statements in this section are taken from "Hypnosis on Trial" by Elizabeth Stark,* Psychology Today, *18 (February 1984), 2, 34–36.*

2. *original:* "During hypnosis, imagined events can seem as authentic as reality, images can be extremely vivid and there is a heightened level of fantasy."

   paraphrase: Hypnotic images, although a fantasy, are extremely vivid and authentic.

3. *original:* "Most psychologists agree that hypnotised subjects are extremely susceptible to suggestions. The very language many hypnotists use with their subjects encourages guesses."

   paraphrase: The way a hypnotist talks to a subject can reinforce the subject's willingness to guess.

4. *original:* "Hypnotised subjects correctly recalled twice as many items as did unhypnotised members of a control group but also made three times as many mistakes."

   paraphrase: Twice as many hypnotised people remembered correctly and three times as many made mistakes.

5. *original:* "The New Jersey Supreme Court, in 1981, approved guidelines for hypnotists to follow to avoid leading or influencing witnesses."

   paraphrase: In 1981, The New Jersey Supreme Court helped hypnotists stay away from witnesses who were trying to lead or influence them.

C. **Directions:** Reread the section in "To Trust, Perchance to Buy" that is labeled GETTING IN SYNC. Then complete the following summary paragraph using your own words as much as possible.

The first hypnotic technique used by _____ is called " _____ ." The sales person builds _____ with statements that _____ . Using " _____ ," the most basic kind of pacing, the sales person might say " _____ ." Mediocre sales people _____ . When a customer resists the sales pitch, _____ . After agreeing with the customer, the sales person _____ . Less successful agents usually _____ , which makes the customer _____ . The most effective type of pacing _____ . However, good sales people do not pace _____ .

Now reread the SOFT SELL section and write a one paragraph summary. If you have to quote some of the original text, be sure to use quotation marks and to weave it into your own sentence.

TIPS ON WRITING A SUMMARY

1. If you are summarizing an article or a book, report the author's ideas as objectively as possible. Don't insert your own opinions. Be careful not to distort the author's ideas by quoting or paraphrasing information out of context. This can easily happen if you do not outline the main points.
2. After reading the selection carefully, make an outline with the thesis statement, major subdivisions, and as much supporting detail as you have room for. This will vary with the length of the article and the requirements of your instructor. Follow the sequence of ideas as they appeared in the article. If an article is not particularly well organized, you may have to move bits of information to fit them into your outline. Don't spend a disproportionate amount of time on one part of the article and skip over other sections.
3. The heading for your paper should give the author, title, and source of the article.
4. The introduction to your summary should always include the title, author, and thesis, even if you have already put some of this information in the heading for your paper. If you are writing a multiparagraph summary, the introduction should also include a preview of the main points.

Although there are many ways to open a summary, here are two patterns that you can use to get started:

a. The THESIS of (give the title) by (give the author) IS THAT (state the main idea).

Don't introduce the thesis with "how" or "why." These words will convert the thesis into a question, and a thesis must be phrased as a statement.

b. The PURPOSE of (give the title) by (give the author) IS TO (use a verb phrase to state the author's intention).

Examples: The thesis of "To Trust, Perchance To Buy" by Donald J. Moine is that good sales people instinctively use the same techniques as a clinical hypnotist.

The purpose of "Hard Questions About Weather Modification" by Kendrick Frazier is to describe the legal problems that have arisen over weather control.

5. Condense the information by at least one-fourth. Anything less runs the risk of becoming a word-for-word substitution. Your summary should be as concise as possible, so trim any unnecessary words and combine sentences wherever possible.

6. The sequence of paragraphs in your summary should follow your outline. Don't leave gaps in your summary. It should be understandable to someone who has not read the original material. Use transitional expressions (see p. 245) to make connections between sentences and paragraphs.

7. Don't use a quotation to make a point. Make the point in your own words, and then back it up with a quotation if necessary.

8. Usually you do not need a special conclusion for a summary. You can signal the reader that the summary is ending by using phrases such as:

In conclusion, the author . . .
The author's last point is that . . .
The final section of this article describes. . . .

SAMPLE SUMMARY

Lee Pound

"To Trust, Perchance to Buy" by Donald J. Moine
Psychology Today, August 1982, pp. 51–54.

Successful sales people intuitively use many of the techniques that are also employed by hypnotists, according to Donald J. Moine, author of "To Trust, Perchance To Buy." He reached this conclusion after comparing the techniques of top life insurance salesmen with those of a well known clinical hypnotist. Later he confirmed his findings by studying sales people in a number of different fields.

An effective sales person begins by establishing trust through the use of hypnotic pacing. In its simplest form, descriptive pacing, the sales person mirrors bits of information about the customer or says something obvious that the customer will agree with. Objection pacing is used when the customer does not go along with the sales-person. It is important to acknowledge the customer's concerns before trying to overcome them. Nonverbal pacing of the customer's body language and speech mannerisms is even more important. However, top sales agents do not try to pace the beliefs and values of their customers. "They understand that 'talk is cheap' and recognize that there are deeper and more binding ways of 'getting in sync' with the customer."

After the pacing statements put the customer in a positive mood, the sales person begins to introduce suggestions and hidden commands to buy the product. Although there may be no logical connection between pacing statements and the suggestion, good sales people always connect them with an "and" to create an emotional carry over. They also use the customer's name, speak slowly, and make eye contact as they deliver indirect commands. For example: "If you can *imagine yourself owning this beautiful car,* and *imagine how happy it will make you,* you will want to, *Mr. Benson, buy this car.*

The use of parables and metaphors is the final technique discussed by the author. Successful sales agents use stories and comparisons to get the customer's attention, to overcome objections, to make technical information more interesting, and to clinch a sale. Their success depends not just on the story but on the way they tell it, linking statements together in a hypnotic rhythm.

Moine concludes by pointing out that other persuaders—"politicians, laywers, even preachers"—use these same hypnotic techniques.

EXERCISE

A. Comment on how you would improve each of the following beginnings in a summary:

1. The thesis of this article is that technology alone is inadequate to solve the problems created by the population explosion.
2. The title of the article is "Hard Questions About Weather Modification." The author is Kendrick Frazier. The thesis is that we are unprepared to cope with the problems that may result from weather control projects.
3. The thesis of Elaine Cotlove's article, "Pass/Fail Grading," is how we need to change the grading system.
4. Kendrick Frazier's provocative article, "Hard Questions About Weather Modification," is full of interesting facts about a new problem that we face in today's ever changing society.
5. The thesis of "The Sugar Story" by Fred Rohe is why people should avoid the use of sugar.
6. In "Meeting Energy Needs," Joyce Harley argues that nuclear power plants are needed to provide energy until other alternatives become technologically feasible. I think that she has overlooked some alarming dangers of nuclear power plants and some alternatives that are already practical.
7. The thesis of "Facing Your Future" by Lee Crowley is to explain the need for career education on the high school level.

B. This exercise will help you practice trimming unnecessary words from the rough draft of a summary. Imagine you are sending a telegram at 5 cents a word. How can you economize by simply omitting words? Go through these sentences and simply cross out any words that are not absolutely essential:

1. A rainfall that falls on one farmer's land may ruin and destroy another farmer's crops.
2. "If you dump only so much as one snowflake of snow that I didn't ask you for," a resident who lives in the small mountain town of Silverton, in the Colorado Rockies, told the committee members on the panel, "you are denying my civil rights as a citizen."
3. Because the high mountain highway that goes from Silverton to Ouray in the Rockies is highly vulnerable to dangerous avalanches of snow, which create a driving hazard for travelers between towns, no seeding in that particular area of the mountain basin will be conducted at this point in time.

C. Now look at the rough draft of a summary paragraph below. It is 203 words long. Can you reduce this summary to 100 words or less without destroying the meaning or omitting anything essential? Besides crossing words out, you may want to rearrange and condense:

According to Harlan Cleveland in an editorial called "The Management of Weather Resources," the present history of our time today is sprinkled with instances and examples of new, innovative technologies running ahead of the social, economic, environmental, international, and institutional thinking that should properly accompany them. It is precisely because the science and technology of weather resource management are still situated at such an early stage that there is an excellent chance in this new field of the management of weather resources to do things right. As of this moment, however, there is no one who is in charge of the future of weather resource management. This is a 20-year problem that we are still tackling with 5-year projects. Those people who are experimenting in the sky have a moral obligation to go beyond just guessing what will happen afterward and what changes they may be causing in the environment that weren't anticipated beforehand. Moreover, and in addition, these people who are experimenting with weather management should do so in open consultation with the many other peoples of the world in other countries, not all of whom are Americans, who might be likely to be affected by the changes that occur.

Adapted from "The Management of Weather Resources," Science Magazine, 201 (August 4, 1978), 4354, 399.

Summary Checklist

_____ Heading contains necessary information on source of the article.

_____ Introduction gives author (if available), title, and thesis.

_____ Paragraphs are organized around topic sentences and are clearly related to the outline.

_____ Sequences of ideas makes sense. Transitions have been used to show the connection between ideas.

_____ References to terms, names, etc. are explained.

_____ Summary is primarily paraphrase. Information is clear and accurate.

_____ Quotation marks are used around phrases and sentences which come from the article.

_____ Quotations are integrated into the text.

_____ No personal opinions are expressed.

_____ Paper has been carefully proofread for errors.

5. AIMING AT A THESIS OF YOUR OWN

Review: What Is a Thesis?

THE THESIS IS an assertion or claim about the subject. As your research progresses and you focus on a particular aspect of the subject, you should begin to draw some conclusions and to make connections. "What is the point of all this?" you should ask yourself. The point is your thesis statement. That statement is likely to change several times during the research and writing process as you refine your thoughts about the topic.

In the strict sense of the word, a thesis is an original insight. For example, a graduate student in speech pathology wanted to investigate the effect that eye contact had on a listener's reaction to a stutterer. After setting up a test situation and recording the results, the student concluded that poor eye contact, not stuttering by itself, caused a negative reaction in the listener. This was an original insight with important implications for therapists who work with stutterers.

It is not necessary to conduct primary research of the type just described to form an original thesis. Library research offers many possibilities for pointing out relationships that you think are important and significant. A student might read about different methods that have been used to treat stutterers and make a connection between advances in knowledge about stutterers and changes in therapeutic approaches.

At this stage in your education, you are not expected to come up with a totally original slant on your subject. However, your thesis should reflect your thinking about that subject. A thesis is more than a rehash of what you have read and taken notes on. It points to some meaning in these facts and ideas, some perspective that your reading has caused to form in your mind. Your thesis should reflect what you believe is interesting and important.

We want to stress that the type of research paper we are showing you how to write is more than just a summary. At this point you should reread the sample research papers in the back of this book and pay attention to the way that the writers interpreted and commented on the information they gathered. Although you cannot decide on the final shape of your thesis statement until you have completed your research, it is important for you to get a feel for what a good thesis statement is like. If you have a clear idea of what you are aiming for, your research will be more meaningful and you will avoid limiting your subject to something so cut and dried that it does not lend itself to interpretation.

A Warm-Up Exercise: Getting a Hunch

A thesis of your own usually does not emerge automatically from your information. If it does, be cautious. You might simply be swallowing some-body else's prefabricated idea. If, on the other hand, you draw a complete blank, try out some possibilities in your head. You have nothing to lose by experimenting, and at this stage are not yet committing yourself.

One way to start is with a research question like the ones on p. 17. For example, the topic of *teenage pregnancy* can be approached with a research question like one of these:

1. Does fear of pregnancy discourage teenagers from sexual experimentation?
2. Is ignorance about sex a deterrent against sexual activity?
3. Does access to contraceptive devices encourage sexual activity?
4. Does sex education lead to sexual activity among teenagers?

In each case the research question evokes the response of "Maybe" or "It depends." Then the question leads to an opinion (or thesis) which can be supported with facts you find in your reading.

For instance, here are some possible thesis statements which could an-swer the first research question above ("Does fear of pregnancy discourage teenagers from sexual experimentation?"):

Possible Thesis Statements

Fear of pregnancy as a deterrent against sexual activity among teenagers varies with their attitudes toward abortion and access to it.

or

Fear of pregnancy as a deterrent against sexual activity among teenagers only operates among those who know enough anatomy to understand and antici-pate the cause and effect relationship.

or

Any possible deterrent effect of pregnancy is overruled by teenagers' curiosity about sex and peer pressure to experiment.

Another way to aim at a thesis is to look at some data and ask yourself: "I wonder if _____ ," and then fill in the blank. For example, you might read some statistics about teenage pregnancy and discover that every year about 10 percent of American teenage girls, mostly unmarried, get pregnant. Start off, "I wonder if teenagers get pregnant because _____ ," and then fill in the blank. Try out several versions. Jot them down on scratch paper. For any idea that doesn't seem too silly, move on to a second fill-in-the-blank: "I suspect that _____ ." If you feel you could possibly find some proof to back up your suspicions, you can be confident that you are on the right track to creating a good thesis.

EXERCISE

Directions: Here is the beginning of an article, "Why Teenagers Get Pregnant," by William A. Fisher, in *Psychology Today,* Volume 17, March 1983, pp. 70–71:

> Each year, 10 percent of American teenage girls (mostly unmarried) get pregnant—alarming proof that use of contraceptives by teenagers has not kept pace with their increased sexual activity. Even well-informed young people who have easy access to contraceptive devices often fail to use them.
>
> Some time ago, social psychologist Donn Byrne hypothesized that one major psychological barrier to teenage contraception was erotophobia, or fear of sex. Over the past six years, several studies that my colleagues and I have done have confirmed that hypothesis.

Reprinted from Psychology Today Magazine, *Copyright © 1983 American Psychological Association.*

1. What was the author's original research question?

2. What was the author's original hunch to fill in this blank: "I suspect that

_____"?

3. Underline the words in this passage that identify the author's thesis.

The Invisible Frame Method

A writer's thesis statement expresses a considered interpretation or confident opinion of the topic. Therefore, one way to make sure that your thesis meets that basic rule is to mentally put I THINK THAT in front of your statement and see if it fits.

I THINK THAT	retarded children need special toys.	Retarded children need special toys.
I THINK THAT	zoning laws are unfair to homeowners.	Zoning laws are unfair to homeowners.
I THINK THAT	studying religion in public schools would help prevent people from joining crazy cults.	Studying religion in public schools would help prevent people from joining crazy cults.

Why should this frame be invisible? In other words, why shouldn't you name yourself in your thesis? Because it is distracting. You want your reader to think about your ideas, not you. So don't name yourself, just launch right into the idea.

GUIDELINES FOR A THESIS STATEMENT

1. The thesis must be a complete sentence. By definition, a thesis makes a claim about a subject. You have to stick your neck out and make a point. Therefore, a description of the subject is not sufficient.

    Subject: The accuracy of weather predictions.

    Thesis: I THINK THAT the accuracy of weather predictions has improved.

Make an assertion about each of the following subjects:

   a.   The future of the American family.

   b.   Job opportunities for women in the business world.

   c.   The increase of fast food restaurants.

   d.   The consumption of alcoholic beverages.

A word of caution. Be prepared to change your thesis if it makes you uncomfortable or if you won't be able to support it. You may start a research project with a ready-made thesis that you believe—for instance, "The United States should not sell wheat to communist countries"—only to find as you read more and takes notes about the subject that you don't really feel that way. So be prepared to change your mind and your thesis in light of new information. Remember, it's your thesis. You can do what you want with it and change it any way you want to get your point across.

2. A thesis must be an assertion, not a question. A question may be used effectively in your title or introduction as a way of creating interest, but a thesis is a statement that answers the question.

Question: Why are people hooked on credit cards?

  Thesis: Credit cards are popular not only because they are a convenient substitute for money but because consumers have been brainwashed into thinking the credit card is a status symbol.

3. The thesis must be a generalization or an opinion, not just a statement of fact. A fact is something that can be verified as true or false; an opinion is something that must be supported or proved.

  Fact: Each year hail destroys 1 percent of America's crops.

Opinion: The application of weather control technology is essential to increase the food supply for our expanding world population.

A word of caution: Do not overgeneralize or assert more than you can prove in your paper. What would a writer have to know in order to support adequately the opinion statement about weather control?

4. Thesis on a controversial subject should not be wishy-washy. You may feel that there are good arguments on both sides, but you should make some assessment of the issue.

Weak: Abortion is a controversial issue.
or
Women should have the right to control their bodies, but, on the other hand, abortion is murder.

Better: The controversy over abortion stems as much from economics as from religious values.
or
Although abortion is not ethically desirable, it is a practical necessity in our society.

5. A thesis should make a point, not just *promise* to do so. For instance, if you write this as a thesis, "There are two main reasons why government should support solar energy," then you have made a promise to tell your reader what these two reasons are. So you should start out saying why in the first place, that is, in the thesis itself: "Government support for solar energy will provide jobs and lessen our dependence on foreign oil suppliers."

Promise: A good nurse must have three important qualities.

  Better: A good nurse must have intelligence, independence, and compassion.

6. Ideally, a thesis should be stated as a single sentence that not only gives the main idea—

    "The construction of nuclear power plants should be halted."

    but also indicates the major subdivisions of your paper—

    "because they are *more dangerous* and *more costly* than most people realize."

7. Learning to combine a group of related ideas into a single sentence takes a bit of practice. Look at the thesis sentence on credit cards:

    Credit cards are popular not only because they are a convenient substitute for money but because consumers have been brainwashed into thinking that the credit card is a status symbol.

    Can you tell how many ideas have been combined in that sentence?

EXERCISE

Directions: Combine each set of related ideas into a single thesis statement. Try writing more than one version for each set of statements because your own thesis will probably go through several versions.

A.
  1. Soap operas attract viewers from all walks of life.
  2. Soap operas deal with contemporary problems.
  3. The plots of soap operas are full of old fashioned suspense.

Version 1:

Version 2:

B.
  1. Nuclear power plants are opposed by some people.
  2. They claim the plants are dangerous.
  3. There is always a chance of human error.
  4. The back-up systems have not been adequately tested.

Version 1:

Version 2:

C.
1. A growing number of people support the return of the death penalty.
2. They are angry about the upsurge in murders.
3. Many of the murders are premeditated acts by professional criminals.

Version 1:

Version 2:

D.
1. TV stations are trying to sell the news.
2. They are trying to make the news exciting.
3. They use a crew of attractive, young reporters.
4. The reporters have an informal, chatty style.

Version 1:

Version 2:

EXERCISE

Directions: Evaluate the following thesis statements as good, fair, or poor.

1. The educational benefits of children's television programs, such as Sesame Street and Electric Company.
2. Although there are many reasons for the increase in divorce rates, two factors stand out.
3. The U.S. government has done nothing to stop the rise of medical costs.
4. I think that citizens should support fluoridation because research has shown that it is effective in reducing tooth decay and does not cause harmful side effects.
5. Six players suffered serious injuries in just one Sunday of professional football, and many more were hurt in high school and college matches.
6. The reasons why alcoholism has increased among teenagers.
7. Fad diets are so dangerous that people are dying.
8. Recent breakthroughs in computer technology are revolutionizing the operation of offices, factories, and classrooms.
9. A federal study of 46 cities, published May 1978, showed no difference in the cancer rates between cities with fluoridated drinking water and cities without it.
10. What is behind the rising cost of automobile repairs?

MINI-RESEARCH EXERCISES

A. **Directions:** Read the following three paragraphs which are taken from different sources. Notice that the term "subject" refers at one time to a *person* and at another time to *hypnosis.* After reading the selections, fill in the blanks in the list of important facts, using your own words as much as possible.

(1)

Hypnotic suggestibility is much harder to achieve when the hypnotist does not have the confidence of the subject because the hypnotist does not merely make suggestions, but must talk the subject into acting. If the subject does not trust the hypnotist, nothing may happen. Hypnotic suggestibility also depends on the type of person being hypnotized. People who are used to following instructions and taking orders, such as grade school children, are usually the best subjects for hypnosis (Trotter & McConnell, 1978, p. 99).

(2)

Indeed, most students of the subject insist that there must be developed a special kind of trust relationship between the subject and the operator. One common test of the susceptibility to hypnosis is to stand behind the prospective subject and ask him to permit himself to fall voluntarily to see what it feels like to 'let go.' If the subject steps back to break his fall, he almost invariably turns out to be a poor hypnotic subject for that particular operator (Jaynes, 1976, p. 394).

(3)

Early investigators assumed that women enter hypnosis more readily than men, but this has not been borne out in most studies; similarly, hypnotizability is not especially related to intelligence nor to education. There does appear to be a significant relationship with age, ability to respond, reaching a peak before puberty, stabilizing in the early adult years, and declining in very old age. . . . There is evidence that hypnotizability is greater among individuals who seem generally well adjusted (Orne & Hammer, 1974, p. 138).

Important Facts

1. Hypnotizability refers to ＿＿＿＿＿＿＿＿＿＿＿＿＿＿＿＿＿ .
2. ＿＿＿＿＿＿ , ＿＿＿＿＿＿ , and ＿＿＿＿＿ do not seem to affect a person's hypnotizability.
3. ＿＿＿＿＿＿＿＿＿ and ＿＿＿＿＿＿＿＿＿ do affect hypnotizability.

4. Perhaps the most important factor affecting hypnotizability is _____ .

5. One test of this trust is _____

    _____ .

B. **Directions:** Read the next set of three sources. Decide on the common topic of all three and write your own list of important facts. Decide on a topic sentence that pulls together these facts and makes a point about them. Then write several more sentences combining the information from your list. Again, use your own words as much as possible.

(1)

If I ask you to taste vinegar as champagne, to feel pleasure when I jab a pin in your arm, or to stare into darkness and contract the pupils of your eyes to an imagined light, or to willfully and really believe something you do not ordinarily believe, just anything, you would find these tasks difficult, if not impossible. But if I first put you through the induction procedures of hypnosis, you could accomplish all these things at my asking without any effort whatever (Jaynes, 1976, p. 379).

(2)

Some strange tales have been told about hypnotism and the power of suggestion—tales of people performing unnatural acts while hypnotized or people becoming slaves to a master hypnotist. While people have been known to do some odd things while hypnotized, they usually won't do anything they couldn't be talked into doing under normal circumstances (Trotter et al., 1978, p. 99).

(3)

. . . a number of controlled studies . . . call many earlier extravagant claims about hypnosis into serious question. It now seems quite unlikely that the hypnotized person can transcend his waking potentials, in physical strength, perceptiveness, learning ability, and productivity. Similarly, it seems most improbable that hypnotized people can be compelled to do what they would be most unwilling to do in the waking state. . . (Orne et al., 1974, p. 138).

Common topic:

List of important facts:

Topic sentence:

C. **Directions:** Read the next set of three sources. Decide which of the fol-
    lowing conclusions could be supported by information from these
    sources. Then use the appropriate conclusion as a topic sentence and
    write a paragraph in which you use information from all three sources to
    explain the topic sentence. Use a combination of direct quotation and
    paraphrase in your paragraph.

    Possible conclusions:

    1. Some researchers believe that hypnosis is an unusual or altered state of
        consciousness.
    2. Some researchers believe that hypnotism is a normal human experience
        which can be explained by concepts from social psychology.
    3. Some researchers believe that there is a relationship between abnormal
        psychology and hypnosis.
    4. Some researchers believe that we will never be able to fully understand
        hypnosis.

(1)

Other theorists stress the social or interpersonal interactions that
hypnotic behavior involves. They emphasize how an actor willingly
and unwittingly permits a director to guide him into living a part,
how a patient may be relieved of a headache if given a pill that is
actually pharmacologically inert (a placebo); how an uncommitted
person becomes an enthusiastic supporter of crowd feeling at a demonstration; how a spectator flinches and jabs along with his favorite
fighter; and how a student changes his views to those of an admired
teacher. Hypnosis is held to consist of nothing more than events like
these, there being no need to assume additional special states such as
the inhibition of parts of the brain. Hypnotic events are results of
interpersonal influences in which various abilities, skills, and response propensities are brought into play (Orne et al., 1974, p. 135).

(2)

Concepts derived from abnormal psychology—such as trance, som-
nambulism, and dissociation—are misleading and do not explain the
overt and subjective responses. Responsiveness to test suggestions is
a normal psychological phenomenon that can be conceptualized in
terms of constructs that are an integral part of normal psychology,
especially of social psychology. Social psychology conceptualizes
other social influence processes, such as persuasion and conformity,
in terms of such mediating variables as attitudes, motivations, expec-
tancies, and cognitive processes. In the same way, the mediating

variables that are relevant to explaining responsiveness to test suggestions include attitudes, motivations, expectations, and cognitive–imaginative processes (Barber, 1979, p. 223).

(3)

In many cultures trance states mark a *rite de passage*. As an illustration we cite one of Benedict's studies. She has described how, among the Plains Indians, an individual will experience many of the phenomena, including hallucinations, which are usually subsumed under the term hypnosis. The content of the hallucinations is relatively constant within groups but highly variable between groups. The role of the tranced subject is perceived from interaction within his own group (Sarbin, 1950, p. 263).

Topic sentence (conclusion):

D.   **Directions:** Read the following selections. Write a paragraph based on a comparison of the information in all three sources. Underline your topic sentence. Use a combination of paraphrase and direct quotation.

(1)

. . . Since the time of the Abbé Faria (1819), hypnosis has been associated with sleep. The term hypnotism invented by Braid, comes from the Greek word hypnos, meaning sleep. . . . None of the hypotheses that postulate a similarity between hypnosis and sleep have received convincing scientific support (Chertok, 1967, p. 193).

(2)

Ivan Pavlov, the Russian physiologist, came to view sleep as reflecting widespread inhibitory processes in the brain and concluded that hypnosis is a similar inhibitory state in which there remain a few centers of neural excitation. His views enjoy wide acceptance among Soviet and eastern European workers who also tend to use prolonged periods of sleep in psychiatric therapy (Orne et al., 1974, p. 134).

(3)

Pavlov's theory and other theories linking sleep and hypnosis were effectively refuted by [a study] which demonstrated that the knee jerk and the involuntary reaction to a signal were not appreciably disturbed by hypnosis. Williams (1965) investigated behavior in sleep and hypnotic states and observed that sleeping and hypnosis can be readily distinguished in the laboratory. Das (1965) also reported a number of EEG studies showing only partial inhibition of cortical activity under hypnosis. This finding supports the notion that hypnosis and sleep are distinct from one another. . . (McCabe, Collins, & Burne, 1978, p. 49).

E. **Directions:** Read the following selections. Write a paragraph based on a comparison of the information in all three sources. Underline your topic sentence. Use a combination of paraphrase and direct quotation.

(1)

Despite active empirical study of hypnotic phenomena, there is no single generally accepted explanatory theory. Some theorists . . . think of hypnosis as a state of altered consciousness . . . in which a person tends to respond to suggestions automatically and uncritically. While this view does not ignore increased suggestibility, it still holds that a subject not at the moment responding to a suggestion may nevertheless be in a trance state. . . (Orne et al., 1974, p. 135).

(2)

Any S[ubject] who has experienced deep trance will unhesitatingly describe this state as basically different from his normal one. He may be unable to explicate this difference, but he will invariably be quite definite and certain about its presence. Thus, one of the characteristics of hypnosis is that in deep trance the S[ubject] experiences the state as discontinuous from his normal waking experience (though not always in the intermediate stages of trance). Hypnotic trance differs from pathological states which may also be discontinuous, in that the S[ubject] enters and leaves the state in accordance with previously established rules of the game (Orne, 1959, p. 297).

(3)

An altered state of consciousness is a cognitive state different from the waking state. While some ASCs occur naturally and commonly, others are induced by various psychological maneuvers or by pharmacological changes that can be measured. ASCs can be recognized subjectively by the individual himself as different from the waking state. . . . The outside observer can sometimes also recognize that the individual in an ASC acts differently. However, more frequently, subjectively very vivid altered states do not translate themselves into objectively measurable behavior. . . .

The major ASCs comprise medium and deep hypnosis, psychedelic states, classical Eastern meditation, and states of mystical rapture. . . (Fromm, 1979, p. 83).

F. **Directions:** Using information from any combination of the sources in the preceding exercises, write paragraphs to support the following assertions:

1. Hypnotism could be a dangerous tool in the wrong hands.
2. Athletes and students could benefit from hypnosis.
3. Hypnotism is not completely understood.

SOURCES FOR MINI-RESEARCH EXERCISES

Barber, T. X. (1979). Suggested hypnotic behavior: The trance paradigm versus an alternative paradigm. In E. Fromm (Ed.), *Hypnosis: Developments in research and new perspectives* (pp. 217–269). Hawthorne, NY: Adline Publishing Co.

Chertok, L. (1967). Theory of hypnosis since 1889. *International Journal of Psychiatry, 3*, 193.

Fromm, E. (1979). The nature of hypnosis and other altered states of consciousness. In *Hypnosis: Developments in research and new perspectives* (pp. 81–103). Hawthorne, NY: Adline Publishing Co.

Jaynes, J. (1976). *The origin of consciousness in the breakdown of the bicameral mind.* Boston: Houghton Mifflin.

McCabe, M. P., Collins, J. K., & Burne, A. M. (1978). Hypnosis as an altered state of consciousness. I: A review of traditional theories. *Australian Journal of Clinical and Experimental Hypnosis, 6*, 1, 39–54.

Orne, M. T. (1959). The nature of hypnosis: Artifact and essence. *Journal of Abnormal and Social Psychology, 58*, 277–299.

Orne, M. T., & Hammer, A. G. (1974). Hypnosis. *Encyclopaedia Britannica*, (15th ed.). 1974.

Sarbin, T. R. (1950). Contributions to role-taking theory: I. Hypnotic behavior. *The Psychological Review, 57*, 5, 255–269.

Trotter, R. J. & McConnell, J. V. (1978). *Psychology: The human science.* New York: Holt, Rinehart and Winston.

6. ANALYZING AND EVALUATING INFORMATION

IN THIS CHAPTER we will go into a fuller explanation of the thesis and the way to develop a sound argument to support your ideas. We will help you to sharpen your analytical skills and explain how to write a type of paper that is commonly assigned in college: the reaction paper. The reaction paper, as we explained earlier, is closely related to the research paper because it requires you to evaluate information, form an opinion, and then develop an argument to support your position.

As you recall from the section on summarizing, the thesis of an article is different from the topic. The topic is just another word for the subject, yet the thesis is an *interpretive* statement about the topic. We stress interpretive because the thesis cannot be a simple factual statement. How can you tell the difference? A factual statement is one that can always be tested. It may turn out to be wrong, but there is a way to check it out.

Example: Crop damage from hailstorms in the U.S. runs about $700 million a year.

Crop damage may really be more or less than that, but this statement is a factual statement because we could test it by getting the figures from the Department of Agriculture or the insurance industry.

On the other hand, an interpretive statement must be proven by presenting an argument that follows logical criteria. There is no quick way to test an interpretative statement.

Example: Solar energy can provide 25 percent of the nation's energy needs by the year 2000.

That statement looks factual at first glance because of the numbers, but it involves a projection into the future. No reference will tell us whether the estimate is correct. Instead, we would have to examine the writer's arguments and information before we could decide whether or not we agree. In general, a statement of fact does not leave much room for disagreement. Here are some factual statements:

135

1. The National Weather Service had 5,000 employees in 1978.
2. The National Weather Service's 12 to 18 hour predictions are 85 percent accurate.
3. Mount McKinley is the highest peak in North America.

Can you argue with any of these statements?

We do not want to mislead you into thinking that fact and opinion are absolutely distinct. The truth of factual statements depends upon the state of knowledge at any time. Everyone knows the story of Galileo's efforts to convince others that the sun, not the earth, was the center of our solar system. So widely held was the belief in the earth as the center that it was regarded as a fact. Therefore, we should think of fact and opinion as points on a spectrum and try to distinguish the degree to which a statement is debatable.

EXERCISE

Directions: Describe where on the fact–opinion spectrum each statement would fit. Remember that a factual statement does not have to be true. If the statement is factual, what sources would you use to check it? If it is an opinion, what arguments or facts would you use to support it?

1. Women constitute 40 percent of the work force in the U.S.
2. Men have a shorter life expectancy than women in the U.S.
3. The life expectancy for women in the U.S. is 58.
4. Men are stronger than women.
5. There are more women than men in the U.S.
6. Children's books present stereotypes of women, limiting their careers to a narrow range.
7. The women's lib movement has destroyed family life.
8. Biological differences are responsible for the different roles that are expected of men and women.
9. College is more important for men than women.
10. More females than males graduate from high school.

USING FACTS AND OPINIONS

All writing is a blend of fact and opinion. Opinions are needed to interpret the facts and make them meaningful; facts are needed to support opinions. In taking notes for your research paper, make sure that you do not record and use an opinion as if it were a fact. As you read, train yourself to distinguish facts and opinions. When you read an opinion, be prepared to anticipate supporting reasons. When you read facts, be prepared to relate them to other facts and to interpret their meaning in light of the author's opinions, whether explicitly stated or only suggested.

EXERCISE

Notice that the blank in the following sentence can be filled in with many possibilities:

"Weather modification is ———————————— ."

Possibilities:

a.   in its infancy
b.   alarming some people
c.   sometimes the cause of unplanned side effects
d.   irresponsible
e.   accompanied by complex problems
f.   progressing
g.   a good idea
h.   a bad idea

For each of these possibilities, indicate whether the resulting sentence is a fact or an opinion. What might a reader expect to follow each of these completed sentences? Can you suggest some ideas?

Now match each of these completed sentences to the best versions below. In each case be ready to defend your choice of following sentences.

Example: h. a bad idea. "Weather modification is *a bad idea.*"

This version is an opinion. The reader would expect some reason.

The best following sentence that fits is C (see list that follows): "Increased run-off derived from precipitation modification could cause even greater problems than that of an inadequate water supply."

"Weather modification is *a bad idea. Increased run-off derived from precipitation modification could cause even greater problems than that of an inadequate water supply.*"

Following sentences:

A.   The scale now being examined is of individual clouds and small cloud systems.
B.   There is the first tantalizing evidence that the intensity of hurricanes might someday be reducible.
C.   Increased run-off derived from precipitation modification could cause even greater problems than that of an inadequate water supply.
D.   The judgment of a National Academy of Sciences panel in 1966 still has to prevail: "We cannot now predict with certainty all the important consequences of such acts."
E.   Heavy mountain snow that looks good to reclamation officials and thirsty down-basin residents might not have quite the same appeal to the mountain rancher with a cabin below an avalanche-prone ridge.

F.   "If you dump as much as one snowflake I didn't ask for," one resident complained, "you are abridging my rights as a citizen."
G.   Practically all the major issues—regulations, public–private relations, federal–state responsibilities, international questions, federal organization—have yet to be resolved.

Your Own Writing

In your own writing there are two ways to use opinions honestly: (1) attribute opinions to their authors, and (2) qualify them clearly as opinions.

1. An opinion attributed to its source:

Weather modification developments will take place within the next few years, according to a recent National Research Council report.

This technique also lends you the opinion-maker's authority:

In a major policy address on "Sun Day," 1978, the President himself claimed that solar energy could provide 25 percent of the nation's energy budget by the year 2000.

2. A statement clearly qualified as an opinion:

Within a few years, the technology of modifying weather *may* be applied on a large-scale basis. (Notice the writer used *may*, not *will* be applied.)

Here are some of the words that are commonly used to signal an opinion:
probably
perhaps
some
maybe
seems
may, might–could, would–should

Read the following statement. How has the author qualified it as an opinion?

Weather modification over homogeneous areas of land does not seem to cause many harmful effects.

Here is another version. What has been added?

National Research Council scientists claim that weather modification over homogeneous areas of land does not seem to cause many harmful effects.

Here is still another version. What is wrong with it?

Weather modification does not cause harm.

EVIDENCE AND LOGIC

Almost every book and article has a thesis, either stated or implied, that determines what information will be included and how it will be presented. Even textbooks have a slant on their subject. Therefore, even if a book or an article does not seem to present an argument, we can still think of content as the case an author is developing to support a thesis. You should always try to determine the slant an author has on a subject. Make an effort to find out if the author is considered a reputable authority. Sometimes you can make a rough assessment of the author's prestige by checking the publisher. For example, the *New York Times* maintains stricter standards than the *National Enquirer*. Likewise, a magazine like *Atlantic* prides itself for a record of accuracy and substance in its articles. *Who's Who in America* provides brief sketches that might help you to determine an author's expertise and possible slant on a subject.

Distinctions and Guidelines

Let's consider what makes a logical argument different from other kinds of mental activity. Our minds are constantly active: receiving information, sorting and storing it, projecting into the future, reminiscing about the past, making decisions and plans. Clearly, there is a difference between the process that takes place when a person looks at the clouds and decides it will rain, and when one looks at the clouds and sees a horse. In the first instance one is using the clouds as evidence for an inference the person is making about a future event. This process is labeled logical thought and is the basis of the scientific method.

There are two complementary forms of logical thought: induction and deduction. Induction involves making a generalization about a number of particular instances and deduction involves applying a generalization to a specific case. For example, on a number of separate occasions you observe that when a certain type of cloud is in the sky, it usually rains. This leads you to draw the conclusion that if a certain cloud is present, it is likely to rain. You have formed a generalization and you will now apply that generalization to specific instances. Now when you see those clouds, the generalization will come to mind and you will grab an umbrella before you leave the house.

Logical argument is designed to improve the state of knowledge; rhetorical arguments are designed simply to persuade an audience. Advertising relies on rhetoric, employing devices that appeal to our emotions, to our fears and fanatasies, in order to sell us a product.

A familiarity with the common errors in logical thinking will enable you to assess a writer's argument, even when you do not know much about the subject yourself.

Errors of Inductive Reasoning

1. *Lack of support for the conclusion.* The writer who simply claims that "everyone knows," or "experiments prove," or "leading scientists agree," without providing any specific names or facts, has not proved anything.

2. *Use of unreliable support.* Evidence can be considered unreliable if it is out of date or if it is based on the work of a person whose reputation is questioned or whose attitudes are biased. You may not be able to make this kind of assessment without checking other sources.

3. *Use of irrelevant authorities.* A person who is an expert in one area may be quoted on a subject outside his or her field. Movie stars and professional athletes are frequently used to endorse deodorants and politicians.

4. *Hasty generalization.* Writers are open to this criticism if they fail to consider a sufficient number of cases before arriving at a conclusion. You should also try to determine if the cases they used were typical or exceptional. When writers ignore facts that contradict their positions, it is called "card stacking."

5. *Overgeneralization.* This problem is closely related to the one above. In making a generalization or interpretation, the writer is grouping specific instances into a category. There are elaborate formulas that specify proper sampling techniques. Without that special knowledge, you can still use common sense to question a writer's sampling procedure. For example, can a writer who interviewed a dozen runners, none of whom smoke, claim that most athletes are nonsmokers?

6. *Oversimplification of cause and/or effects.* A doctor who listens to your symptoms (effect) and concludes that you have Mongolian Flu (cause) is using inductive reasoning. The problem with cause–effect analysis is that there is rarely a simple and direct connection between two things. For example, if you take the medicine prescribed by the doctor and feel better, how do you know that the medicine was responsible? When a writer is dealing with human behavior or social issues we must look very carefully at his or her analysis of cause and effect. Likewise, if a writer narrows the choices for action and suggests that we must do X or Y will happen, the writer may be oversimplifying the situation. For example, advocates for nuclear power have claimed that if we do not build more plants, we will freeze in the dark. What alternatives may they be overlooking?

7. *Abuse of analogies.* An analogy is a comparison between two or more items. Analogies are useful in explanations because they enable a writer to compare a new idea with one that the reader already understands. Comparing the narrator of a short story with the lens of a movie camera might help a student to understand point of view. Although analogies can illustrate a concept, they cannot prove an argument because they are based on similarity; rarely do we find two instances that are identical. The differences may be more important than the similarities. Of course, analogies can be a powerfully persuasive device. When the government announced plans to build a dam that would have backed up water into a section of Grand Canyon, conserva-

tionists ran an ad that asked: "Should we flood the Sistine Chapel to bring tourists closer to the ceiling?" The Sistine Chapel contains priceless art work, just as Grand Canyon contains imcomparable natural beauty. Advocates of the dam claimed the analogy was unfair, but conservationists won public support for their efforts to save the canyon.

Errors of Deductive Reasoning

1. *Faulty premise*. The major premise is the generalization that is being applied to the specific case. An analysis of deductive reasoning looks like this:

Major premise (A generalization)	Doctors are politically conservative.
Minor premise (A specific case)	Harold is a doctor.
Conclusion	Therefore, Harold is politically conservative.

Obviously, if the generalization that forms your major premise is unsound, the rest of the argument is all wet. Most major premises are formed through a process of induction, but sometimes they may be value statements based on religious principles; you then have to decide whether you share those principles. Martin Luther King relied on such a value statement when he defended his program of civil disobedience. In "Letter From a Birmingham Jail" he claims that "one has a moral responsibility to disobey unjust laws." His argument follows along these lines:

Major premise	One has a moral responsibility to disobey unjust laws.
Minor premise	Laws that enforce segregation are unjust.
Conclusion	Therefore, one has a moral responsibility to disobey laws that enforce segregation.

2. *Hidden premise*. If a writer fails to state the generalization on which an argument is based, it may be because the generalization is commonly accepted. However, sometimes a writer hides the premise because he or she cannot prove it. A writer who argues that you should not buy a certain type of car because it is made in Japan is hiding the premise that cars made in Japan are inferior.

Here are a couple of frequently heard jibes. What is the hidden premise in each?

If you're so smart, why aren't you rich?
When all else fails, try what the Captain suggests.

3. *Unwarranted conclusion.* Even if both premises in a deductive argument are valid, the conclusion may be false. Unwarranted conclusions can occur if the writer shifts the meaning of key terms in the argument or if the writer fails to follow other rules about the application of generalizations to specific cases. Here is an example of a writer making an unwarranted conclusion:

> Critics of nuclear power plants claim that a serious accident would be more devastating than an atom bomb. However, a nuclear power plant cannot explode like a bomb. The reactors used in nuclear power plants are fueled by small, scattered elements which are incapable of combining to form the critical mass needed for an explosion of a nuclear power plant.

The problem with the reasoning here can be described in two different ways. First, there is a difference between saying that "a nuclear power plant cannot explode like a bomb" and claiming that "there is no need to worry about the explosion of a nuclear power plant." The terms have changed during the course of the argument. Second, we must realize that explosions can take place in different ways. Creating a critical mass is not the only means to cause an explosion. The failure of cooling systems in a nuclear power plant could result in an explosion.

Logical argument is intended to appeal to our intellect, not our emotions. Any argument that uses inflammatory language or personal attacks against individuals is very weak. A writer who has facts as a back up does not have to resort to these tactics.

EXERCISE

The following article will give you a model of how arguments are presented and it will also test your ability to spot logical errors. Following this exercise, the section on writing a reaction paper will show you how to compose a critical analysis of an argument.

Read the article and try to answer the following questions:

1. What is the author's thesis?
2. What data or information is used to support the thesis?
3. What assumptions or values are involved?
4. What type of reasoning is used?
5. Is the language objective and unemotional?

HOT ENOUGH FOR YOU?

Marian Kester

As if we don't already have enough problems, the weather has been acting up. If there's one thing we'll never abide it's something with a mind of its own. And *destructive?* It's just plain malicious mischief the way these hurricanes and earthquakes home in on population centers and valuable real estate. Can you imagine some volcano trying to erupt in your backyard all over your garage and the new redwood deck? Yet it's happened to some people! The weather's gone wild just like crime in the streets and the cost of living. But help is on the way.

Weather acts up when elements build up under *pressure.* So the way to go would seem to be to let them let off steam—safely, under controlled conditions. We could wipe out the threat of storms with more conscientious cloud-seeding (there are exciting new possibilities for the use of mercury compounds in this area), and forbid flooding with more systematic damming of our waterways. The shining example in this area is the once-mighty Colorado, now harnessed from top to bottom for the benefit of mankind. The lowest of the dams catches what's left of the flow so only the merest trickle almost—but not quite—makes it to the old Colorado's mouth in the Golfo de California. Now *that's* resource management! And as for drought, there's a heck of a lot of water just waiting to be pumped sitting around twiddling its thumbs in the water table.

Fires, for example, can be prevented, thereby saving thousands of acres of valuable timber yearly. Chemical clouds can be sprayed from cropdusters that will literally make trees non-inflammable. That hypothetical volcano we mentioned above can be dealt with, too. The technology already exists to tap into surly pockets of magma and siphon it off where it can be supercooled. Once again, the principle is *diversion,* controlled decompression.

"Hot Enough for You?" by Marian Kester appeared in the East Bay Express, *September 9, 1983, and is reproduced here with permission of the author.*

Earthquakes are a stickier wicket. The faults in the crust that they exploit to do their dirty work appear to be more complex and extensive than seismologists once thought (*cf.* the Coalinga tragedy). The latest plan in the exciting field of earthquake suppression is this: each locality will keep vibration-sensitive animals caged in a lab, wired for "sound"—the sound of an oncoming quake. When all the epicenters are located, tons of concrete will be poured in around them to halt further slippage. In more remote areas demolition squads will go in and relieve the pressure on the relevant fault in one fell swoop. We like our Earth the way it is; we don't need any more mountain ranges. If you don't mind my quoting a "red" on this topic, it was Leon Trotsky who wrote in 1924 that "nature will become more artificial. . . . Man will occupy himself with re-registering mountains and rivers, and will earnestly and repeatedly make improvements in nature. In the end, he will have rebuilt the earth, if not in his own image, at least according to his own taste. We have not the slightest fear that this taste will be bad" (*Literature and Revolution*). Right on, Leon. You read it here second.

Surprisingly, the one natural phenomenon mankind has least control over is the tornado, along with its cousin the waterspout. We simply don't know yet what makes the damn thing work. Once we do, though, we'll trip it up before it gets out of the cradle. The truth about tornadoes is, they're ugly as *well* as vicious. Obviously we'll still let the more scenic volcanoes in isolated areas put on a show as long as tourist dollars demand. But the stubborn tornado has no redeeming social value I can think of (except as a plot device in *The Wizard of Oz*).

You might argue that meteor showers are pretty, too, but don't underestimate the damage they have the potential to do. For one thing, it's a very bad idea to have foreign matter entering our atmosphere from God knows what contaminated reach of space. Like the hand you stick in your mouth, who *knows* where that meteor's been? It might have space fungus on it; it might give off harmful rays. For another thing, while a little bit of cosmic debris may be OK, there are *huge* chunks of junk zooming around out there—everything from comets and asteroids to maverick moons and even dead planets! Let one of those things hit us and it'll rip the sheet of gases right off the globe. The Earth will stop dead in its tracks and we'll all kick the bucket so fast it won't even be funny. Fortunately, although few people are aware of it, there is a group of scientists already putting their heads together around this threat and it's just a matter of time before we have it licked. The numbers are looking good. Rest assured, some very qualified individuals are "watching the skies" for you.

Someday soon, then, thanks to scientific weather management, we all will live in a comfortable, air-conditioned environment, free of extremes and unexpected cataclysms. Modern people aren't like the Bantus; we don't wait around for nature to attack, we make pre-emptive strikes. In addition to voting for President, we'll someday soon vote on what weather we'd like. Now *that's* democracy! If we decide to give the little chickadees some snow to frolic in, we can always whip some up on the machine. There's really no limit to the control we can enjoy. As antagonism gives way to cooperation with human desires, a new era in the relationship between mankind and his weather is dawning.

Some of the foregoing is fantasy and some all too actual. Yes, I'm trying to kid you. Weather Management, sadly, does exist, yet another unswallowable idiocy to stick in one's craw. The most amazing defect, or rather one of the many amazing defects, of the meteorological ideology is its belief that even if we *could* "manage" the weather and control the climate, we'd do a decent job of it. I see no grounds for this belief, Trotsky notwithstanding. We can't tell if the ozone layer's shot or not. We don't know whether the climate is in a cooling or warming trend. We've only been keeping records for about fifty years ("Record-breaking heat wave hits Northeast! Hottest temperatures since July 12, 1947!"), whereas the evolution of atmospheric conditions on this melting, matting, moulting planet is a subtle, infinitesimal process which has had eons to play with. Robert Ardrey notes (*African Genesis*): "For a creature whose life span is three score and ten, any real comprehension of a million years is too much to ask. But if we cannot truly understand the term, we may at least gain a certain respect for it. . . . What is demanded is humility, not mathematics. . . . The Pleistocene was the time when the weather went mad, the time of the glacial onslaughts, and we are still in its strange embrace. . . . The Pleistocene is larger than all our logic, and we are tiny, civilized minds clinging to its windward marches, the blast of the future watering our noses while to our flapping coat-tails clings the specter of accident."

Nor do meteorologists have any training in how *pollution* is affecting weather patterns and climatic trends; they display complete ignorance of pollution's impact in their daily reports. "Oh! It's out of our field!" But as anyone who's ever trusted a weather man knows, they must be a fickle, vainglorious breed of hardened, unrepentant sinners. A cynical chuckle—"Well, let's try again tomorrow!"—and they're off and running once more. Even a dead clock is right twice a day. You sure don't need a weatherman to know which way the wind blows. In short, meteorology as a science compares unfavorably with palmistry. It must even bow to astrology. Remember that comet, Kohoutek? Scientists' predictions of its size, duration, and global effects turned out to be about as accurate as spiritualists' predictions that it heralded the Second Coming.

Absolute Zero is −459.670°F. That's a million times colder than the point where water freezes, and 10,000 times colder than the coldest region of the universe, intergalactic space. Typically enough, the only place Absolute Zero occurs is artificially in labs like the Tech Institute's at Northwestern. Even Nature refrains from such frigidity. Ironically enough, humans themselves can tolerate only a tiny range of temperatures, approximately ten degrees wide with 70°F at the midpoint, before they start to break down. That sliver of a range is richly represented on this phenomenal planet, this balmy little sphere where everything possible seems to have been arranged—at least for the time being—so that warm-blooded, oxygen-breathing life should thrive. Green plants, a perfect gaseous shield against lethal cosmic radiation, just the right type of sun at just the right distance—we could not have picked a likelier spot. Perhaps it picked us. What more do we want? Don't ask. Ten years ago, the astronauts gazed down from space and beheld our planet, milky blue. Last year they reported it looked gray. Ten years from now they'll probably be able to smell it halfway to the moon.

A strange inversion of values seems to have taken place. Instead of seeing temporal human authority as questionable and mutable, people now view it as absolute, massified; while acts of God and nature such as flood, fire, earthquake, storm, drought, wind, and volcanic eruption are viewed as "outrages" to which a stop must immediately be put. You can't fight city hall but you *can* thumb your nose at natural law. The recent headlines, "Alicia Rips Into Texas," "Alicia Slams Into Houston," flatter us, as if tropical storms had some kind of animus toward humans, bore some kind of grudge against civilization and its works. I guess that's why it's called the *Pathetic* Fallacy.

Of course, the media barge around the earth behaving like American tourists in Greece in order to sell papers by dramatizing people's dull lives and intimating to them that Something's got it in for us. On the radio, mindless reporters gasp about El Nino, the Santa Anas, "freak lightning," flash floods in the desert. "Flash floods? In the desert? Holy Toledo!" Never mind that flash flooding allows the deserts to renew their life cycle. People don't like surprises and they don't like deserts, even the impressive ones they create themselves ("The natural desert of Arizona is a place of beauty and inspiration. The man-made desert of the Oklahoma dustbowl is a place of desolation and despair"—geographer Raymond Dasmann in *The Last Horizon*.) But people don't like rainy days, either. If we could vote on the weather, boy, we'd *never* get rained on.

"Most likely," Trotsky opined, "thickets and forests and grouse and tigers will remain (after nature yields finally to man's artifice), but where man commands them to remain." I can't even copy out that sentence with a straight face. And around the same time Trotsky penned his opinion, Paul Valery was theorizing that the universe is shaped like the human head! Shaped like a monkey's paw, more likely. Aw, for crying out loud, wild weather is one of the last exciting, adventurous things left that can happen to us. I mean, what else is there? Elections? Let's just keep voting on the President and not on the Pleistocene.

WRITING A REACTION PAPER

A reaction paper takes a major step beyond the summary. The summary is an objective dissection of the article's ideas. Your own ideas do not appear. A reaction paper goes further; it includes the article's ideas and also your own response to them and your evaluation of them. Other terms for a reaction paper are critical analysis and review. The subject of a reaction paper can be either an article or a full-length book. We want to remind you again that your research paper is an extended reaction paper; the difference is that you will be evaluating several sources instead of just one.

The process of writing a reaction paper involves the use of the analytical skills just discussed. You may also want to locate additional information if you have been assigned a reaction paper on an unfamiliar topic. A simple means of locating additional information is to talk to other people. Perhaps your friends or classmates have some personal experience relevant to the topic. Some of them may have read something in the newspaper or seen a TV show on the subject. If you can't get a little help from your friends, turn to one of the indexes and locate additional articles. Check *Book Review Digest* if the reaction paper is assigned on a book. The *Digest* is bound by year and organized by the author's last name. The entries contain four or five summaries of reviews that were published when the book first appeared. Each summary contains information that will enable you to locate the full review if you want to read it. Also, abstracts give summaries of articles published on various subjects.

The right attitude will help you write a good reaction paper. A *skeptical appreciation* is best: *appreciation* because the author did go to some trouble to construct his or her article and must have thought it would be important in some way, and *skeptical* because you want to measure the author's ideas against your own and your experience. Think of yourself as saying to the author: "OK, show me. What's the big idea here? Why do you think so? So what, anyway?"

After you have read the article actively in this way, you can respond in many different ways. For instance, you may agree with the author completely, and in that case will want to add more supporting details. You may agree with the thesis in principle, but find the support inadequate or illogical. You may disagree with the thesis and want to provide counter-evidence. You may find the logical argument convincing but want to take issue with ethical or moral assumptions. You may find the scope of the article too narrow and want to draw out further implications. In any case, your major responsibility is to respond actively.

EXERCISE

Respond actively to each of the following observations. Brainstorm. Free associate. How do you feel about each of them? Do you think it is a good thing? A bad thing? What else does the sentence make you think of?

1. Tomorrow's secretary will probably work at home using a computer terminal, never leaving the house.
2. The half-million dogs in New York City produce 20,000 tons of excrement and one million gallons of urine each year.
3. Nudity is now allowed on many public beaches.
4. Runaway wives now outnumber runaway husbands.
5. Some researchers claim a 90 percent success rate in determining the sex of children before they are born.
6. Donald Duck has been banned in Finland because the cartoon provides a bad model of family life.
7. Four thousand deaths and 4 million sick days were caused in 1978 by auto emission pollution.
8. At least one out of three marriages today will end in divorce.

Steps in Writing a Reaction Paper

1. Read the article carefully, underlining key passages.
2. Make an outline of the article so that you can clearly see the major arguments and supporting details. If your reaction is based on a misunderstanding of the article, it will not be valid.
3. Decide on your general reaction. Do you agree or disagree? Should you try to find more information on the subject? Were your ideas changed as a result of reading the article? Does the author use good reasoning and up-to-date information? Were reliable authorities quoted? Does the author define terms and use them consistently?

4. Make notes of your reactions on a separate sheet of paper.
5. Talk to people about the article and your ideas to get their perspective on the subject. Try to find other articles on the subject. Your paper should not be just a summary of the article, nor should it be a series of vague personal opinion statements.
6. Consider both sides of the argument if you are writing on a controversial subject. Your paper should acknowledge the opposing arguments and counter them. Sometimes the opposing arguments may be valid, but are of secondary importance as you evaluate the pros and cons. Nevertheless, it is important for you to acknowledge their existence. Failure to do so implies that you have not understood the issue or thought carefully about it.
7. Make an outline for your paper. A reaction paper should be organized to develop *your* thesis, which will be a statement of your evaluation of the article. You should also include enough summary information to make your paper understandable to someone who has not read the original article.
8. Write the paper following this pattern of organization:

Introduction	Identify the author, title, and thesis of the book or article. State your reaction.
2nd paragraph	Summarize one of the major support points. Give your evaluation of it.
3rd paragraph	Summarize a second main point. Give your evaluation.
4th paragraph	Summarize and evaluate another point or bring in new ideas on the subject.
Conclusion	Restate *your* reaction and summarize *your* points only in a long paper.

9. Provide enough signals to let the reader know when you are summarizing and when you are reacting. Keep repeating phrases such as "according to the author," "the author claims," "the article explains."
10. Stick to an assessment of the article. Do not wander away from the text or get off the subject.
11. Maintain a consistent position. Do not start your paper by agreeing with the author and then change to disagreeing at the end. If you agree with some points and disagree with others, state that in your introduction, but indicate whether you lean toward agreement or disagreement.

EXERCISE

A. Read the following reaction paper on "Hot Enough for You?" Answer the following questions:

1. Where does the writer state his own reaction to Kester's article?
3. How does the writer support his criticisms of Kester?
4. Does the writer provide enough summary of Kester's article so that a person who has not read "Hot Enough for You?" would be able to follow the reaction paper?

5. What are some of the expressions the writer uses to clue the reader as he switches back and forth between summary and analysis?

6. Where does the writer quote Kester directly? How is the quote worked into the paper? Should the writer have used more quotations? Fewer quotations?

7. Has the writer used facts or opinions from any other source?

B. Find an article in which an author takes a strong position on some issue. Write a reaction paper in which you evaluate the writer's information and reasoning.

SAMPLE REACTION PAPER: A RESPONSE TO "HOT ENOUGH FOR YOU?"

Michael Rivera

In "Hot Enough for You?" author Marian Kester criticizes scientific weather management. She is worried about two problems. First, we do not have enough information in order to make accurate predictions about weather, let alone make wise choices about controlling it. Second, we tend to see weather, in particular, and nature, in general, as a hostile force competing with us. Although there is certainly merit in Kester's position, especially her admirable moral sense, it is hard to agree wholeheartedly with her argument and its implications.

Kester is angry about what she sees as human ignorance and arrogance, and is quite sarcastic. She thinks, instead, that we should appreciate the drama of weather, and cooperate with nature rather than control it. Her argument against using available technology to control the weather is based on ethics rather than economics. She never mentions the money cost and does not specify how advanced the research and development of these technologies are now. Most people would probably agree in criticizing the examples Kester gives: spraying forests with chemicals to make them fireproof, and dealing with volcanoes and earthquakes. Just because the technology theoretically exists does not mean that we should do it. But readers would probably agree with Kester for a different reason. The technology would cost too much to put into practice and might not work. Kester, on the other hand, sees interfering with natural processes as immoral. One major problem with Kester's argument is knowing where to draw the line. Should we never interfere with nature? From its beginnings in Mesopotamian irrigation to today's gene splicing, Western civilization has been based on understanding and controlling nature. Would Kester give up all the real benefits of our technology, from electricity to polio vaccines? That is the really hard part of this debate, and there is no easy answer.

Everyone would agree with Kester's first point about our igno- rance. There is so much we do not know about nature. However, Kester overstates her case about weather forecasting. For her, "me- teorology as a science compares unfavorably with palmistry. It must even bow to astrology." It is unfair for her to give as an example the mistakes about the comet Kohoutek, because that was a matter for astronomy, not meteorology. Also, although Kester does not admit it and may not know, apparently the accuracy of National Weather Service forecasts really is improving, especially short-term predic- tions about temperature.

Without drawing much attention to it, Kester does identify one good reason for our ignorance—the specialization of experts. For example, she remarks that meteorologists are not trained to under- stand pollution and therefore cannot see the bigger picture of what is happening. This is surely a growing problem in every field.

Kester's second point, about human arrogance in wanting to tame nature, is more controversial. We all control the effects of weather, at the least by wearing clothes to keep us warm in winter or by seeking shade in summer. We develop drought-resistant corn and irrigate our fields. It is true that mankind has sometimes made terrible mistakes, causing accidents and unplanned side-effects. But should we just give up trying? Is it all interference or meddling?

Kester sees the culprit in the media who turn nature into melo- drama. Yet she personally also wants drama, what she calls "wild weather . . . one of the last exciting, adventurous things left." This seems inconsistent. Her article does jump from point to point. Bring- ing in Leon Trotsky's comments from 1924 is exotic. But Kester does cite reputable scientists, including geologists and anthropologists.

To fault Kester for logic is probably unfair. She is angry and passionately involved in warning us. Her exaggeration is unavoid- able. She raises a number of important issues in indirect ways, and makes each of us think about where we stand on them. It would be nice, for instance, to know for sure whether it was going to rain or not when you were planning a picnic. But how could we all agree on what kind of weather we wanted, even if we were absolutely sure we could make it happen? Not knowing what the weather will bring is a small, but real, excitement for each of us every day. I hope we keep it this way.

ARGUING A CASE—FOR OR AGAINST

In developing an argument you are trying to persuade someone or some group that your ideas or values make sense. You have probably begun to develop some ideas about the topic you have been researching. In this section we want to give you an opportunity to test out some of those ideas and rehearse them with an audience before you use them in your formal research paper. In addition to describing and illustrating the steps in constructing an argument, we will explain how to use an informal system of acknowledging your sources.

The first step is to decide how strong a position you want to take on your subject. Suppose you have been researching the effectiveness of vitamin supplements. The information you have uncovered might be conclusive enough for you to argue that vitamins can help the body to fight everything from the common cold to cancer. On the other hand, you might decide that the facts do not support most of the claims that are made for vitamin supplements.

As you are mulling over the facts, you also want to keep in mind the importance of finding a position that is worth arguing. Some aspects of your subject may be so universally accepted that there is no point in developing an argument about them. For example, everyone agrees that child abuse is terrible. Almost everyone now agrees that it is a serious social problem. However, there are different opinions about how we should respond to this problem. Concentrate on an aspect of your topic where there is some disagreement and develop a position.

Finding your position or thesis depends partly on your sense of an audience. You need to estimate just how much your audience already knows about the subject. For example, many psychologists already know that the use of hypnosis in police work poses certain dangers. However, a general audience might not be aware of the problem. For a less informed audience, then, your argument might be aimed at convincing them that there is a problem. For an informed audience, you might develop an argument to support a solution to the problem.

Once you have settled on a position, you must analyze the reasons for your position and list them. Next, you must select facts, details, and examples which support your position. Sometimes it helps to start writing down your ideas without worrying about organization. Just write your thoughts and feelings as freely as possible until you have stated everything that is on your mind. Then you can review what you have written and pull out your major points.

Suppose you were opposed to the use of hypnosis in criminal investigations. A list of your arguments and support points might look like this:

ARGUMENTS	SUPPORT POINTS
1. Hypnosis leads to lies.	Murder trial in illinois
2. Hypnosis does not improve memory.	Freud's scepticism
	Hypnosis increases suggestability.
	Leading questions can alter memory.
3. Convinces jury.	Hypnosis can induce false certainty.

After you have identified the reasons for supporting your position, you must think of all the counter arguments that might be raised against you. Sometimes you can tell what the pros and cons of an argument are from your reading on the subject. Other times, you will have to brainstorm to imagine the objections someone might pose. You must also be honest and open minded enough to identify any facts which do not fit your position.

Counter Arguments

1. There are cases where hypnosis has provided police with new clues.
2. Police usually get corroborating evidence.
3. Police hypnotists are trained to avoid leading questions.
4. Lawyers often coach witnesses.

Your next step is to see if you can find weaknesses in the counter arguments or additional facts which will weaken those counter arguments. As you carefully assess the pros and cons, you may find yourself modifying or changing your position. That is all right. A change in your position may mean that you are doing a thorough job of thinking through an issue.

Once you have carefully considered the pros and cons, you must develop a strategy for presenting your argument.

The Introduction

Catch the reader's attention. You can do this by:

Using a startling example or case history
Giving some of the history of the issue
Quoting an authority on the issue
Asking a series of questions

State or imply your position. If your position is controversial and your audience is skeptical or hostile, you may not want to state your position.

Instead, you may decide to let the force of your facts and reasoning lead the audience to the same conclusion that you have reached.

The Body

Present arguments and counter arguments. There are at least two possible strategies here. If you have found a few opposing points that you cannot refute, the best strategy is to mention them briefly and then go on to develop the arguments in support of your position. On the other hand, if you have been able to refute most of the counter arguments, then your best strategy might be to build each paragraph around a counter argument and your refutation of it. The sample argumentative paper uses this strategy.

Present proposals and recommendations. First, you need to demonstrate that your proposals are directed at the real causes of the problem. Next, you should show that the proposal is practical. Finally, you should consider any disadvantages in your proposal.

The Conclusion

End on a strong note. Save a compelling reason, fact, example, or quote for the end of your paper.

ACKNOWLEDGING YOUR SOURCES

When you are presenting an argument, it is helpful to let your audience know the source of your information. Good sources of information from reliable and unbiased authorities add weight to your argument. In a formal research paper you would follow one of the accepted systems of documentation to show where you obtained your information, but in the argumentative paper you can use an informal method called a running acknowledgment. To use this method you identify the source within the text of your paper. You can include an author's name, qualifications, or title of the publication.

Example: Opponents of forensic hypnosis, such as Dr. Martin Orne, president of the International Society of Clinical Hypnosis, argue that there is no scientific evidence to prove that hypnosis improves recall.

Example: Officer Millie Markman of the New York Police Department points out that forensic hypnotists are trained to ask very open-ended questions.

Example: According to an article in a recent issue of *Psychology Today*, hypnotic techniques are used by many people who are trying to persuade others.

Example: The facts presented in this paper come primarily from publications produced by Independent Research Associates, which has established a reputation for reliable information on alcohol and drug abuse.

EXERCISE

Some topics are more controversial than others. However, you can almost always find some issue in your readings that you feel strongly about and that you could argue a case for or against.

This exercise requires you to write an argumentative paper about an issue associated with your topic. Use an informal method of documentation (running acknowledgment) to identify the specific sources of your information.

Here is an opportunity for you to stick your own neck out and make clear just where you stand on some issue that you feel is important. Your main job is to persuade the reader that your position is right.

The sample argumentative paper that follows will give you a model of what your paper should look like.

SAMPLE ARGUMENTATIVE PAPER: THE VERDICT COMES IN ON FORENSIC HYPNOSIS

Peg Van Patten

On July 15, 1976, shocked townspeople of Chowchilla, California, learned that twenty-six children had not returned home from elementary school. Their school bus had been abducted by three gunmen. The children and bus driver, forced into a buried trailer body, bravely dug their way out the next day. However, a serious problem remained: there were no clues to the identities or whereabouts of the three masked kidnappers. Subsequently, hypnosis was tried on bus driver Ed Ray, enabling him to recall all but one of the license plate numbers of the men's van. The information ultimately led to the apprehension of the trio.

This success story is frequently cited by advocates of forensic hypnosis because hypnotic recall provided the key that solved the crime. However, there is growing controversy about police use of hypnosis. Arizona and Minnesota have banned its use in court; New Jersey has limited admissibility; six states are yet undecided; and in Massachusetts a convicted killer was granted a new trial because testimony based on a hypnotic session was used.

Although the potential for abuse always exists, forensic hypnosis should be permitted under carefully controlled conditions. The track record of forensic hypnosis is quite impressive. Hypnosis produced new leads in 77% of the cases studied in Los Angeles, and 91% of the informational items were later corroborated.

Opponents of forensic hypnosis, such as Dr. Martin Orne, president of the International Society of Clinical Hypnosis, argue that there is no scientific evidence to prove that hypnosis improves recall. It may be true that research has not been able to document improved recall, but there are numerous examples from police files. In addition to the Chowchilla case, a middle-aged North Carolina woman remembered under hypnosis a murder that took place when she was nine years old. In Los Angeles, a woman who had witnessed a murder while intoxicated was at first unable to give any sort of description. During hypnosis, she described the murderer "right down to the stripes in his pants and the dots in his tie." The composite drawing that resulted led to an arrest.

Dr. Orne is also fearful that leading questions may be asked of a hypnotized person. He claims that improper questioning can feed information to a witness. This is a real danger, but it is one that forensic hypnotists are well aware of. Officer Millie Markman of the New York Police Department points out that forensic hypnotists are trained to ask very open-ended questions. "Mustaches are very hard," she states. "I can't ask if he wore one, because that suggests he did."

Dr. Orne and other psychiatrists and psychologists have presented a resolution, often read at trials, which calls for the ban of forensic hypnosis by law officers and insists that only they and their colleagues are qualified to perform it. Other organizations backing this position are the Society for Clinical and Experimental Hypnosis and the California Attorneys for Criminal Justice. The organizations fear that subjects under hypnosis reliving repressed experiences may become emotionally agitated and require medical assistance. However, this fear has proved groundless. On the contrary, subjects often feel calmer after recalling hypnotically traumatic events. For example, many rape victims haunted by nightmares often get their first peaceful night's sleep after hypnosis. Hypnotic suggestion enables a witness to view the crime scene as though it is a replay of a television or movie documentary on a screen. The witness is told that the film may be slowed down, speeded up, or stopped at will. Either the witness or the hypnotist may choose to "freeze" the action just before a traumatic event. In addition, a victim may be told that he or she may allow his part in the film to be played by a favorite movie star, thus minimizing personal terror. To date there have been no lawsuits filed claiming harm done to a witness from hypnosis.

Another objection expressed by the psychiatrists is the worry that fantasy presented convincingly by a subject may be viewed as fact. In answer to this charge, Dr. Martin Reiser, head of Los Angeles Police Department's "Svengali Squad," declares, "We know by corroboration when we're getting facts and when we're not . . . in 80 to 90 percent of our cases we are able to get subsequent corroboration of a composite drawing of suspects, license numbers, or vehicle descriptions. And so, this charge is patently ridiculous."

The Society for Clinical and Experimental Hypnosis also asserts that police officers do not have sufficient training to qualify them to perform hypnosis and offers its membership list as a guide for attorneys and courts in choosing a hypnotist. The only requirements for belonging to S.C.E.H., however, are paying dues and being a physician, psychologist, or dentist: training in hypnosis is not even included. Training undergone by officers in places like the Law Enforcement Hypnosis Institute takes 48 hours, as opposed to a usual 16 to 20 hours for the medical profession. Frank J. Monaghan, founder of the Hypnosis Institute of Fort Worth (Texas), regards the medical professionals as "interlopers." He remarks that "the investigative hypnotist does not regard himself as qualified to practice medical hypnosis or psychotherapy any more than he should regard physicians as professional investigators." Sergeant Diggett, staff hypnotist for the New York Police Department, suggests a less altruistic motive of the psychologists: He estimates that the 400 interviews conducted by himself and Officer Markman meant that New York psychologists lost out on a potential $80,000 in consultation fees.

The final objection of psychiatrists and others is the charge that law enforcement officers represent only the prosecution and may bias a witness in their eagerness to get convictions. However, law officers never hypnotize defendants, only witnesses and victims. Furthermore, hypnosis is usually only used when no suspects or leads are available. There have been cases in which the information from hypnosis cleared a suspect. For example, a rape victim in Terrell, Texas, realized under hypnosis that the man charged with the crime was a look-alike, not her assailant. There have been instances in which defendants have requested hypnotism: Allen Lewis, who confessed to pushing a girl on the subway tracks in New York, and Peter Reilly, who became a cause célèbre in Connecticut after confessing to the grisly murder of his mother, were given new trials when hypnosis revealed that they had been coerced into confessing. Many believe that when Reilly, a teenager, was questioned for three days without proper food and sleep, he spontaneously entered a state akin to hypnotic trance, during which his interrogator suggested that he might have argued with his mother and killed her.

Law enforcement hypnotists point out a classic example of a psychiatrist bungling a hypnotic interview: the New Jersey case of *Sell* vs. *Hurd* (1980). Dr. Herbert Spiegel, a renowned expert in clinical hypnosis, made many technical errors which resulted in the testimony being disallowed and the case being dismissed. Mrs. Jane Sell had been attacked with a knife while asleep; suspects included her husband and her ex-husband. First, Dr. Spiegel did not tape the interview. Second, he encouraged the victim to fantasize by asking her to "imagine" what happened. Furthermore, he led the witness by asking, "Is it David? Is it Paul?" rather than the objective question, "Who is it?". Spiegel later defended himself by describing his purpose as "primarily therapeutic, namely, attempting to treat her traumatic neurosis." Recently, Dr. Spiegel was quoted as saying "the police officer is infinitely more skillful in interrogating witnesses than any psychiatrist."

In conclusion, there is potential for abuse in forensic hypnosis, just as there is in any witness interrogation and recall. Certain guidelines can be established to minimize problems. First, hypnotists should work only with witnesses and victims in videotaped sessions. They should be given only the barest essentials of the case. Also, the information that results must be backed up by corroborating evidence. Finally, the hypnotist must be an experienced criminal justice professional, trained in interrogation procedure and psychology.

EXERCISE

The purpose of an argumentative paper is to convince the reader. Because this notion of the audience that needs to be persuaded is so important, we include the following peer review sheet as an opportunity for you to try out your argument with an audience and get some specific response to your ideas and to your paper.

Directions: Work in pairs, exchanging your papers. When you get your partner's paper, read it and fill out this "Peer Review Sheet."

Argumentative Paper
Peer Review Sheet

Writer's name _____

Reviewer's name _____

1. Is the issue or problem made clear in the introduction? State the issue in your own words.

2. Where does the writer state his/her position? Copy the position statement on this sheet.

3. What arguments are given to support the writer's position? List the arguments.

4. What opposing arguments does the writer mention? List them. Can you think of any opposing points that the writer does not consider?

5. Does the writer agree with any of the opposing arguments? If so, list them.

6. What arguments or evidence does the writer use to show the fallacies of the opposing side?

7. Does the writer present sufficient facts, examples, or case histories to support his/her opinions and claims? If not, where are additional facts needed?

8. Are the connections between ideas clear? Are there any places where you cannot follow the writer's reasoning?

REFINING YOUR BIBLIOGRAPHY

So far you have been tracking down sources of information for your paper and keeping a record on bibliography cards of what you have found. Soon you will be working in depth with these sources, reading them in detail and taking notes. Now is the time for weeding some out. You need to decide which sources you really want to get to know and which to screen out. There are two ways to do this, one by forming your own general impression, the other by consulting authorities you trust.

The same thing happens when you meet new people. You quickly form a general impression of what they are like on the basis of their appearance and behavior. And you may change your mind later. To get even more information about them, so you know whether or not to invite them to a party, for example, you might ask some mutual friends for their opinion, too. This way you find out about their reputation.

The next assignment requires you to form an initial impression of your sources in two ways: First, to describe them by summing them up briefly, and, second, to evaluate them by offering your first impression opinion. Just as with people, you may change your mind later on longer acquaintance; but you must begin somewhere and this step will move you on comfortably to the next steps.

An Annotated Bibliography

Professional researchers and librarians learn a special format for this activity. You don't need to worry about that now. What you are aiming at, however, is to provide several sentences for each of the sources you identified back on Worksheet 6, your preliminary bibliography.

Begin by identifying the source with complete bibliographical information. Then write one or two sentences to *summarize* the main point or points of the source objectively. Then add one or two more sentences to *evaluate* how good or useful you think it is likely to be.

Here are four examples of annotated bibliography items, prepared by a student working on a research paper about genetic engineering. Notice that this student has used quotations from the original source as a short cut to make his points.

Articles:

> Dembart, Lee. "Fears on DNA Studies Fade, but Won't Die," *Los Angeles Times,* April 12, 1980, Part I, p. 1 ff. Dembart claims that fears of "Andromeda Strain" are unfounded. There is an interesting quote by James D. Watson, codiscoverer of DNA, who says over the genetic controversy, "I think the whole thing is lunacy. . . . I helped raise these issues, but within six months I was acutely embarrassed. There's no evidence that anyone has gotten sick from any of this." On the other side, Dembart quotes Robert Sinsheimer, who acknowledges

fears are less justified than originally thought, but also suspects that genetic engineering could conceivably result in a new route for the transmission of cancer. This seems like a pretty balanced, up-to-date overview of the whole issue.

Rich, Vera. "Soviet Claims," *Nature*, July 3, 1980, pp. 6–7. The Soviet newspaper *Pravda* claims that the U.S. is working on "ethnic viruses." They are supposed to be bacteriological weapons which would selectively attack members of particular races or ethnic groups. This ridiculous claim could at least be used to demonstrate the paranoia generated by the government's hush-hush attitude toward this issue.

Books:

Howard, Ted, and Jeremy Rifkin. *Who Should Play God?* New York. Dell, 1977. According to its dustjacket, this book "lifts the cloak of secrecy from genetic experiments" and explores, among other things, "who is performing the research and who profits from it." It's clearly anti-genetic engineering; its chapter titles give a good idea of the direction and flavor of the book, for example, "Eugenics," "Eliminating 'Bad' Genes," "Bio-Futures," "Scientists and Corporations." This looks like the place to go for the social arguments from the political left wing.

Wade, Nicholas. *The Ultimate Experiment: Man-Made Evolution.* New York. Walker and Company, 1977. This seems to be a more balanced book than Howard and Rifkin's, for example, the chapter: "Assessing the Hazards." The book explains the significance of the Conference at Asilomar in 1975 which set guidelines for genetic research, I think. There is a description of *E. coli* bacteria which all the sources refer to. Wade admits that estimating dangers is still largely guesswork; he raises issues but remains noncommital. He does make a point of distinguishing genetic engineering from other technologies. One interesting point I stumbled across here: "Despite the yodeling about medical benefits, the most important contributions of the gene splicer's craft may well come from some unexpected quarter, such as in the adaptation of microorganisms to convert sunlight into machine-usable forms of energy." Thus genetic engineering *may* be connected with solar power and the whole dilemma of fuel.

The bibliographical material on genetic engineering was compiled by Professor Malcolm Kiniry from student work generated in his English III class at UCLA, 1983.

EXERCISE

For each of the following annotated items, identify the two main parts: (1) the summary of what it is about; and (2) an evaluation of its worth or usefulness.

1. Bresler, Robert J. "The Bargaining Chip and SALT." *Political Science Quarterly,* volume 92, 1977, pp. 65–88. Bresler explores the dangers and advantages of using bargaining chips during strategic negotiations. He points out that the U.S. uses this ploy often. The article is good because it examines a not often mentioned aspect of SALT.

2. Burt, Richard. "The Scope and Limits of SALT." *Foreign Affairs*, volume 56, 1978, pp. 751–776. From a pro arms control point of view, Burt points out the substantive limitations of SALT II: the failure to address the issues of MIRV, cruise missiles, and new technology. This article is a good liberal critique of SALT II.
3. Gray, Colin S. "SALT: Time to Quit." *Strategic Review*, volume 4, 1976, pp. 14–22. Gray takes the view that SALT was of dubious worth and that SALT II is definitely bad for the national security of the United States. He calls for the discontinuation of SALT before further damage is done. Gray presents an excellent conservative critique of SALT.
4. Kinter, W. R., and R. L. Pfaltzgraff. "Assessing the Moscow SALT Agreements." *Orbis*, volume 16, 1972, pp. 341–360. The authors hold the conservative view that SALT cannot halt the slipping nuclear advantage of the United States. They conclude that the United States needs a national reassessment of defense policy. They further conclude that the only utility of SALT is in developing a dialogue with the Soviets. This is a good conservative critique of SALT I.
5. Kruzel, J. "SALT II: The Search for a Follow on Agreement." *Orbis*, volume 17, 1973, pp. 9–18. Kruzel favors SALT. He points out that SALT II is concerned with converting the interim agreement of SALT I into a permanent treaty and also with both quantitative and qualitative reductions. This is a useful overview of the early SALT II negotiations.
6. Lodal, Jan. "SALT II and American Security." *Foreign Affairs*, volume 57, 1979, pp. 387–410. Lodal takes a favorable view of SALT II. He argues that SALT II enhances American national security by preserving our technological advantage and at the same time limiting Soviet arms development. He presents a good liberal defense of SALT II.
7. Scoville, H. "Beyond SALT I." *Foreign Affairs*, volume 50, 1972, pp. 488–500. Scoville presents a pro SALT view which argues that SALT I was only the first step and that SALT II is necessary to complete the process. He offers a fine liberal argument for SALT II.

The annotated items on SALT were prepared by Professor Patricia Chittenden for her Library and Information Science 110 course at UCLA, 1984.

Discovering a Source's Academic Reputation

Not all your sources come from libraries. But there is a good chance that books you may want to use have already been professionally reviewed, and these reviews help establish the book's reputation. So consulting these reviews is a handy short cut.

Where do you find reviews of your book sources? Look in the reference section of your library for specialized guides to book reviews. These guides list the reviews alphabetically by author of the book reviewed. Some have title and subject indexes and a few include a reviewer index. In order to locate a book review, you need to know the book's date of original publication. This indicates when the book could have been reviewed.

Here are the main guides for book reviews:

Book Review Digest
Book Review Index
Current Book Review Citations
New York Times Book Review Index, 1896–1970

In addition, professional journals often include reviews of new books and important articles. Usually the index you are using will identify these reviews. Here is an example from *Psychological Abstracts:*

suggestive nature of trance experience & future of hypnosis as "shared
    delusion", comment on D. E. Gibbons's article, 9701
suggestive nature of trance experience & future of hypnosis as "shared
    delusion", comment on D. E. Gibbons's article, 9702

WORKSHEET 11

Annotating Your Bibliography

Name _____   Date _____

Directions: Look at your preliminary bibliography, Worksheet 6. Pick two articles and two books from it. Annotate the two articles in the space below. Follow the format illustrated in the preceding exercise and in the examples on pp. 163–164.

Article 1:

Article 2:

For each of your books, find and read a review.

Book 1:   Which guide did you use to find out about the review?

Where was this review published? (that means, in what other book or magazine)

Annotate your book in the space below. Follow the format illustrated in the examples on p. 164.

Book 2:   Which guide did you use to find out about the review?

Where was this review published?

Annotate your book in the space below. Follow the format illustrated in the examples on p. 164.

7. RECORDING INFORMATION WITH A NOTE CARD SYSTEM

MANY STUDENTS, WHEN they are required to read several sources at once, feel swamped by words. Everything begins to blur. One book or magazine article seems just as good, or as bad, as the next. One of your most important goals as a student is to develop a kind of x-ray vision so that when you read several sources you will be able to see the logical structure beneath the blur of words, notice the main points, see how they are supported, and, also, observe how they are related to other sources. Like learning anything, this x-ray skill takes practice. You have already been practicing with single sources. And because research papers involve more than single sources—that is, multiple sources—now is the time to move on. It is not enough just to read each separate source for meaning. When you prepare a research paper you need to integrate facts and ideas from different books and articles.

This requirement to integrate source material is all-important. Trying to avoid it results in the most common flaw in college research papers: a research paper that presents information from one source in a paragraph or two, and then moves on to present information from another source, and then another, one by one, instead of combining related points. In this case the writer does not demonstrate any individual, independent, or personal perspective on the subject; the paper just parrots information.

COMPARING AND CONTRASTING

Before we discuss note taking, we would like you to practice the process of finding similarities and differences between two writers. Here are two paragraphs taken from different sources. In some ways they overlap; in other ways they are different. Read them.

1. From a column by Kendrick Frazier in *Science News:*

    At this point weather modification is so much in its infancy that
    the future social and legal issues are just beginning to emerge. Few
    people have been affected so far. But many responsible persons feel
    that the time to examine the issues is now, before the capability to
    cause widespread effects is developed. The most fundamental ques-
    tion regarding weather modification is: Should it be done?

2. An anonymous article in *The Futurist,* entitled "Making Weather Fit the
    Crops":

    Scientists predict that weather modification will become common
    within the next several years. It will take a great deal more research
    before the local weatherman will be able to announce rather than
    predict the weather. But the increasing sophistication of modification
    techniques is making such an occurrence more likely.

EXERCISE

1. These two paragraphs are basically about the same subject. What subject?

2. Do these two writers agree on anything at all?

    (a) What do they agree on? (Your own words):

    (b) Copy the phrases of sentences expressing or implying this agreement:
    1.

    2.

3. What do these two writers disagree about? (In your own words):

4.   What words or phrases signal these things they disagree about? Copy them:

1.

2.

Now fill in the following paragraph:

According to both (author of 1) ———————————————— and the

anonymous writer of (title of 2) ———————————————

weather modification is (what they agree on *in your words*) ——————

_____ .

However, they also disagree. They disagree about (in your own words)

_____ .

For example, in 1 (writer's name), ————————————————

maintains that (quote his main point) ————————————————

_____ .

But the writer of (title of 2) ————————————————

is more interested in (quote it)

_____ .

The Point of This Exercise

This kind of synthesis is not too difficult if you are working with only small bits of data and can keep looking back at them. However, if you are working with long reading passages—books and articles—it is just impossible to keep all the data in your memory.

To supplement your memory, to keep track of your ideas, and to help organize them, you can use a note card system.

TAKING NOTES

Each writer's approach to taking notes is slightly different. The spectrum ranges from chaotic to highly disciplined. Some writers prefer to read extensively and take only occasional notes, which they use to help them relocate information that they want to quote or paraphrase. We are going to stress a more orderly recording process: note cards. The note card approach is used not only by academic researchers, but also by highly respected journalists, such as John McPhee. According to the editor of the *John McPhee Reader*, he takes extensive notes while interviewing people. Later, these notes are typed and read to spot any areas that need further research. After he has filled in the missing information, McPhee studies the complete set of notes to identify the subdivisions of his topic. He writes the labels of his subdivisions on index cards, "fans them out and begins to play a sort of writer's solitaire, studying the possibilities of order." Once he decides on a structure, he makes a folder for each subdivision. Then McPhee goes back to the typed notes, cuts them up, and sorts them into the appropriate folders. Each folder becomes the raw material for one section of his article.

Are Note Cards Necessary?

We don't blame students for believing that note cards are a fetish of English teachers. You probably know people who have written successful research papers without using note cards. They seem superfluous, and cumbersome; they make a difficult task seem more complicated. However, our experience has convinced us that note cards have some important benefits and we would like you to try the system at least once. Then you will be free to decide for yourself whether to continue.

How Note Cards Will Help You

1. They will improve the content of your paper by making it less likely that you will rely on long quotes strung together by an occasional sentence of your own. The system we suggest requires you to strictly limit the amount of information on each card.
2. They will improve the organization of your paper by making it easier for you to integrate information from different sources. Unless you use note cards (or have already developed good organizational skills) you run the risk of writing a paper that is just a series of separate summaries. This is the most common flaw in undergraduate research papers.

There are two points to learn about note cards, a hard one and an easier one:

The easier one is what a note card looks like.
The hard one is deciding what information to take out of your reading and how to
   record it on a note card.

What a Note Card Looks Like

1. It looks like all your other note cards. That is, it is the same uniform size, not
    torn sheets of paper. Buy 5″ × 8″ index cards or make your own by recycling
    ordinary letter size paper (from the wastepaper basket perhaps?), folding it
    from top to bottom and cutting it in half to give you two note cards. This
    recycling is not only ecologically sound, but if the paper already has some-
    thing written on the back you will not be tempted to write on two sides of a
    note card (which tends to complicate everything).
2. It has the same parts filled in as your other note cards. It uses the same
    pattern. The standard format for a note card includes this information:

    Your borrowed information (your note). Put only one idea on each card.
    An exact reference to the page(s) where you got this information. That maga-
       zine or book can be indicated by the author's name (if you are using only
       one source by that author) or, if there is no author, by the title. You can
       abbreviate this bibliographical information, too, because you already have a
       bibliography card somewhere else where you previously recorded all the
       important data and the complete details for each of your sources.
    A subject label that you put at the top of the note card. Where do you get this
       subject label? You dream it up yourself by asking "What is this note I have
       just written down about?" The trick is to come up with a descriptive label
       that is as precise as possible without copying out the whole noted idea
       again. You will need these subject labels later to group your note cards and
       sort them into piles. The process of creating labels becomes easier as you
       progress in your research. Gradually, you will begin to see how your topic
       is subdivided.

Example of the Pattern for a Note Card

```
┌──────────────────────────────────────────┐
│          SUBJECT LABEL HEADING            │
│                                           │
│   Your recorded idea, that is, your       │
│   note, perhaps quoted, but probably      │
│   paraphrased.                            │
│                                           │
│   the source (probably author's name)     │
│   and page number                         │
│                                           │
└──────────────────────────────────────────┘
```

Remember to put only one idea on each note card. Don't worry if that idea may be only one or two words. For example:

```
+------------------------------------------+
|                                          |
|          minimum technique               |
|                                          |
|     wet finger = wind direction          |
|                                          |
|    Thompson, p. 57                       |
|                                          |
+------------------------------------------+
```

Stupid Note Cards

The technique for making stupid note cards is to treat note cards like little pieces of paper and copy long, continuous passages from your sources. This will completely defeat the purpose of note cards which is to wean you from relying entirely on other people's ideas.

Adding Your Comments to Note Cards

The extra space on a notecard can be very useful when you want to comment on an idea you are borrowing and recording.

Danger: Make sure you separate your own comments and don't mix them up with your source. A convention like square brackets is a help, or using a specially colored pen.

```
+----------------------------------------------+
|                                              |
|        cricket chirps--measure temp.         |
|                                              |
|   "Count the number of chirps in 14 seconds  |
|   and add 40.  The result is the temperature |
|   in degrees Fahrenheit."                    |
|                                              |
|   me--you'd need a stopwatch.  So why not buy|
|   a thermometer in the first place?          |
|                                              |
|   Franz, p. 121                              |
|                                              |
+----------------------------------------------+
```

We strongly encourage you to put your reactions on note cards as you record information. The little flashes that occur while you are reading frequently are forgotten unless you jot them down. Furthermore, we want to stress again that the purpose of the research is to help you answer an important question about your subject. Your goal is to formulate some conclusions about the subject and then to use the notes as a way of explaining and supporting your ideas.

What to Take Out of Your Reading and Put on a Note Card

1. Any main ideas that may be related to your research question or topic.
2. Any particularly interesting supporting details. What does "interesting" mean here? Interesting to you. When you read a passage some details will stick in your mind because they connect to your own personal experience. Somebody else might not react the same way. Those details that you respond to are noteworthy.

You should also ask yourself why they strike you as particularly interesting. If you can bring these hidden reasons up to the surface, they may give you some direction about developing your own thesis on the subject.

As you can see, selecting information from your reading to record on a note card requires reading the source first as well as reconstructing an outline of the ideas in it so you can identify the parts you need.

At first, you will find yourself taking quite a few notes because the subject is new to you. However, as you read more and become more informed, and as you narrow your topic and it becomes more familiar, you will probably take fewer notes per reading. In any case, always make sure you put only one idea on each note card.

REVIEW: QUOTING AND PARAPHRASING

In general, you should paraphrase the original. That means you should boil it down and put it in your own words when you transfer the information from your reading to your note card.

You should quote only in a few special situations:

1. When the original is worded so elegantly, perfectly, memorably, powerfully, that you don't want to change its effect at all by messing with it.
2. When you just can't paraphrase it and do justice to the meaning, even though you have tried.
3. When the original is very provocative or unusual, and you want to borrow the prestige and authority of the original words to run defense for yourself, in case your reader may not agree with this point.

Remember that quoting means copying the exact words of the original and putting them inside double quotation marks.

Changes You Can Make When Quoting

If it does not change the meaning at all, you can omit some words within the part you quote. You must indicate that you have discarded some of the author's words by replacing those words with a special punctuation mark called an ellipsis, which looks like three dots:(. . .).

Plagiarism

There are two types of inadequate paraphrasing that can constitute plagiarism. Study the example of an original passage and the two inadequate paraphrases of it that follow.

Original passage from "Weather Forecasts: Fair, Gradual Clearing, Rising Accuracy," *Changing Times,* February 1978, p. 45.

> Thunderstorms are forecast and tracked with good accuracy, but it is something else to predict the lightning, tornadoes and floods that go with them. Most tornadoes are less than a quarter of a mile and erratic. Tornadoes and flash floods can usually be forecast only two to six hours ahead, and then only for a broad area.

Poor Paraphrase #1: This version replaces individual words with synonyms, thereby suggesting that the student has not fully understood the material.

> Thunderstorms are predicted and followed with beneficial exactness, but it is otherwise to forecast the lightning, tornadoes and floods that accompany them. The majority of tornadoes are fewer than 500 yards across and random. Tornadoes and sudden floods can habitually be predicted only 120 minutes to a quarter of a day beforehand, and then only for a wide section.

Poor Paraphrase #2: The sentence order has been changed around, but the words are the same.

> Scientists very accurately forecast and track thunderstorms, but predicting their lightning, tornadoes and floods is something else. Covering less than a quarter of a mile, most tornadoes move erratically. Scientists can usually forecast tornadoes and flash floods only two to six hours ahead of time, and they can do that for a broad area only.

Here is a good paraphrase of the original passage:

> Although scientists can predict thunderstorms, they have trouble pinpointing the time or specific location for any accompanying lightning, tornadoes or floods.

SAMPLE NOTE CARDS

Direct Quotation

Use this method if the information is difficult to paraphrase or if the author's choice of words is particularly memorable.

Improving accuracy of short-range forecasts

"In forecasting high and low temperatures a day
ahead, the Weather Service missed by 4.9°F in 1966,
averaging the forecasts in all states except Alaska
and Hawaii. By 1976, that had been cut to 3.6°.
For temperature forecasts 36 hours ahead, the error
was reduced from 5.6° to 4°...."

"Weather Forecasts: Fair...", p. 46

Paraphrase

Prediction of violent weather--tornadoes

Tornadoes are harder to predict than hurricanes
because they are smaller and develop very quickly.
The Weather Service alerts people if conditions
are likely to produce tornadoes (tornado watch) or
if a tornado has been reported (tornado warning).

"Weather Forecasts: Fair...", p. 46

Combination of Paraphrase and Quotation

This method is frequently used when some of the information in a paragraph is difficult to paraphrase.

Deaths due to violent weather--tornadoes

"In 1926 one tornado killed more than 600 people in
Illinois, Indiana, and Missouri--part of...'tornado
alley'."
      There was an average of one death per tornado
before 1953 when the Weather Service began tornado
alerts.
      Now "... the death rate has declined to about one
for every seven tornadoes."

"Weather Forecasts: Fair...", p. 46.

(Notice that quotations within quotations have single quotation marks.)

EXERCISE

1. Provide headings for the following note cards:

━━ ━━ ━━ ━━ ━━ ━━ ━━ ━━ ━━ ━━ ━━ ━━ ━━ ━━

Dr. Reid Bryson--University of Wisconsin--
studying "changes in the intensity of sunlight"
and atmospheric changes caused by movements of
the North Pole.

purpose of research--make long-range forecasts
(several months) that give general indication
of temp. and precipitation.

"Weather Forecasts: Fair...", p. 47.

━━ ━━ ━━ ━━ ━━ ━━ ━━ ━━ ━━ ━━ ━━ ━━ ━━

Tornado warnings issued by the Weather Service
have decreased the number of deaths per
tornado. Before 1953--one death per tornado.
Now--one death for every 7 tornadoes.

"Weather Forecasts: Fair...", p. 46

---

2. Find information to make note cards with the following headings. The
    article begins on p. 89.

Use direct
quotation

results of Moine's 1981 research

Use para-
phrase

> *storytelling by salespeople*

Use a com-
bination of
paraphrase
and direct
quotation

> *influential techniques used
> by salespeople*

SAMPLE NOTE CARDS FOR ONE ARTICLE

There is no one perfect way to transfer information from an article (or book) onto note cards. What one student chooses to select and record may be different from another student's choice. It depends on what this student has already read, recorded, and knows. What the student selects also depends on the purpose in reading the article and on the possibilities the student senses in the thesis as it develops. However, seeing what one student has done with one particular article can suggest ways for you to work with your sources.

Here is an article, "Wind, Weather and Work," with the student's underlining of important concepts. On one side you will find the thoughts that went through the student's head while reading the article. On the other side, you can see the note cards which record important information. Study this example. Ask yourself if you would think the same thoughts and make similar note cards. If not, what would you change? After all, this student's work is just one way of doing this assignment. There are other ways just as good.

WIND, WEATHER AND WORK

How the atmosphere affects our lives

BY CLAIRE GERUS

I have enough folklore sayings.

> *Some men 'gainst Raine do carry in their*
> *   backs*
> *Prognosticating Aching Almanacks.*
> *Some by painful elbow, hip or knee*
> *Will shrewdly guess what weather's like to*
> *   be*

ALTHOUGH JOHN Taylor wrote these words over 300 years ago, Canadians like John Boyd, a Toronto-based public relations writer in the city, confirms that sensitivity to the weather is still with us. He dreads the approach of winter: "That's when my arthritis acts up," he groans. Marjorie Blackhurst, an oil company executive, claims she knows when a "double low" is on the way. "I wake up feeling achy and stifled," she explains. "It's unfailingly when we're being hit by two low-pressure systems." Joe Richards from Sydney, N.S. knows his asthma's in for it when low-ceiling weather arrives. And at Toronto's Migraine Foundation, the switchboard lights up like a Christmas tree when the barometer plunges.

I don't need any more specific examples of health complaints. Besides, these all come from Canada.

Weather and health. As Dave Phillips, a meteorologist with Environment Canada's Atmospheric and Environment Service in Toronto, says: "Get any group of people together and the two topics they're bound to discuss are the <u>weather</u> and their <u>health</u>." Today, <u>a new branch of science, biometeorology,</u> is exploring <u>possible connections</u> between the two. In <u>1976</u>, the <u>World Health Organization</u> became concerned with the need for global research in this area, declaring it "a matter of urgency." Since then <u>major breakthroughs</u> have come from <u>Europe</u>, the <u>Soviet Union</u>, <u>Japan</u> and the <u>United States</u>.

This seems important. I've never heard of this new science. Is it just the author's opinion? No, the W.H.O. thinks so, too.

```
biometeorology: health + weather
"a new branch of science"
- 1976 W.H.O. called it "a matter
      of urgency"
- imp. advances in US, USSR, Japan,
      Europe

Gerus, p. 29
```

So far, Canadian involvement has been limited to spotty, unco-ordinated research. One frustrated government insider explains: "Even if you do find someone else working on a project similar to yours, trying to get through the red tape to co-ordinate your efforts is nearly impossible."

More about Canadian problems. I don't need this.

Dave Phillips offers an explanation for the lack of interest. "There's resistance among physical scientists to tackle it because it's hard to get clean, precise data. When studying a headache, for example, there are any number of factors that could be causing it."

"Wind, Weather and Work" by Claire Gerus appeared in Financial Post Magazine, *December 1979, and is reproduced here with permission of the author.*

The <u>Swiss</u> have spent years, despite these considerations, investigating the effects of weather on human beings. They've found that <u>roughly 30 percent of the world's population is vulnerable to atmospheric changes.</u> These "<u>weather sensitive people</u>" feel impending changes so keenly they're <u>literally human barometers</u>, experiencing a range of symptoms from mental depression to barely tolerable physical pain. In fact a study by the Swiss Meteorological Institute in 1974 of nearly 800 complaints by people sensitive to weather changes, revealed that fatigue, ill-humor and headache were the most frequent reactions, with more acute symptoms further down the scale. <u>Three-quarters of sufferers were women</u> between the ages of 13 and 60.

This is new to me. Seems like a good revealing and specific example. I like the numbers. I feel comfortable with figures.

Why are women the ill-fated majority? Thanks to a lucky genetic break for men, the <u>male sex hormones</u> are <u>also</u> the <u>anti-stress hormones</u> for pain, infection, trauma and <u>cold.</u> Women, who possess fewer of these hormones, are more susceptible to such forms of stress.

Overactive thyroid can also be triggered by weather-sensitivity. For these men and women, extreme temperature changes can be more than merely unsettling; they can bring on nearly intolerable pain.

I'm glad the author gave more information here to explain the statistics, but I find it hard to believe. I'd better make a note, though. Is this author a man or a woman? This medical problem seems rather extreme, involving only a few people.

You don't have to be weather-sensitive to be sensitive to the weather, however. Meteorologist Phillips and the AES are just completing an eight-month pioneer research study in co-operation with the Migraine Foundation in Toronto. Three hundred local <u>migraine</u> sufferers were observed for possible links between their condition and weather changes, with physicians closely following their progress. "We received scores of letters from doctors asking if there was any link between migraine and the weather," says Phillips. There was. Attacks tended to occur when the <u>barometric pressure fell below 29.9</u>, with <u>wind on the face</u> another factor in bringing on headaches.

This is about Canada again, but lots of people do have headaches, so this is good evidence.

Existing medical conditions, besides migraine headache, have also been shown to be caused by seriously aggravating weather changes:

● A five-year study of admissions in three Texas hospitals between 1946 and 1951 revealed that <u>myocardial infarcts</u>, known to precede heart failures, occur most frequently with sudden temperature changes caused by arrivals of polar or tropical air masses.

● Studies done at an ophthalmic clinic in Basel, Switerland, during the '30s, '40s and '50s, revealed that 80 percent of <u>glaucoma</u> cases were linked with the arrival of cold air masses.

● Dr. Solco Tromp, Europe's foremost biometeorologist, and director of the Biometeorological Centre in Leiden, Holland, has found that the frequency of <u>asthmatic</u> attacks increases during the passage of fast-moving cold fronts, especially after periods of moderate temperatures.

● A five-year study at Philadelphia General Hospital between 1949 and 1953 found that the highest number of <u>bleeding ulcer</u> complaints occur in March and April and October and November, corresponding to the greatest shift in temperature in those years.

The author lumps all these medical conditions together with bullets in a sort of outline, rather than discussing them in detail like the migraine headaches, so I'll lump them altogether, too, on one note card.

Swiss findings: "weather-sensitive people"

30% of people
"literally human barometers"
3/4 = women (p.31)

Gerus, pp. 29, 31

---

why women = "weather-sensitive"?

male sex hormones = anti-stress
                    hormones
          (against cold)

[me: I don't believe this]

Gerus, p. 31

---

migraine headaches

- caused when barometric pressure
      below 29.9

- also caused by wind in face

Gerus, p. 31

---

misc. medical conditions

- myocardial infarcts (before heart
                            failure)
- glaucoma (eye)
- asthma
- bleeding ulcers

Gerus, p. 31

I don't need any more information about history.

I wonder if this is true, and how many doctors the author is talking about, but if it is true, it's imp.

I'll ignore this stuff about Canada, but it would be interesting to Canadians.

This is really important -- the scientific reason!

I'm glad the author provides this explanation. It helps to have the explanation from this Univ. of Calif. scientist. I believe it.

Wouldn't you know there is supposed to be a solution. I wonder if this machine really works?

NONE OF THIS would have surprised Hippocrates (460 to 357 B.C.), our first physician, who wrote: "One should be especially on one's guard against the most violent changes of the seasons and unless compelled, one should neither purge nor apply cautery or knife to the bowels until at least 10 days have passed."

Even today, doctors in central Europe refuse to operate when they learn that a hot, dry wind known as the "Foehn" is imminent, as people are more vulnerable to upset at that time. And Calgarians blame the Chinook, Canada's western version of this wind for everything from the common cold to Alberta's high divorce rate. These unexpected blasts of warm air, known as "witches' winds," arrive in late winter and wreak havoc with human beings, as colds, infections, suicides and high accident rates soar with their onset. Researchers believe that the high numbers of positively charged air particles, or ions, accompanying the winds, could be the cause. Because our bodies contain a natural balance of positive and negative charges, any surplus of positive ions creates stress. Microbiologist and experimental pathologist Albert Krueger of the University of California has discovered that, in response, our bodies release a specific anti-stress hormone called serotonin. Overproduction of this hormone, called "the ultimate downer" by doctors, can inhibit our absorption of oxygen and produce sleeplessness, migraine with vomiting, respiratory problems, depression and heart pain.

Krueger also points out that office workers, who complain of similar symptoms, are continually exposed to environments conducive to the build-up of positive ions, thanks to air conditioning, synthetic fabrics, furniture and cigarette smoke, all known inhibitors of negative (beneficial) ions.

One solution which is gaining popularity is the office negative-ion generator, which restores the normal quantities of these beneficial charges to the air. Two Canadian manufacturers, both based in Montreal, are currently vying for new converts. Peter Slocum, marketing manager for Bio Tec, says, "We're doing 10 times the business we did last year. People are a lot more concerned about the environment they're working in." People who work in doctors' offices, health spas, and large high-rises with windows that don't open are buying them because, as Slocum explains, "they diminish the effects of crosslink infection spread by close contact with others, and by air conditioning."

Bill Lee, president of rival Elcar International Ltd., agrees that "the majority of our clients want to improve their environments." Among Elcar's clients are Xerox, The Royal Bank, the Ontario Ministry of Culture and Recreation, and British Columbia's Simon Fraser University. Both firms offer a variety of negative ion generators, from a tiny version that fits into your car lighter at around $100 to a $500 model which covers an area of about 18,000 cubic feet. Sales this year were good, claim Lee and Slocum, with combined sales for 1979 probably hitting 25,000 in Canada alone. Foreign export markets are picking up as well. "With the smog situation in Los Angeles, we're constantly kept busy sending down more units," says Slocum.

---

don't operate: wind conditions

Eastern European doctors
- before the "Foehn" (hot dry wind)
- because patients weak then

me: [is this like the Santa Anas?]

Gerus, p. 31

---

reason for bad wind: positive ions

e.g. "Foehn"

- bad wind carries many positive ions and body reacts to them

"any surplus of positive ions creates stress"

Gerus, p. 31

---

why positive ions are unhealthy

Albert Kreuger, Univ of Calif. microbiologist & pathologist

- says ions cause body to release too much "serotinin" (anti-stress hormone)
= "the ultimate downer" (p.31)
- example: office workers suffer (p.33)

Gerus, pp. 31, 33

---

negative-ion generator machine

- machine produces good ions to counteract bad ions

- producing companies are successful

- example: in Los Angeles (smog)

Gerus, p. 33

Fred Soyka, Toronto-based author of *The Ion Effect*, predicts that in time negative ion generating machines will be included in the design of new buildings' standard heating and cooling systems. Israel, Japan and England are already placing these devices in homes and offices, and two South African banks and a Swiss textile mill have reported higher staff morale, fewer mistakes, and lower absenteeism. (Absenteeism costs Canadian companies $14 million, with 130 million days lost due to illness.)

This is just one person's opinion -- a journalist's prediction.

While the pros and cons of "the ion effect" are being debated, <u>other weather research</u> is focusing on <u>magnetism</u> as a possible <u>culprit in health problems.</u> At the National Research Council in Ottawa, Olivier Heroux of the biological sciences department, has studied the effects of <u>sunspot activity on white rats.</u> In an article in *Science Dimension* (Vol. 2) in 1978, titled "Is Stress Regulated by the Sun?" Dr. Heroux suggests that there could, indeed, be a link. By placing his animals in a "cold chamber," with heat, light and temperature strictly controlled, he found that, for some reason, a periodic drop in resistance to colds would occur. After eliminating a wide range of possible causes, he finally admitted that <u>sunspot activity,</u> which affects the <u>earth's magnetic field,</u> could be the culprit. Every spring and fall, the rats' resistance dropped simultaneously with the time the earth's position allows highest penetration of solar particles into our atmosphere. Although reluctant to claim a cause-and-effect relationship ("it may be that geomagnetic activity is linked to something else"), he does suggest that a <u>connection exists between the seasonal activities of his mice and the sun.</u>

This experiment sounds important, but I wonder if they can use these studies about rats to explain human health?

Meanwhile, researchers S. R. C. Malin of Britain and B. J. Srivastava of India, reported in the Feb. 22, 1979 issue of *Nature* magazine "a high correlation" between periods of high sunspot activity, and increased admissions to hospitals in two cities in India.

Yes, I guess they can use rats this way to indicate similar human problems, at least in this one case.

The <u>implications</u> of these experiments in biometeorology could be enormous. If scientists can pin down which weather factors coincide with illness, they can direct our efforts at discovering why. For now, it appears that more sophisticated techniques in weather forecasting will, at least, offer more personal information to the public. Future weathermen, says Dave Phillips, will likely be consultants who, along with physicians, can help the public in general and specifically those with health problems, to cope with future weather trends. "We'll even tell them which <u>areas of the country to avoid</u> if they're planning to travel," predicts Phillips.

Lots of people travel, so this seems important.

Certainly there may be a demand for such a service. <u>Weather-consciousness is on the rise.</u> An <u>Associated Press</u> survey has shown that <u>nine out of 10 readers want more personalized weather reports.</u> Pollution indexes have been with us for years. Comfort indexes are on their way. Why not an index relating our health to the rain or snow outside?

Yes, I agree there's an increasing interest in weather and more useful weather forecasts. I'm more interested, but that may be because I'm doing this research paper.

```
health & sunspots (magnetism)

- experiment with rats showed
  connection: greater the sunspots,
  lower the rats' resistance to colds

⌈me - but are people similar to rats⌉
⌊      in this respect?            ⌋

- from article in Science Dimension,
                      1978 re sun & stress

Gerus, p. 33
```

```
health & sunspots

another example: when high sunspot
  activity, more patients into
  hospital in one case in India

- from article in Nature, 1979

Gerus, p. 33
```

```
biometeorology - practical effect

- advice to travelers: "which areas
    of the country to avoid"

Gerus, p. 33
```

```
biometeorology - practical effect

"more personalized weather reprots"

(like pollution index, but about
    comfort)

Gerus, p. 33
```

Exercise

Make a set of note cards based on an article you will use for your research paper.

1. Make at least 10 cards.
2. Limit the information on each card to a few facts about one idea.
3. Label each card with a subject heading at the top.
4. Indicate the source and page number at the bottom of the card.

8. ORGANIZING YOUR NOTES AND SYNTHESIZING YOUR INFORMATION

REVISING YOUR NOTE CARDS

AT THIS STAGE you should have a disorganized heap of note cards. One temptation is to keep on making note cards forever in order to put off this next step. This temptation is understandable because you often know that there is some excellent book or magazine article on your subject that you are waiting for someone to return to the library or to be sent through Interlibrary Loan. However, after you have read or made note cards on a reasonable number of sources you just have to say to yourself, "OK, that's it. On to the next step." The problem then becomes what to do with this mess of note cards. The first thing to do is to go back and look at your cards, one by one. It doesn't matter in what order. The purpose of this step is to make sure that only one idea or set of facts is recorded on each note card. If necessary, rewrite some of your note cards (you don't need to consult the original source). For example, what could be improved in this note card?

```
                        weather signs

153     clues:
16 and 52   animals (birds and bats)
                --height they fly
                --higher better (air pressure)
153     plants (grass wet with dew = good)
153     sky--smoke rising = good
                halo = rain
                setting sun--red in west good
                        yellow/grey = bad
16      smells--low pressure, bad weather
                smells leak out

Ross, pp. 16, 152, 153
```

Although there is no perfect answer to the question "How many different note cards are needed for these different ideas?," ideally more than one is needed. How many note cards would you recommend splitting this example into?

This is a real note card prepared by someone writing a real research paper, and the reason this note card was prepared this way, honestly, was because the researcher did not read the article through first before taking notes, but just jumped around randomly.

Also make sure that the subject headings you have put at the top of each note card accurately label the idea recorded. What could be improved about the following note card?

> <u>weather</u>
>
> "Pitted against your favorite TV weatherman, with his radar and weather satellites, the <u>Old Farmer's Almanac</u> still is right as rain."
>
> Grosswirth, p. 63

How could you change this note card for the better? Remember that the label should identify the noted idea as precisely and narrowly as possible without actually repeating it.

Go through all your own note cards to make sure they are in as good shape as possible.

Now what? In a word: outlining.

Before you actually start in writing your paper you need some sort of pattern to follow that will indicate the logical relationships of your ideas, and the order you will present them in. You make up this pattern, or outline, from the subject labels on your note cards.

You will start by sorting your note cards into piles according to their labels, in other words, by grouping together note cards with related ideas.

EXERCISE

Take the following subject heading labels and group them. In other words, which ones go together?

1. Sherry nut cake with lemon frosting
2. Green bean salad
3. Eggnog
4. Chilled cucumber soup
5. Seabass poached with shrimp sauce
6. Muscat wine punch

7. Curried lima beans
8. French onion soup
9. Clam chowder
10. Tablecloth
11. Lemon meringue pie
12. Company fish casserole
13. Marinated mushrooms with artichokes
14. Spicy summer squash
15. Cheese
16. Champagne cocktail

This exercise is trickier than it might look at first. There are several different ways to group these labels:

1. You could group them according to courses in a meal or recipes in a cookbook. In this case you are creating pigeonholes for them to fit into:

   Beverages
   Appetizers
   Soup
   Salad
   Entree
   Dessert

2. You could perhaps group them according to ingredients:

   Dishes prepared with wine
   Dishes not prepared with wine

3. You could also group them according to temperature:

   Hot dishes
   Room temperature dishes
   Cold dishes

4. What else can you think of to divide up and group these labels? Color? Or which ones you would like to eat better, or consider preparing?
5. And what do you do with the label "Cheese"? Don't you have to be more specific before you can work with it at all? Like cheese fondu, or cheddar cheese slices with apple pie, or macaroni and cheese?
6. And what do you do with "Tablecloth"? It doesn't seem to belong here at all.

What Did You Learn from This Exercise?

These labels are like labels on note cards. Just as you had to juggle these labels around in different ways, you must also be prepared to juggle around your note card subject headings: juggle them, rewrite them so they are more specific, make up categories for them, and maybe even ignore or throw some out. It depends on your thesis (more of that in a minute).

EXERCISE

Here are some real note cards in a real research paper for you to practice on. We will give you the whole note cards, not just the subject heading labels. The labels alone would be enough at this stage for the person who actually wrote these note cards. But the labels might not be enough for someone else who hadn't had the chance to read the sources themselves.

Cut these note cards apart carefully and shuffle them around into piles. What different groups do you get?

climatologist's job

observe long-term changes in weather

Anderson, p. 10

---

situation--up for grabs

"In the long term, climate is cooling off--or is
it warming up? As for tomorrow's weather, even
the world's biggest computer can't say for sure
what it will be."

Anderson, p. 10

Von Neumann & computer

machine called MANIAC

(Mathematical Analyzer, Numerical Integrator and
    Computer)

blizzard

Anderson, p. 30

195

<u>$ savings for accurate prediction</u>

"Dr. Vernon Suomi of the University of Wisconsin
estimates that a really accurate three-day forecast
would result in savings of $86-million a year just
for growers of wheat in the state of Wisconsin."

Anderson, p. 30

<u>tree-ring research</u>

good weather = thick annual ring around tree trunk

Lab. of Tree-Ring Research, U. of Arizona
e.g., 4,000 year-old bristlecone pine trees

Calder, p. 36

<u>technological breakthroughs</u>

1643--"Toricelli invented the barometer and
      meteorology became vaguely scientific"
1843--telegraph, mod. meteorology began
    --forecasting possible now
1930--radiosonde (balloons)
1960--computer, satellite

Calder, p. 56

<u>errors in mod. computer-model forecasting</u>

45% of errors--"computing procedures"
20%--not enough data on worldwide weather
35%--ingorance of natural processes, e.g.
    cloud to rain

Calder, p. 62

<u>N'l Weather Service</u>

5,000 employees
predictions getting slightly better
  (e.g. temperatures), but still way off

<u>Changing Times</u>, p. 46

<u>instrument kit</u>
Heathkit, Benton Harbor, MI 49022
"everything needed for a wind speed and direction
indicator, indoor/outdoor thermometer readings and
barometer--all mounted when completed in a simulated
wood console suitable for wall or desk display."
--12 hours to assemble (author)
helpful suggestions, e.g. don't do it all at once

Dillon, p. 70

cricket chirps

"an accurate thermometer. Count the number of chirps in 14 seconds and add 40. The result is the temperature in degrees Fahrenheit."

(me--you'd need a stopwatch, so why not buy a
        thermometer?)

Franz, p. 121

Grandma's "folkloristic wisdom"

"... it is reassuring to learn that we can all be neighborhood weather prophets if we only pay a little attention to what Grandma has been saying for years."

(me--but we won't necessarily be right)

Franz, p. 121

---

biometeorology: health + weather
"a new branch of science"
- 1976 W.H.O. called it "a matter
        of urgency"

- imp. advances in US, USSR, Japan,
        Europe

Gerus, p. 29

Swiss findings: "weather-sensitive
people"

30% of people

"literally human barometers"

3/4 = women (p.31)

Gerus, pp. 29, 31

---

misc. medical conditions

- myocardial infarcts (before heart
                          failure)
- glaucome (eye)
- asthma
- bleeding ulcers

Gerus, p. 31

---

why women = "weather-sensitive"?

male sex hormones = anti-stress
                      hormones
               (against cold)

    me:
  [I don't believe this]

Gerus, p. 31

don't operate: wind conditions

Eastern European doctors

- before the "Foehn" (hot dry wind)

- because patients weak then

    [me!
       is this like the Santa Anas?]

Gerus, p. 31

---

migraine headaches

- caused when barometric pressure below 29.9

- also caused by wind in the face

Gerus, p. 31

---

reason for bad wind: positive ions

e.g. "Foehn"

- bad wind carries many positive ions and body
        reacts to them

"any surplus of positive ions creates stress"

Gerus, p. 31

why positive ions are unhealthy

Albert Krueger, Univ. of Calif.
    microbiologist & pathologist

- says ions cause body to release too much
  "serotinin" (anti-stress hormone)
  = "the ultimate downer"
- example: office workers suffer (p. 33)

Gerus, pp. 31, 33

---

biometeorology - practical effect

"more personalized weather reports"

(like pollution index, but about comfort)

Gerus, p. 33

---

biometeorology - practical effect

- advice to travelers: "which areas
    of the country to avoid"

Gerus, p. 33

negative-ion generator machine

- machine produces good ions to
      counteract bad ions
- producing companies are successful
- example: in Los Angeles (smog)

   Gerus, p. 33

---

health & sunspots (magnetism)

- experiment with rats showed
   connection: greater the sunspots,
   lower the rats' resistance to colds

[me - but are people similar to rats
      in this respect?]

- from article in Science Dimension,
                  1978 re sun & stress

Gerus, p. 33

---

health & sunspots

another example: when high sunspot
   activity, more patients into
   hospital in one case in India

- from article in Nature, 1979

Gerus, p. 33

Old Farmer's Almanac

"Pitted against you favorite TV weatherman, with
his radar and weather satellites, the Old Farmer's
Almanac still is right as rain."

Grisswirth, p. 63

Old Farmer's Almanac--secret

"A 184-year-old formula, the key to the Almanac's
predictions, is still being kept secret by the
book's editors."

Grisswirth, p. 65

sky color

"Evening red and morning gray,
Help the traveler on his way;
Evening gray and morning red
Bring down rain upon his head."

"There is, therefore, a real physical basis for,
and much truth in, the proverbs that declare one
result to follow the red sky of the morning, and
quite another that of the evening."

--dust, condensation, etc.

Humphreys, p. 32

clouds--"reliable warnings"

"High clouds,... having required much cooling to form, obviously do not contain enough humidity to produce any considerable rain or snow."

"The higher the clouds, the finer the weather."

Humphreys, p. 50

clouds--adage

"In the morning mountains,
 In the evening fountains."

"When the clouds appear like rocks and towers
 The earth's refreshed by frequent showers."

Humphreys, p. 53

principles of accurate prediction

"The secret of good forecasting lies in keeping the senses carefully tuned in to the environment."

Ross, p. 16

weather signs

153 "clues"
16 and 52 animals (birds and bats)
          --height they fly
          --higher better (air pressure)
153 plants (grass wet with dew = good)
153 sky--smoke rising = good
        halo = rain
        setting sun--red in west good
                      yellow or gray = bad
16 smells--low pressure, bad weather
                smells leak out
Ross, pp. 16, 152, 153

best signs--winds and clouds

"The best guide to future weather is the wind
   direction..."
"The best aids to forecasting the weather of the
   immediate future are certainly the clouds..."

Smith, p. 706

"folk art of forecasting"

"... for thousands of years forecasting was a folk
   art practised primarily by sailors, farmers,
   hunters, fisherman."
"... an educated guess."
"... amazingly accurate."

Thompson, p.10

definition "weather"

"The essence of weather is change."
    --wind
    --pressure
    --moisture

Thompson, p. 16

---

minimum technique

wet finger = wind direction

Thompson, p. 57

---

forecasting data

wind direction
barometric pressure

Thompson, p. 58

adage--clouds

"In the morning mountains/ In the evening fountains."

Thompson, p. 81

clouds

3 main ingredients in weather: heat
                               wind
                               water

only 1 visible--water/clouds

Thompson, p. 81

arthritic pains

Univ. of Pennsylvania School of Medicine 2-year
study of 30 arthritic patients.
"... when researchers simulated approaching storm
conditions--gradually dropping pressures from 31.5
to 28.5 inches and boosting humidity from 25 to 80
per cent--the results were astonishing. Eight out
of 10 patients reported stiffness and swelling in
their joints, and some reproted the symptoms within
minutes of the change."

Thompson, p. 112

219

clouds: $ research

More $ spent on cloud research now than any
other meteorological aspect.

Thompson, p. 82

microweather

"another kind of weather, which exists on a small
    and often personal scale."
"... the weather that affects us most directly ..."
"always local, even minute, but it is significant
    nontheless."
e.g. moving out of the sun into shade

Thompson, p. 114

technological breakthroughs

1780--hair hygrometer, Horace Benedict
        de Saussure
Toricelli--barometer

Thompson, p. 142

<u>computer forecasting</u>: <u>errors Neumann</u>

Dr. John von Neumann
first test 1950 successful, equal to good weatherman
"But later trials produced wildly fictional weather
(e.g., a July blizzard in Georgia) ..."

Thompson, p. 150

<u>ancient weather forecasting</u>

"a matter of reading natural signs in advance"
Aristotle's <u>Meteorologica</u>
Aristotle's pupil Theophrastus--<u>Book of Signs</u>

1. flies bite before storm--false
2. red sunrise and halo around sun or moon = rain
   red sunset = good weather
   --correct 70% = good forecast

Thompson, p. 154

<u>ancient measurements--before 17th C</u>

1. rain--bucket
2. wind direction--weathervanes (finger)

Thompson, p. 154

223

<u>today's prediction--accuracy</u>

12-18 hour--85% right
36 hour = 75% right

Thompson, p. 159

CONSTRUCTING A PROVISIONAL OUTLINE

The next step is to see what your shuffled piles of note cards look like. Record these groups on a separate piece of paper.

For example, the writer of our sample research paper on weather came up with these piles and this description of how the note cards were grouped:

What is weather?
National Weather Service
ancient/modern measurements
machines
Old Farmer's Almanac
sky
wind
folklore
animals
people

As he looked at this description, several things occurred to him: First, some of these piles seemed to go together, logically. For example, *ancient/modern measurements* and *machines* seemed to go together as information about *technology*.

Second, some piles overlapped, like *folklore* and *Old Farmer's Almanac*.

Third, some piles looked like they should be split up. The pile on *people*, for instance, seemed to split into *healthy people* and *sick people*.

Fourth, some cards seemed to fit equally well into several piles. Information about *Grandma* could fit under *folklore* or under *people*.

At this point, just do the best you can, shuffling, rearranging, and experimenting with different groups. This process is not just a mechanical outlining exercise. It will also be automatically helping you in another important way— it will help you decide what you want to say about all this information. In other words, it will be helping you clarify your own thesis.

At this point, the writer of the sample paper then revised his piles of note cards. To get a more complete, clearer picture, he then added supporting details to his description of each group, like this:

What is weather? (change in wind, air pressure, moisture)
National Weather Service (employees, not always right, why important, climatologist)
technology (kit, ion generator, hygrometer, barometer, computers, bucket, weathervane, tree rings, balloons)
folklore (ancient art, Grandma, *Old Farmer's Almanac*)
sky (color, clouds)
wind (direction, finger, positive ions, Foehn)
animals (crickets, rats, birds, bats)
people (microweather, weather-sensitivity, women)
illness (operations, arthritis, migraines, miscellaneous)
biometerology (new science, travelers, comfort forecast)

Now it seemed to the writer that some of these groups looked like main headings that included other groups as parts. For instance, *people* and *illness* seemed to be parts of *biometerology*. *Sky, wind,* and *animals* seemed to fall under their own heading, which had to be made up and provided for them: *nature.*

In any case, there usually is no one, perfect way of arranging note cards and grouping them in piles. You just have to experiment and try out different versions to find one you like best.

Matching a Provisional Outline to a Thesis

Now is the time for fine-tuning, for adjusting your thesis, if necessary, to fit your supporting material (your note cards). It is also the time for adjusting your notes. Practically speaking, that often means throwing some note cards out—a painful thing to do for some people who spent a long time and lots of energy making these cards in the first place.

For example, at this point, the writer of our sample research paper had to ask honestly, "Do I really want to get into the history of weather forecasting? What kind of point can I make about this history? What point about the subjects do I want to make anyway?" If the writer couldn't think of any point to make about this history, and therefore didn't need that information about the history of ancient measurements or technological breakthroughs, the only thing to do was to throw out those note cards.

Our writer ended up with this thesis, which did seem to fit the other note cards: "In addition to consulting a National Weather Service forecast, there are some reasonably accurate ways to find out the weather yourself."

The next step is to develop a formal outline, that is, to arrange these groups as main ideas, indent their supporting details, and add the correct symbols.

Review Outlining

You have already practiced outlining (pp. 94–106) when you reconstructed the logical skeleton of an article. Remember that this outline or logical skeleton of a piece of writing does two things:

1. It shows the relationship of ideas—main ideas and their supporting details. Symbols indicate how these ideas are related to each other (I, II, III, or 1, 2, 3, 4, 5, or a, b).
2. It shows the order of these ideas.

You may say at this point, "OK, my groups of note cards represent main ideas; but what order do I put them in?"

Think of the reader. What would be the clearest order for the reader of your paper? You want the reader to understand and be convinced. So, arrange the order of your groups of ideas with the reader in mind. What order will be most helpful for the reader? Do it that way.

Here is what the writer of our sample research paper came up with. Notice that the thesis and the outline now go together.

A SHORT TOPIC OUTLINE

Thesis: In addition to consulting a National Weather Service forecast, there are some reasonably accurate ways to find out the weather yourself.

   I.   National Weather Service
         A. Value
         B. Accuracy
  II.   Own Instruments
 III.   *Old Farmer's Almanac*
  IV.   Nature
         A. Sky
             1. Color
             2. Clouds
         B. Wind
         C. Animals
   V.   Biometerorology
         A. Healthy people
         B. Sick people

A LONGER SENTENCE OUTLINE

Thesis: In addition to consulting a National Weather Service forecast, there are some reasonably accurate ways to find out the weather yourself.

   I.   National Weather Service predictions are not always available.
         A. They are valuable, especially to farmers who need forecasts.
         B. NWS predictions are getting better, but they aren't perfectly accurate.
  II.   You can make your own instruments.
 III.   You can consult the *Old Farmer's Almanac*.
  IV.   You can consult nature.
         A. The sky reveals weather.
             1. Folklore sayings about sky color are generally accurate.
             2. Clouds are the best "clues."
         B. Wind direction is also significant.
         C. Animals indicate weather patterns.
   V.   Biometeorology links weather and human health.
         A. Many healthy people respond to kinds of weather.
         B. Some sick people suffer from weather.

9. DRAFTING THE PAPER

Drafts

THE STEP-BY-STEP APPROACH in this book may give you the misleading impression that writing a research paper is a tidy, if not a totally mechanical process. True, these techniques are the ones that most writers rely on to produce research papers. However, they are only guidelines to a process that is at times frustrating, creative, and messy. As guidelines, they can help by giving you direction, but, as you know from your work so far, you must be prepared to make constant adjustments as you proceed: adjusting your own curiosity and interest to fit a manageable topic; adjusting your topic to fit the material you find; adjusting your thesis statement to the evidence in your sources; adjusting your outline to your note cards, and your note cards to your outline. At this stage you will need to adjust the sentences and paragraphs that you start composing on paper to the ideas you have in your head and to the ways that you would like them to appear and sound to a reader. This means getting something down on paper that is necessarily going to be less than perfect, and then revising it, often several times. In this rough draft stage you will find yourself changing words, rearranging sentences, adding some parts, and throwing out others.

There are several principles that will govern the choices you make as you revise your drafts. First, your audience's expectations will affect your style and word choice. A research paper is, of course, an academic assignment, and academic disciplines tend to have their own writing conventions, rather like etiquette. This means that you have to recognize these expectations and adjust your own writing so that it is appropriate and conforms to them. This principle is particularly true of word choice and tone. The social sciences, for instance, aim at objectivity and detachment. Social scientists favor the passive voice to eliminate the intrusive presence of a researcher: They favor neutral descriptive words. Notice the deliberately clinical tone of the sample paper on hypnosis for a psychology class.

A second principle that will affect the drafting of your paper, particularly when you are writing a report instead of a thesis paper, is you own sense of style. If your main job is not so much to persuade your reader of a point as it is to engage the reader's interest in some information, then you often have an opportunity to revise for what sounds best to you. The writer of the sample paper "Do-It-Yourself Weather Forecasting," (see pp. 289–297) for example, clearly enjoyed playing with information, trying out various sentence patterns and word choices, engaging himself as well as his reader. The subject is obviously not as serious as the other papers', but it is just this difference that allows room here for a personal voice. And what is appropriate in one paper would not be appropriate in another.

If you are writing a thesis paper rather than a report, you must pay attention to the development of a good argument. Your job is to convince your reader that your thesis (the conclusion you reached about your subject) is sensible. You accomplish this goal by presenting your reasons and backing them up with information and ideas that you discovered in your research. The greatest danger at this point is to just write out facts and opinions that were expressed by other writers.

One of the most important skills in writing a research paper is being able to lead into and away from the facts and ideas that you have obtained from other writers. We will show you a number of patterns for doing this, but right now we want to give a warning: NEVER QUOTE OR PARAPHRASE WITHOUT PROVIDING A CONTEXT. In other words, do not throw undigested chunks of data at the reader. You must always say something about the borrowed facts and ideas.

In addition, you want to make each of your ideas clear to the reader. To do this you need to separate your main points from each other, which you do with paragraphs. You also need to provide logical bridges between ideas by providing transitions (special words and phrases within and between paragraphs) that show how these ideas are connected to one another and to your thesis. Introductions and conclusions require special kinds of paragraphs, which we will describe at the end of this chapter.

This chapter deals with these techniques:

1. Constructing paragraphs
2. Incorporating sources
3. Providing transitions
4. Developing an introduction, conclusion, and title

CONSTRUCTING PARAGRAPHS

A rough draft or even several rough drafts are necessary before you type the final version. At the rough draft stage your job is to fit together your material in paragraph form, making fine adjustments and adding comments to show the reader how your ideas fit together. Before we give directions on how to construct paragraphs, we want you to complete the following exercise.

EXERCISE

1. Begin by reading the article on the following page.

HOT/COLD COUPLES

"We quarrel about it once a day—at least," says Catherine Harris, a New York City police captain's wife of 34 years. "She likes the hot weather and I like the cold," says WABC-TV weatherman Storm Field of his wife. "My wife has the narrowest range for temperature tolerance of anyone I have ever known in my life," admits Chuck Scarborough, WNBC-TV anchorman in New York City.

Being thermally incompatible with your mate is no laughing matter. As Nick Charney, founder of *Psychology Today* magazine says, "This is more important than people give it credit for. It's particularly important for lovers." Though never listed as grounds for divorce, psychotherapist Dorothy Minkow agrees, "It can cause stress on any relationship."

An informal *New York Daily News* poll of 100 individuals suggests that 75 percent of us regularly disagree with our families over temperature. "If you put people in a laboratory lying nude or dressed in shorts and you ask them to dial the temperature they prefer, you get differences of up to ten to fifteen degrees Fahrenheit," says Dr. Joseph Stevens, a psychologist and a heat expert with the Pierce Foundation Laboratory in New Haven, Connecticut. A lot of it has to do with our varying metabolic rates, he explains. "And you have tremendous differences in activity levels and the way people dress." Your mood counts, too.

Is there a cure for the common cold/hot couple? Not really, says sufferer and writer Dick Brass. "Dress warmer if you're cold and lighter and looser if you're hot. Try to keep more active if you're cold and slow down if you're hot. You can also get a dual control electric blanket," he adds.

2. Gather and jot down at least seven pieces of information about the subject from this passage. They don't have to be sentences:

    A.

    B.

    C.

    D.

    E.

    F.

    G.

3. How are all, or most of, these pieces of information similar or related to each other? Write *one* sentence that will pull together most or all of these pieces of information into a main idea.

4. Using the pieces of information in 2, write 4 or 5 sentences that will help to describe or explain the sentence in 3.

    A.

    B.

C.

D.

E.

The Point of This Exercise

If you combine 3 and 4 you have a paragraph—nothing else will function as one. This is the process that happens automatically when you write a paragraph. (*P.S.* The paragraph you have just composed is also a summary of the passage.)

Paragraph Structure

Paragraphs are logical units, composed of sentences, and set off from each other by an indented beginning. They are composed of a "topic sentence" that communicates the paragraph's main point, such as the sentence you wrote for 3, and other sentences that back up the main point with supporting detail, such as the sentences you wrote for 4. Paragraphs are building blocks of essays, just as sentences are building blocks of paragraphs.

Good writers and good readers always approach a piece of writing expecting a certain structure. You should keep this sense of structure in mind when you approach a reading assignment, or a writing assignment like your rough draft.

To help you, here is a chart for people who like charts, and an analogy for those who prefer that kind of description.

An Essay (or a Chapter)	A Paragraph	A Sentence
is composed of a thesis statement and main ideas	is composed of a topic sentence and sentences of supporting details	is composed of a subject and verb and other modifying words

In this chart, notice that an essay (or chapter) is made up of two logical parts: a thesis and main ideas. So, too, a paragraph is like a miniature essay, and its two parts (the topic sentence and the sentences of supporting details) have the same relationship to each other as the two parts in an essay have. A sentence also is made up of its two essential parts: (1) its subject and verb, and (2) the other words in the sentence that develop the subject and verb. All these logical units—sentence, paragraph, and essay—have the same logical shape or structure of their parts. Their parts fit together in the same way; they are symmetrical.

An Analogy (or Comparison). Many of you know how Russian dolls sometimes come cleverly packed one inside the other. So, too, sentences are packed inside paragraphs, and have the same shape and the same division into parts. Paragraphs are packed into essays. (And essays, or chapters, are packed inside books.)

To get back to you writing your rough draft of the research paper, you already have an outline telling you the order in which you are going to take up the main ideas. Depending on how long your paper is, and how detailed your outline is, you can often expect to spend one paragraph on each major idea or each major subdivision.

For example, here is part of the outline for the sample research paper on weather:

II. You can make your own instruments.
III. You can consult the *Old Farmer's Almanac.*
IV. You can consult nature.
    A. The sky reveals weather.
      1. Folklore sayings about sky color are generally accurate.
      2. Clouds are the best "clues."
    B. Wind direction is also significant.
    C. Animals indicate weather patterns.

Now turn to p. 292 and notice how, in the research paper itself, main point II became one paragraph. Main point III also became one paragraph. But main point IV was split into four paragraphs to accommodate all the information. Like Russian dolls, details 1 and 2 are logically related to (are all inside) point A, just as points A, B, C are all logically related to (are all inside) main point IV.

How many sentences should there be in a paragraph? There is no easy way to tell. There should be at least two, though. If you want to write a one-sentence paragraph, watch out; there may be something wrong. That one sentence would be either a main point ("topic sentence") without any supporting details, or it would be a supporting detail just floating around, not connected to any point. Occasionally a writer will use a one-sentence paragraph as a means of highlighting an idea. However, if one-sentence paragraphs were used frequently, they would lose this special effect. If you find yourself writing a paragraph of more than, say, ten sentences or so, you probably need to split them up into smaller logical units (like the Russian dolls).

EXERCISE

Here is a list of information. Each piece of information comes from a separate note card, and it all comes from one pile of note cards:

Insect-eating birds, e.g., swallows, fly low before a storm.
Frogs croak (me—with joy?) before a storm. They are more comfortable in moist conditions apparently.
Air pressure decreases before a storm.
Humidity increases before a storm.
Insects fly lower before a storm because it is harder for them to fly in low pressure conditions.
Barnyard ducks are supposed to quack before a storm. (Me—like frogs?—more comfortable).
Some people begin aching as a low pressure front moves in.
Locusts are thought to know where it will rain. They are blown along by the wind until the wind converges with another, causing rain.
Arthritis, rheumatism, and corns give some persons pain in stormy conditions.

1. What do you think the subject label was for this pile of information?

2. How are these pieces of information related to each other? Write *one* sentence that will pull this information together into a main idea:

3. Using all the pieces of information above, write four or five sentences that will help to describe or explain the sentence in 2:

    A.

    B.

    C.

    D.

    E.

INCORPORATING AND ACKNOWLEDGING SOURCES

According to the outline you made, you know that you will be weaving certain borrowed facts and ideas into your paper at particular places and in particular paragraphs. But how exactly do you go about weaving them in?

You have a choice, which boils down basically to one of four posibilities, all correct:

1. *A simple quotation.* You simply quote the borrowed data documenting the quotation, of course.

   Example: The basic principle is "the higher the clouds, the finer the weather."

   In this case you rely entirely on a parenthesis or a footnote to indicate where you got this information. Documentation will be explained in detail in Chapter 10.)

2. *A quotation with a running acknowledgment.* Here you quote your borrowed data, but you introduce it with "a running acknowledgment" that indicates in the text of your paper where you got the idea.

   Example: Dr. Vernon Suomi, a scientist at the University of Wisconsin, claims that "a really accurate three-day forecast would result in savings of $86-million a year just for growers of wheat in the state of Wisconsin."

   In your running acknowledgment you can include not only the author's name but also qualifications and, if you like, the title of the source where the information comes from:

   Example: According to W. J. Humphreys, who quotes this saying in his *Weather Proverbs and Paradoxes*, weatherlore about sky color has "a real physical basis . . . and much truth."

3. *A simple paraphrase.* Here you just paraphrase the borrowed data, with no running acknowledgment, relying on the documentation alone to indicate the source:

   Example: These official forecasts are improving.

4. *A paraphrase with a running acknowledgment.*

   Example: You can even make your own instruments from a kit, which took J. Dillon only 12 hours, according to his recent article, "Build Your Own Weather Monitor," in *Motor Boating and Sailing.*

How Do You Choose Among These Four Options?

Sometimes it helps the reader to judge your argument better and faster if you provide a running acknowledgment, indicating the quality of your borrowed data (the expert's qualifications, the title of the source). At other times a running acknowledgment just gets in the way. Think of your reader.

Be prepared to experiment as you compose your rough draft. Devise some running acknowledgments, and then read the result. Perhaps you like it? If so, leave it in.

A hint: Most college students do not use enough running acknowledgments.

Some Phrases to Use for Running Acknowledgments

Here is an example used earlier:

Dr. Vernon Suomi, a scientist at the University of Wisconsin, claims that "a really accurate three-day forecast would result in savings of $86-million a year just for growers of wheat in the state of Wisconsin."

Instead of "Dr. Vernon Suomi claims" you would write:

Dr. Vernon Suomi points out
              concludes
              warns that
              notes
              refers to
              proposes
              believes
              makes the case for
              analyzes
              observes that
              reports
              agrees (disagrees)
              discusses
              adds
              writes
              states
              explains that

Or, you could start off with something like:

In the words of Dr. Vernon Suomi,
As Dr. Vernon Suomi observes,
As Dr. Vernon Suomi sees the problem,
According to Dr. Vernon Suomi,

Placing Running Acknowledgments in a Sentence

You have three choices, all of which are correct:

1. You can begin the sentence with the phrase for the running acknowledgment:

    Dr. Vernon Suomi, a scientist at the University of Wisconsin, claims that "a really accurate three-day forecast would result in savings of $86 million a year just for growers of wheat in the state of Wisconsin."

2. You can insert the running acknowledgment phrase in the middle of the sentence:

    "A really accurate forecast," according to Dr. Vernon Suomi, a scientist at the University of Wisconsin, "would result in savings of $86 million a year just for growers of wheat in the state of Wisconsin."

3. You can place the running acknowledgment at the end of the sentence:

    "A really accurate three-day forecast would result in savings of $86 million a year just for growers of wheat in the state of Wisconsin," says Dr. Vernon Suomi, a scientist at the University of Wisconsin.

Punctuating Quotations

Exact words of the original are put within double quotation marks:

The basic principle is "the higher the clouds, the finer the weather."

If the exact words of the original contain a built-in quotation, double quotation marks go around the whole excerpt you borrow from the original, and single quotation marks now go around the original's built-in quotation:

According to medical researchers, "Patients suffering from arthritis can respond painfully to 'microweather,' which is a small, local differential in air pressure and humidity."

Periods and commas go inside quotation marks.
Colons and semicolons go outside quotation marks.
Question marks go inside or outside quotation marks depending on whether the whole sentence is a question, or only the quoted part.

She asked, "How many people saw the eclipse of the sun?"

Did he actually promise, "There will be a party at my house after the final exam"?

Placing Long Quotations on the Page

A quotation that is longer than three lines is handled differently. It has no quotation marks and it is indented as a block. See the sample papers for illustrations.

To sum up this section, here is a series of examples showing how the same idea, taken off the following note card, could be incorporated into a research paper.

<u>sky color</u>

"Evening red and morning gray,
Help the traveler on his way;
Evening gray and morning red
Bring down rain upon his head."

"There is, therefore, a real physical basis for, and much truth in, the proverbs that declare one result to follow the red sky of the morning, and quite another that of the evening."

--dust, condensation, etc.

Humphreys, p. 32

A quotation: Sky color is an accurate sign. "There, is therefore, a real physical basis for, and much truth in, the proverbs that declare one result to follow the red sky of the morning, and quite another that of the evening."

A quotation with running acknowledgment: Sky color is an accurate sign. W. J. Humphreys records several folklore sayings about sky color in *Weather Proverbs and Paradoxes* and concludes that they have "real physical basis . . . and much truth."

A paraphrase: Sky color is an accurate sign. Folklore sayings about red and gray skies are, in fact, scientifically accurate.

A paraphrase with a running acknowledgment: Sky color is an accurate sign. W. J. Humphreys records several folklore sayings about red and gray skies in his *Weather Proverbs and Paradoxes,* and concludes that they are, in fact, scientifically accurate.

EXERCISE

A.   Indicate whether each of the following sentences, taken from a research paper, incorporates its source as (1) a simple quotation, (2) a simple paraphrase, (3) a quotation with a running acknowledgment, (4) a paraphrase with a running acknowledgment.

1.   Dr. W. Henry Lambright, a Syracuse University political scientist completing a book-length study of the subject, characterizes the results as a case of "muddling through."
2.   Dr. Archie M. Kahan, the project's manager, believes the social concerns about the Colorado pilot project can be resolved by mutual discussion.
3.   The goal is to increase summer runoff by adding to the snowpack accumulation over a 3,300-square-mile area of the San Juan Basin.
4.   The Soviet Union "definitely spends more money on weather modification than any other country in the world."
5.   There is the first tantalizing evidence that the intensity of hurricanes might some day be reducible.

B.   Read "Hot/Cold Couples" again (see p. 235).

1.   Now examine each of the 17 sentences in the article and indicate how the author has incorporated each source, that is, which of these four possibilities:

A bare quotation
A quotation with a running acknowledgment
A paraphrase
A paraphrase with a running acknowledgment

2.   Do you agree that each choice is best? Would you like to suggest any alternatives that seem preferable to you?

PROVIDING TRANSITIONS

You know how the ideas fit together in your research paper because they are your ideas. You have been working with them carefully—reading, taking notes, making an outline, and so on. However, your reader doesn't have this benefit. The reader won't know how your ideas are connected unless you include guidelines, like traffic lights, indicating the flow of your argument. These words and phrases that you insert into your sentences and paragraphs are called "transitional expressions." Your sentences and paragraphs may be grammatically correct without them, but adding them will improve the clarity of your paper tremendously. Most college students do not use enough of these expressions. Using them is not difficult. It is only a matter of using the right ones, and remembering to use them in the first place.

Here, for example, is a grammatically correct paragraph without enough transitional expressions:

The weather in any one month or season might help to predict the weather in seasons to come. This hope has so far proved illusory. Weather lore is full of pious attributions of predictive powers to various saints' days. Few survive a rigid test. Recent Soviet research has reopened possibilities of this type in their search for indicator days, or "forerunners." These appear to show weather circulation characteristics similar to those predominating in the ensuing season. It is possible that some of the ideas of the ancients were not so far from the truth.

Now here is the paragraph as it was originally written in the *Encyclopaedia Britannica* with all its transitional expressions:

The weather in any one month or season might help to predict the weather in seasons to come. But this hope has so far proved illusory. Weather lore is full of pious attributions of predictive powers to various saints' days, but few survive a rigid test. Nevertheless, recent Soviet research has reopened possibilities of this type in their search for indicator days, or "forerunners." These appear to show weather circulation characteristics similar to those predominating in the ensuing season, and it is possible, therefore, that some of the ideas of the ancients were not so far from the truth.

What exactly has been added? Go back and underline the additions.

Transitional expressions show the logical order and relationship of ideas. Here are the most common kinds of logical relationship expressed by transitional expressions, and some of the words for them. You can probably add some more synonyms for each category yourself:

1. Indicating order in time: first, second, third, next, last, finally, then, subsequently, ultimately.
2. Adding something: and, in addition, moreover, additionally, also, too, furthermore, not to mention, besides.
3. Contrasting two somethings: but, however, nonetheless, on the other hand, yet, conversely, on the contrary.
4. Drawing a conclusion: therefore, consequently, in conclusion, to conclude, summing up, accordingly, evidently.
5. Emphasizing something: indeed, surely, in fact, it is clear that, certainly, in particular, to repeat.
6. Bringing in an example: for example, namely, to illustrate, for instance.

EXERCISE

Fill in the blanks in the following sentences, which were taken from an *Encyclopaedia Britannica* article, with an appropriate transitional expression.

1. Workers on land and at sea are very conscious of wind direction and change; ———————————— , city dwellers tend to forget.

2. Weather lore can be considered to be divisible into seven categories. ———————————— , the beliefs concerning the sky are scientifically sound. ———————————— , the continuity of weather patterns and indicator days, ———————————— Groundhog Day, are less reliable than the shorter-term forecasts of the first group.

3. Weather lore has a long history. ———————————— it is probably true to say that weather lore was an integral part of early religion.

4. Insects have been credited with forecasting powers. Locusts ———————————— , have been thought to know where it will rain in the world's deserts.

5. Abnormally good visibility often correctly forecasts rain to come; ———————————— , abnormal acoustics are less reliable.

6. Competent knowledge was of the greatest importance in those parts of the world where the weather was the most variable and the seasons least dependable. Most of the existing stock of weather lore, ———————————— , comes from the temperate regions of the world; it is relatively absent in the tropics where the climate is more stable.

7. The best aids to forecasting the weather of the immediate future are ———————————— the clouds.

Other Transitional Devices

Besides using these special words and phrases by inserting them into your rough draft, there are three other noteworthy techniques of providing connections to help your reader follow your argument.

1. Using these words that automatically refer back to a previous idea:
    this, that, these, such

Examples:
At a later stage of civilization, the sailor and navigator became skilled in weather forecasting. *This* was of necessity because failure to understand the weather led to almost certain death in distant seas.

Weather lore is full of *such* examples, some reasonable, some fanciful.

In general, *these* beliefs are less reliable than the shorter-term forecasts of the first group.

2. Using loose synonyms (including pronouns) for words in preceding sentences. Synonyms are equivalents referring to the same thing or person.

Examples:
The fifth type includes the lore based on the unproven belief that *nature* is more intelligent than man. In truth, *plants and animals* do react promptly and predictably to current weather.

(nature = plants and animals)

Lacking the distraction of birds, beasts, and plant life, the old *seamen*, especially in the great sailing era of the last century, became expert in weather prediction. *Mariners* also were adept at the use of the barometer.

(seamen = mariners)

Plants react quickly to their environment. *They* are indicators of weather rather than prognosticators.

(plants = they)

3. Using the same words can connect the ideas in sentences with an echo effect.

Examples
Many *cycles* can be found in any series of past weather. The least illogical *cycles* are associated with the sunspot *cycle*.

In the past, certain weather *sequences* in months or seasons have occurred often enough to be recognized and embodied in weather lore. In later years these *sequences* disappeared, but the beliefs remained.

PREPARING AN ABSTRACT

Some academic disciplines prefer an abstract, or summary of your paper, rather than an outline at the beginning of your paper. You can make an abstract of your paper by converting your outline into paragraph form or by using the techniques of summarizing that were discussed in Chapter 4. The abstract should be a true summary of the key ideas and arguments in your paper, not just another version of your introductory paragraph. The abstract should be placed after your title page. Here is an example of an abstract of the sample paper on weather forecasting. Also, check the sample paper on hypnosis (pp. 307–317) for another example.

Abstract

In addition to consulting a National Weather Service forecast, there are some reasonably accurate ways to find out the weather yourself. It is important to know about these other methods because the National Weather Service forecasts are not always accurate or available at the time that we need them. Forecasting instruments can be built easily and cheaply from kits. The *Old Farmer's Almanac* provides guidance on long term weather patterns. You can interpret natural signs in the condition of the sky, the direction of the wind, and the behavior of animals. Folklore sayings are often reliable aids to interpreting these signs. Finally, you can study the ways in which weather affects human health.

THE INTRODUCTION

An introduction usually consists of one paragraph, occasionally several paragraphs, and has the same basic function as the title: inform and interest. Here are some of the approaches you can try for your introduction. As you examine them, try to identify the thesis statement.

1. *Ask a question or a series of questions to focus your reader's attention on the subject.*

    Are we in for another ice age? Should we believe the weather prophets who claim that a cooling trend in the world's temperature over the last thirty years signals the end of the favorable conditions on which we have come to depend? Will we find our growing season shrinking as our world population expands? We had better find out some answers, because guess who is coming to dinner by the end of the century? Five billion people. And many of the world's population are already starving. Better long range forecasts and even possible global weather modification contingency plans will be necessary to feed all these people.

2. *Use a quotation from your reading.*

    "The history of our time is sprinkled with instances of new technologies running ahead of the social, economic, environmental, international, and institutional thinking that should accompany them."[1] This reminder comes from a panel of scientists who were asked to give Congress advice on the federal government's role in weather modification. Given the pressure in local areas for certain types of weather modification, like cloud seeding in arid regions, it is important for the government to study the issue, particularly the question of liability for the unforeseen consequences of such action.

3. *Use dramatic facts or examples.*

    Although research on weather modification is practically nonexistent, weather control projects, especially cloud seeding, are on the increase and should be regulated by a federal agency. Between 1974 and 1977 the number of projects rose from 74 to 88, and the land area affected expanded from 154,000 square miles to 260,000 square miles.[1] Add to these figures the more than 200 people who were killed when a dam broke in Rapid City, S.D. in 1972.[2] Many residents blamed a rain-making experiment for this catastrophe. The worst part was that few citizens even knew about the experiment until afterwards, although they were the ones who had to suffer the consequences.

4. *Stress the importance of your topic.*

    When experiments with cloud seeding began a generation ago, scientists and farmers were enthusiastic about the future of this new technology. Since that time, however, people have begun to question

the wisdom of changing the weather without full and open considera-
tion of the ecological changes which might occur. One scientist, speaking at a conference on weather modification, warned that increasing
the rainfall could cause rapid soil erosion in the arid regions because of
the "instability of the soil and the sparseness of the vegetation."
("Weather Forecasts" 46) In turn, food production would be affected,
and since we all eat, we all have a vested interest in ensuring that the
growing cloud seeding industry develops responsibility and is properly controlled.

5. *Summarize an event or give a short anecdote.*

When Jim Johnson of Topanga Canyon, California, took off one
morning in his plane full of silver iodide, he did not know what a flood
he was about to unleash, a flood of angry calls and letters from residents below who did not appreciate the extra raindrops.[1] Johnson was
not very concerned about them. He was just doing his job, doing what
he was paid for—to make it rain. Johnson is just one of many people
involved in a growing new industry—cloud seeding. So far this industry has not been controlled by any regulatory agency, but the time has
come for such action.

6. *State your thesis in a provocative way.*

The problem of feeding the undernourished masses of the world
will not be solved by improved farming methods, weather control or
even birth control. Currently we possess the means of feeding every
human being in the world were it not for an economic system which
encourages waste in the wealthy nations while at the same time foster-
ing agricultural colonialism in the poor countries. "Europe, for example, imports one-third of the African peanut crop to feed its live-
stock,"[1] and land in Latin America is used to raise beef and crops such
as coffee, cocoa, and sugar for export.

7. *Give a bird's-eye view of what is to come by previewing your main ideas.*

The National Weather Service is not 100% reliable. Nor is the
official forecast always available on the spot for people, like campers
and picnickers, who need to know if it is going to rain. But there are
some reasonably accurate ways to find out what the weather will be
yourself. You can buy some of the same instruments the National
Weather Service uses, or even make your own kit. Without spending
any money, you can simply register weather changes through your
senses and observe how plants and animals react. Folklore sayings
offer a way of interpreting these responses, and although not all these
sayings are scientifically accurate, some are, and will allow you to
predict the weather with some confidence.

The Do Nots

1. Do not beat around the bush. Give the reader a clear idea of your topic and your slant on the subject. Weak introductions are a product of not knowing where you want to go with your subject.
2. Do not announce the topic. Avoid statements such as, "This paper will attempt to discuss the controversy over abortion." If you imitate one of the models we just presented, you will not have to fall back on such tedious announcements.
3. Do not make obvious statements, such as "Conservation is a very important topic now that everyone is interested in ecology." How can you tell if something is too obvious? Well, you can try it out on your friends and classmates.
4. Do not use quotations that have become cliches, such as "The way to a man's heart is through his stomach."
5. Do not rely on the title or outline to provide information. The introduction should be capable logically of standing by itself so the reader knows what is going on (the topic and your slant on it).
6. Do not begin with a definition unless you really need one. For example, a paper on euthanasia would have to begin by distinguishing between "active" and "passive" euthanasia. A paper on the hospice movement would have to explain what a hospice is. But don't fall into this old rut: "Webster's Dictionary defines zoning as 'dividing a city into sections reserved for different purposes.'" This definition isn't necessary; it just gets in the way because everybody already knows what zoning is.

THE CONCLUSION

The purpose of a conclusion is to give a note of finality to your paper by restating your thesis, usually in slightly different words. Too often papers just stop instead of coming to a logical end. Here is where you want to leave the reader with a good impression of your argument. You want to make sure that your reader understands your thesis and your reasons for it. You want to drive your point home and clinch the argument. It is worth spending extra time on your conclusion, and the general principle involved is to think especially of your reader.

We recommend two foolproof techniques for winding up your paper with a good concluding paragraph. You can use one or the other or a combination of both. The first technique emphasizes your thesis; it reassures your reader that you know what you are writing about. The second technique emphasizes the main points you used to support your thesis; it provides your reader with a quick review.

Technique 1—Emphasizing the Thesis

Fill in your thesis below and then, quite independently of your paper, think of at least five (ten would be better still) questions that could be made up to fit the statement you have made. Forget about your paper for the moment. Focus just on your thesis. For example:

Thesis: In addition to consulting a National Weather Service forecast, there are some reasonably accurate ways to find out the weather yourself.

Questions:
1. How do you consult a National Weather Service forecast?
2. What is the National Weather Service?
3. How does the National Weather Service forecast the weather?
4. How accurate are National Weather Service forecasts?
5. How accurate are your own forecasts?
6. What ways can you find out the weather yourself?
7. What do you need to do your own forecasting?
8. Why should you bother to try to find out the weather?
9. Which ways of forecasting weather are more accurate?

Your thesis:

Your questions:
   1.

   2.

   3.

   4.

   5.

Your reader probably will develop questions like these while reading your paper, and it is very important for you not to leave your argument up in the air. So in your conclusion, anticipate your reader's questions and then make sure you provide some answers for them, reminding your reader, of course, what your thesis has been all along. For example:

In the meantime, we can all compete with the TV "weather-watch," based on official National Weather Service forecasts. All we need are some data about atmospheric conditions, which we can record with our own senses, or a few common instruments, and some interpretive principles, which we can borrow from the folklore stored in our memories or from the emerging science of biometeorology. In the words of one optimist, "We can all be neighborhood prophets if we only pay a little attention to what Grandma has been saying for years."[29] That doesn't mean that Grandma knew what she was talking about or that we will be right, but the Weather Service is not always right either. If we select our information and sayings carefully, there is more than an even chance that our own forecasts will be correct and that we will be able to predict the weather for our own convenience and comfort.

Now write your own concluding paragraph in which you answer your own questions and restate your own thesis.

Technique 2—*Emphasizing Your Main Points*

Copy your main points from your outline. For example:

1. National Weather Service predictions are not always available.
2. You can make your own instruments.
3. You can consult the *Old Farmer's Almanac.*
4. You can consult nature.
5. Biometeorology links weather and human health.

Your main points from your outline:

1.

2.

3.

Now, restate these main points in slightly different words—that means paraphrase yourself and summarize your own argument. Use appropriate transitional words to express the sequence of ideas, and finish off with your thesis again. For example:

In summary, there are five ways to find out what the weather will be. First, the National Weather Service provides a good forecast, but the people who need it most do not always have access to an official prediction. Second, ordinary instruments available from any hardware store can provide a prediction, as can special meteorological kits. Publications like the *Old Farmer's Almanac* are a third source, and they are sometimes surprisingly accurate, too. A fourth equivalent of instrument readings are the natural signs displayed in sky, wind, and animal behavior. And, last, people, too, both healthy and sick, respond to weather, the study of which constitutes the new science of biometeorology. Therefore, an ordinary person, as well as the official weatherman, can predict with some confidence what the weather will be.

THE TITLE

Let's consider the title. What can a title do?

1. Define the topic.
2. State or imply the thesis.
3. Create interest.

Here is a list of titles. Examine each one in light of the three functions listed above. How much does each title tell the reader?

1. Poor Birds of Paradise: See Haiti and Sigh
2. How Banks Destroy the Economy
3. The Worst American City
4. The Energy Disease
5. Our Feast, Their Famine
6. The Perils of Obedience
7. The Family Out of Favor
8. Harvesting the Dead
9. Airlines: Still the Safest Way to Travel
10. What Have They Done to the Rain?

Good titles usually involve a bit of word play. For example, notice the contrast that is set up in "Our Feast, Their Famine." Choosing words with the same initial sound (alliteration) helps to emphasize the contrast. Can you spot other examples of alliteration in the list of titles?

Another technique is to use words in an unexpected way. Ordinarily we think of the dangers or pitfalls of disobedience. Combining "perils" and "obedience" startles us into paying attention to the title. Do any of the other titles strike you as having an unusual combination of words?

Sometimes a line or phrase that you have read or heard will serve as a suitable title. For instance, "What Have They Done to the Rain?" comes from a 1960's protest song. Review some of the quotes you have used in your paper. Identify phrases that might be possibilities for a title.

EXERCISE

Dream up at least 10 possible titles for your paper. It pays to be silly at this point and let your imagination run wild. Later you can censor the outrageous ideas and discuss your remaining list with friends.

Some Cautions

Now that you have some ideas, here are some suggestions to help you narrow down the range of possibilities.

1. Avoid a bare question unless it is a reference your reader can easily associate with something else, like "What Have They Done to the Rain?" Your job is not only to spark your reader's curiosity; it is also to make a point about the subject, which the title should express. For example, instead of the question "How Safe Is Airline Travel?" your title should reflect your thesis: "Airlines: Still the Safest Way to Travel." Remember the primary purpose of a title is to inform the reader.
2. Avoid the temptation to be so cute or so funny in the title that you confuse your reader. "Junk Food for Thought" in a philosophy paper, or "Montezuma's Revenge" for an American History paper on the Mexican War, are kinds of titles to avoid.
3. A short phrase is better than a complete sentence. A title is one place for sentence fragments. If you feel your title, for instance, "The Sinking Ark," is not enough, add a second half after a colon.

    The Sinking Ark: Endangered Species
    Poor Birds of Paradise: See Haiti and Sigh
    Airlines: Still the Safest Way to Travel

4. Notice the correct punctuation for titles. Your title is never put within quotation marks, underlined, or capitalized in full. Don't put a period at the end.

    Do-It-Yourself Weather Forecasting

Your Rough Draft

Now you are ready to draft a rough version of your own research paper. Begin by building up paragraphs, in the same order as the ideas in your outline. Weave your sources into your writing, with or without running acknowledgments, and provide transitions between ideas in your sentences and paragraphs. After you have developed the body of your paper, work on an introduction and conclusion.

Using a Listener

The readability of a piece of writing is closely related to its success and value. If a listener can understand and follow the presentation of your ideas as you read them aloud, you can then feel reassured that your writing is effective. The following worksheets will give you a structure to use for peer evaluation and self-assessment.

WORKSHEET 14

Peer Evaluation

Name ——————————————   Date ——————————

Peer Evaluator ——————————————————

Read your paper and complete the worksheet by asking the peer evaluator to answer these questions. You can both refer back to the paper as you complete the worksheet.

Introduction

1. Did the opening capture your interest?
2. What is my thesis?

3. Could the thesis be worded more clearly?
4. Should it be stated earlier or later than the point at which I introduce it? Where?

Support

1. What details (such as: examples, statistics, case histories, definitions) have I given to support the main idea?

2. Were all my details connected to the main idea?
3. Should I give more supporting details? Or fewer?

Transitions

1. Did the order of points seem logical?
2. Did you get lost anywhere? Where?

3. Should I include more transitional expressions? Where?

General

1. What parts were most effective?

2. Did I ever seem to be trying to impress you, rather than communicating my ideas? Where?

3. Do I need to provide more definitions of terms? Which?

4. Did I use too many short, jerky sentences, or too many long, complicated ones?

Conclusion

1. Did my conclusion answer the questions that came to mind as you listened to my paper?

2. Is there anything about the end of my paper that leaves you up in the air?

WORKSHEET 15

Self-Evaluation of Draft

Name _____   Date _____

Title _____

1. What have you done to catch the reader's interest?

2. Where is your thesis statement located?

3. What steps have you taken to develop or support the thesis? (list details, examples, case histories, definitions).

4. Do you think you have enough supporting information?

5. Are there any aspects of the paper that do not satisfy you? List any problems on which you need advice.

10. DOCUMENTING SOURCES

YOU HAVE BORROWED a lot of ideas and facts for your research paper, and you must indicate where you got them. Telling your reader where you got them is "documenting your sources." There are two basic formats. Depending on which format you use, you cite this information about borrowed ideas and facts in several places:

1. In footnotes grouped at the bottom of each page as appropriate or collected on a separate page at the end of your paper. This is the *footnote* format.
2. In the text of your paper itself, within parentheses. This is the *parenthesis* format.
3. A bibliography at the very end of your paper where you list the sources you used.

This documentation stage of your research paper project raises three issues: (1) the logical issue of identifying exactly what information is original in a source and therefore needs acknowledging (as opposed to common knowledge); (2) the moral issue of honestly acknowledging the sources you borrow from, and (3) the practical issue of following a correct format consistently in order to identify the sources of borrowed information.

There are several formats, but college students rely commonly on two systems:

1. The *footnote* system has been developed by the University of Chicago and is described in Kate L. Turabian's *Manual* (see card catalog cards, pp. 53–54).
2. The parenthesis system is used by many professional organizations, including the Modern Language Association (MLA) and the American Psychological Association (APA).

Identifying Exactly What Information Is Original in a Source and Therefore Needs Documenting

The rule goes something like this: "Document every idea or fact that is not obvious to someone who is familiar in general with this topic."

It is sometimes hard to apply this rule. When you start researching a topic you may know nothing about it; every idea or fact is new and borrowed. However, once you begin to read about it, you realize that there is a common body of knowledge understood by everyone in this field, and it doesn't need documenting.

However, if in doubt, document it. You cannot have too many acknowledgments.

Honestly Acknowledging the Sources You Use

You must carefully document the sources you rely on; otherwise you run the risk of being accused of plagiarism, which is a kind of cheating. In its most extreme form, a plagiarist hands in somebody else's paper as his or her own—in most colleges, grounds for immediate expulsion. In less extreme forms, a plagiarist copies sections of a source, like a textbook, and tries to pass it off as his or her own work—grounds for certainly failing the assignment, if not the course.

An honest student sometimes runs this risk because certain memorable words or a turn of phrase has stuck in the mind and the student unconsciously repeats it without identifying where it came from. In this case, often even the student can't remember. Careful notetaking is the solution to this problem. Paraphrase your notes in your own words wherever possible, and when you record quotations, do so exactly. In both cases, indicate precise page numbers.

Following the Correct Format for Documenting Sources

There are several different sets of rules, which vary from one discipline and its scholarly publications to other disciplines and their scholarly publications. A well-known ecologist, Garrett Hardin, has complained about these frustrating differences:

> In biology, the speciation process includes the "fixation" of non-adaptive genes (non-adaptive so far as we can tell). Isolation automatically produces differentiation, adaptive or not. In the publishing business something of this sort seems to have happened in bibliographical citations. There are many different systems, an abomination to the author of an interdisciplinary paper, who may have to submit his work to journals following different style-books.
>
> The diversity of citation styles serves little real purpose beyond giving employment to typists. What are the chances of reducing the variety? Surely *nil*. This is something every reformer should ponder over; in miniature, this situation exhibits characteristics of more important malfunctioning units of society.*

Reprinted with permission from Stalking the Wild Taboo *(Second Edition) by Garrett Hardin. Copyright © 1976 by William Kaufman, Inc. All rights reserved.*

Luckily, most college students can rely on one of the two basic sets of rules which we will show you in this chapter.

These rules can be very technical and detailed, and they are undergoing changes as new procedures and technologies affect academic publishing. At this stage in your career, aim especially at using a format system consistently. If you are in doubt, ask your instructor for guidelines and apply common sense yourself to identify sources accurately and adequately. The principle is to make sure your reader could find your original sources on the basis of the information you provide as documentation.

FOOTNOTE SYSTEM

This format relies on footnotes. A footnote comes in two parts: A raised number following your borrowed idea, like this,[3] and then the number again, separated from the text of your research paper with all the information describing where the idea came from, like this:

[3]Martin Grosswirth, "Tired of the Weather Bureau? Try the *Old Farmer's Almanac*," *Science Digest*, 80 (September 1976):65.

Here is an example illustrating how an idea, recorded as a quotation on a note card, could become an idea footnoted in a research paper:

```
            definition "weather"

 "The essence of weather is change."

        -- wind

        -- pressure

        -- moisture

 Thompson and O'Brien, p. 16
```

As part of a research paper, here is a sentence using this idea:

There is always something to discuss, since "the essence of weather is change."[1]

The footnote entry for this idea is:

[1]Philip D. Thompson and Robert O'Brien, *Weather* (New York: Time, Inc., 1965), p. 16.

Where Does the Number Come from and Where Do You Put It?

You number your borrowed ideas consecutively throughout your paper. Start with one, and continue. You place the number itself, slightly raised, just after the borrowed quotation or paraphrased fact or idea.

Where Do You Put the Footnote Information?

Footnotes go at the bottom of pages, each page's references collected at the foot of that page. Footnotes are single spaced at the bottom of their page, with a double space between each one.

Some instructors will allow you to collect all the footnotes, beginning on a separate page, titled Notes, at the end of your paper. In this case, because there is more room, they are double spaced.

As always, check with your instructor about guidelines for specific assignments.

What Does the Correct Footnote Format Look Like?

It depends whether you are referring to a particular source for the first time or not. If not, it is called a "subsequent reference." The most common sources are books and magazine articles. Here are the four most common footnote entries. Notice the order and punctuation of the complete information required. Notice also that the title underlined on the bibliography card is printed in italics. Unless your typewriter can print italics, you should retain the underlining in your footnote.

A bibliography card for a book:

Bibliography

Humphreys, W. J.

Weather Proverbs and Paradoxes

Baltimore

Williams and Wilkins Co.

1923

First footnote reference to this book:

[18]W. J. Humphreys, *Weather Proverbs and Paradoxes* (Baltimore: Williams and Wilkins Co., 1923), p. 32.

A subsequent footnote reference to this book:

>   [23]Humphreys, p. 53.

A bibliography card for an ordinary magazine article (that is, one with a volume number):

```
┌─────────────────────────────────────────────────┐
│                  Bibliography                     │
│                                                   │
│  Dillon, J.                                       │
│                                                   │
│  "Build Your Own Weather Monitor"                 │
│                                                   │
│  Motor Boating and Sailing                        │
│                                                   │
│  volume 134                                       │
│                                                   │
│  December 1974                                    │
│                                                   │
│  p. 70                                            │
│                                                   │
└─────────────────────────────────────────────────┘
```

The first footnote reference to this ordinary magazine article (with a volume number):

>   [6]J. Dillon, "Build Your Own Weather Monitor," *Motor Boating and Sailing* 134 (December 1974):70.

A subsequent footnote reference to this magazine article:

>   [6]Dillon, p. 70.

IBID.—*What It Is and When to Use It*

Ibid. is an abbreviation of a Latin word that means "in the same place." It is used in footnotes as a short cut. If you want to footnote information from a source that you have identified immediately before in a footnote, then you can use this abbreviation. You can only use Ibid. if no other information comes in between Ibid. and your previous footnote to this source. Ibid. means the same source and the same page. If you want to refer to the same source but a different page, add the different page number.

Example

>   [25]Thompson and O'Brien, p. 112.
>   [26]Gerus, p. 31.
>   [27]Ibid.
>   [28]Ibid., p. 33.

Footnote Tips

1. If there is no author, just ignore that part. Don't use Anon. or Anonymous.
2. Use Roman numerals cautiously. Use them only to record original Roman numeral page numbers from your sources (in a preface or introduction).
3. Most magazines have a volume number, and that volume number comes before the date of issue within parentheses. The number following the parentheses is the page number, with no abbreviation "p." However, if the magazine has no volume number, the first footnote entry is different. Here is an example of a first footnote for a magazine article with no volume:

    [17]Claire Gerus, "Wind, Weather and Work," *The Financial Post Magazine*, December 1979, p. 31.

4. An encyclopedia article uses a special format with the special abbreviation s.v. which stands for a Latin phrase meaning "under the word." Follow this model for footnotes to encyclopedia articles. Remember to identify the author's full name, completing initials if necessary.

    [15]*Encyclopaedia Britannica*, 1975 ed., s.v. "Weather Lore," by L. P. Smith.

5. The only Latin abbreviations most students need in their footnotes are Ibid. for an immediately following subsequent reference, and s.v. for an encyclopedia article.

    Other English abbreviations include:

    ed. = editor or edition
    rev. = revised
    p.   = 1 page
    pp. = pages

6. You only need to indicate where you found information, not where the writer got it. If your source quotes a point you want to make, indicate it like this:

    [3]Quoted by Alan Anderson, Jr., "Forecast for Forecasting: Cloudy," *The New York Times Magazine* 10 (29 December 1974):30.

7. Here are patterns for common first footnote situations. For even more detailed information you can consult Turabian's *Manual,* recorded on this bibliography card:

```
                        Bibliography
        REF
        LB
        2369
        .T8     Turabian, Kate L.
        1973    A Manual for Writers of Term Papers,
                    Theses, and Dissertations
                Chicago
                University of Chicago Press
                1973
```

8. The footnote patterns that follow are all for first footnote references. Subsequent footnotes for whatever kind of source need only the author and page(s) if you are using only one source by that author. If you are using more than one source by that author, then include the title after the author's name. If there is no author, for a subsequent reference just write the title of the source and the page(s). Remember the short cut Ibid. for special cases of subsequent reference. Look at the footnotes for our model research paper and you will see instantly how to do subsequent references.

Model Footnotes (First References)

A book with 2 (or 3) authors

   [1]Paul R. Ehrlich and Richard L. Harriman, *How To Be A Survivor* (New York: Ballantine, 1972), p. 28.

A book with more than 3 authors

   [2]Donella H. Meadows and others, *The Limits to Growth* (New York: Universe Books, 1972), p. 82.

A book edited by one person

   [3]Harlow Shapley, ed., *Climatic Change* (Cambridge: Harvard University Press, 1953), p. ix.

A book edited by 2 (or 3) people

   [4]Fraser Darling and John P. Milton, eds., *Future Environments of North America* (New York: Natural History Press, 1966), p. xxiv.

Somebody else's book edited by one person

   [5]Aldous Huxley, *On Art and Artists,* ed. Morris Philipson (Cleveland: Meridian Books, 1960), p. 113.

A revised or subsequent edition of a book

   [6]Paul B. Sears, *Deserts on the March,* rev. 3rd ed. (Norman, Okla.: University of Oklahoma Press, 1967), p. 82.

A translation of a book

   [7]Hermann Flohn, *Climate and Weather,* translated by B. V. de G. Walden (New York: McGraw-Hill, 1969), p. 58.

A book with a corporate author

   [8]National Academy of Sciences/NRC, *The Earth and Human Affairs* (San Francisco: Canfield Press, 1972), p. 17.

A reprinted book

      [9]Arthur C. Clarke, *The Challenge of the Sea* (1960, reprinted ed., New York: Dell, 1966), p. 79.

A government publication

      [10]U.S. Department of Commerce/NOAA, *Heatwave* (Washington, D.C.: U.S. Government Printing Office, 1972), p. 3.

A pamphlet (follow format for a book as much as you can)

      [11]Lowell Ponte, *The New Cold War: American and Soviet Ideas for Dealing with the World's Cooling Climate* (Los Angeles, 1974), p. 2.

      [12]*What's the Weather?* (Public Relations Department, Air France, 683 Fifth Avenue, New York), p. 10.

A book that is a volume in a series

      [13]Reid A. Bryson, *The Sahelian Effect,* vol. 2: *Climatic Modification by Air Pollution* (Madison, Wis.: Institute for Environmental Studies, 1974), p. 239.

An ordinary article from a magazine with a volume number

      [14]M. Franz, "Chirping Crickets, Low-Flying Bats and Croaking Frogs," *Organic Gardening and Farming,* 23 (November 1976):121.

An article from a magazine without a volume number

      [15]Claire Gerus, "Wind, Weather and Work," *The Financial Post Magazine,* December 1979, p. 31.

An article from a newspaper

      [16]George Alexander, "Experts Think World Can Handle Future Population," *Los Angeles Times,* 15 Feb. 1979, sec. 2, p. 12.

An essay published in a book

      [17]James T. Peterson and Christian E. Junge, "Sources of Particulate Matter in the Atmosphere," in *Man's Impact on Climate,* ed. William H. Matthews and others (Cambridge: MIT Press, 1971), p. 297.

An article in an encyclopedia

      [18]*Encyclopedia Americana,* 1976 ed., s.v. "Weather," by Ernest J. Christie.

A poem in a book

[20]W. D. Snodgrss, "April Inventory," *Heart's Needle* (New York: Knopf, 1969), p. 37.

A review of a book

[21]Edward Hoagland, "Without Monkeys," review of *The Wild Boy of Burundi*, by Harlan Lane and Richard Pillard, *New York Times Book Review*, 4 Feb. 1979, p. 11.

Mimeographed material

[22]Charles F. Cooper, "Predicting Ecological Effects of New Technology: The Case of Weather Modification" (mimeographed), a discussion paper prepared for the Center for the Study of Democratic Institutions, Santa Barbara, California, 1 March 1972.

A lecture

[23]Kenneth Boulding, "Bioeconomics: A New Interface," a Symposium honoring Garrett Hardin, UC Santa Barbara, 16 Feb. 1979.

An interview

[24]Personal interview with Garrett Hardin, Professor of Human Ecology, UC Santa Barbara, 16 Feb. 1979.

A film

[25]*Superman*, with Christopher Reeve, Warner Bros., 1978.

A live performance (concert or play)

[26]Jean-Pierre Rampal, conductor, Los Angeles Chamber Orchestra Concert, Music Center Pavilion, Los Angeles, 16 March 1979.

[27]Robert Bolt, director, *A Man for All Seasons*, with Charlton Heston, Ahmanson Theater, Los Angeles, 18 Feb. 1979.

A Record

[28]Paul Simon, "Bridge Over Troubled Water," on Roberta Flack, *Quiet Fire*, Atlantic Records, SD 1594.

A radio or television program

[29]PBS, "New England Potluck Supper," *Julia Child and Company*, 3 Feb. 1979.

Bibliography

Your bibliography is another page at the end. It lists in alphabetical order (according to authors' last names) all the sources you borrowed information from.

The big problem with the bibliography is that you have to use a slightly different format from footnotes. You must get all the information, in the right order, and with the right punctuation, but the format is somewhat different from what you used for footnotes. Remember, you don't have to memorize these rules. Just consult a model for the patterns you need.

The two most common bibliographical entries are for a book and a magazine article. Here are examples illustrating how to take information from a bibliography card and turn it into a bibliographical entry.

A bibliography card for a book:

```
                    Bibliography

    Humphreys, W. J.
    Weather Proverbs and Paradoxes
    Baltimore
    Willimas and Wilkins Co.
    1923
```

A bibliography entry for this book, listed alphabetically under H:

Humphreys, W. J. *Weather Proverbs and Paradoxes.* Baltimore: Williams and Wilkins Co., 1923.

A bibliography card for an ordinary magazine article (with a volume number):

```
                    Bibliography

    Dillon, J.
    "Build Your Own Weather Monitor"
    Motor Boating and Sailing
    volume 134
    December 1974
    p. 70
```

A bibliographical entry for this article, listed alphabetically under D:

Dillon, J. "Build Your Own Weather Monitor." *Motor Boating and Sailing,* 134 (December 1974):70.

Bibliography Tips

1. Do not separate books from articles. They all go together alphabetically according to authors' last names. If there is no author, enter the source alphabetically under its title (ignore "a" and "the" in the title for this purpose).
2. If you have two or more sources by the same author, give the author's name only in the first entry. For a second entry, or more, type 10 hyphens and a period. Continue as usual with the title and so on in alphabetical order.

Example

Ehrlich, Paul R. *The End of Affluence.* New York: Ballantine, 1974.
_____. *The Population Bomb.* New York: Ballantine, 1968.

Here are patterns for other situations you might run into when you put together your own bibliography page(s).

MODEL BIBLIOGRAPHY ENTRIES

A book with 2 (or 3) authors

Ehrlich, Paul, and Richard L. Harriman. *How To Be A Survivor.* New York: Ballantine, 1972.

A book with more than 3 authors

Meadows, Donella H., and others. *The Limits to Growth.* New York: Universe Books, 1973.

A book edited by one person

Shapley, Harlow, ed. *Climatic Changes.* Cambridge: Harvard University Press, 1952.

A book edited by 2 (or 3) people

Darling, Fraser, and John P. Milton, eds. *Future Environments of North America.* New York: Natural History Press, 1966.

Somebody else's book edited by one person

Huxley, Aldous. *On Art and Artists.* Ed. Morris Philipson. Cleveland: Meridian Books, 1960.

A revised or subsequent edition of a book

Sears, Paul B. *Deserts on the March.* rev. 3rd ed. Norman, Okla.: University of Oklahoma Press, 1967.

A translation of a book

Flohn, Hermann. *Climate and Weather.* Translated by B. V. de G. Walden. New York: McGraw-Hill, 1969.

A book with a corporate author

National Academy of Sciences/NRC. *The Earth and Human Affairs.* San Francisco: Canfield Press, 1972.

A reprinted book

Clarke, Arthur C. *The Challenge of the Sea.* 1960; reprinted ed., New York: Dell, 1966.

A government publication

U.S. Department of Commerce/NOAA. *Heatwave.* Washington, D.C.: U.S. Government Printing Office, 1972.

A pamphlet

Ponte, Lowell. *The New Cold War: American and Soviet Ideas for Dealing with the World's Cooling Climate.* Los Angeles, 1974.

What's the Weather? Public Relations Department, Air France, 683 Fifth Avenue, New York.

A book that is a volume in a series

Bryson, Reid A. *The Sahelian Effect.* Vol. 2: *Climate Modification by Air Pollution.* Madison, Wis.: Institute for Environmental Studies, 1974.

An ordinary article from a magazine with a volume number

Franz, M. "Chirping Crickets, Low-Flying Bats and Croaking Frogs." *Organic Gardening and Farming* 23 (November 1976):120–122.

An article from a magazine without a volume number

Gerus, Claire. "Wind, Weather and Work." *The Financial Post Magazine,* December 1979, pp. 29, 31, 33.

An article from a newspaper

Alexander, George. "Experts Think World Can Handle Future Population." *Los Angeles Times,* 15 Feb. 1979, sec. 2, p. 12.

An essay published in a book

Peterson, James T., and Christian E. Junge. "Sources of Particulate Matter in the Atmosphere," in *Man's Impact on Climate.* Edited by William H. Matthews and others. Cambridge: MIT Press, 1971, pp. 294–301.

An article in an ordinary encyclopedia

Encyclopedia Americana, 1976 ed. S.v. "Weather," by Ernest J. Christie.

A poem in a book

Snodgrass, W. D. "April Inventory." *Heart's Needle.* New York: Knopf, 1969, pp. 37–39.

A review of a book

Hoagland, Edward. "Without Monkeys." Review of *The Wild Boy of Burundi,* by Harlan Lane and Richard Pillard. *The New York Times Book Review,* 4 Feb. 1979, p. 11.

Mimeographed material

Cooper, Charles F. "Predicting Ecological Effects of New Technology: The Case of Weather Modification." Mimeographed. A discussion paper prepared for the Center for the Study of Democratic Institutions, Santa Barbara, California, 1 March 1972.

An interview

Hardin, Garrett. Personal Interview. 16 Feb. 1979.

A film

Superman. With Christopher Reeve. Warner Bros., 1978.

A live performance (concert or play)

Rampal, Jean-Pierre, conductor Los Angeles Chamber Orchestra Concert. Music Center Pavilion, Los Angeles, 18 Feb. 1979.
Bolt, Robert, director. *A Man for All Seasons.* With Charlton Heston. Ahmanson Theater, Los Angeles. 18 Feb. 1979.

A record

Simon, Paul. "Bridge Over Troubled Water." On Roberta Flack, *Quiet Fire.* Atlantic Records, SD 1594.

A radio or television program

PBS. "New England Potluck Dinner." *Julia Child and Company.* 3 Feb. 1979.

EXERCISE

1. Make up a first footnote reference to an article in *Changing Times* magazine entitled "Weather Forecasts: Fair, Gradual Clearing, Rising Accuracy." Your borrowed idea comes from page 46 in the February 1978 issue. The issue was in volume 32. The article started on page 45 and was three pages long.

2. Make up a subsequent footnote reference to another borrowed idea from the same page in this article.

3. Make up a first footnote reference to a book entitled *Weather*, written by Philip D. Thompson and Robert O'Brien. It was published in 1965 in New York by Time, Inc. You took this footnoted idea from page 16 and page 17.

4. Make up a subsequent footnote to this book, but this particular footnoted idea comes from page 159.

5. Make up another subsequent footnote to this same book and to this same page (159).

6. Make up a first footnote reference to an article by L. P. Smith in the 1975 edition of the *Encyclopaedia Britannica*. The article was titled "Weather Lore."

7. Now make up a short bibliography listing these three sources (the magazine, book, and encyclopedia) correctly and in the correct order:

TYPING GUIDELINES FOR THE FOOTNOTE SYSTEM

See the model research paper that starts on p. 00 for detailed examples. Here are some rules to consider now:

1. Double space throughout except single space footnotes at bottoms of pages and single space block quotations.
2. Type on one side only of good, white, unruled paper.
3. Leave one-inch margins on sides, top, and bottom of paper.
4. Indent paragraphs 8 spaces. Indent block quotations 4 spaces.
5. Separate footnotes from the text of your paper by typing an unbroken line for 20 spaces immediately under your text, beginning at the left margin.

6.   Each footnote begins on a new line, indented 8 spaces.
7.   Type footnote numbers slightly above the line. Don't punctuate the number or leave a space after it.
8.   Start with the title page, not numbered.
9.   Follow the title page with the unnumbered outline page.
10. The first page of the paper itself begins with the title repeated, and no page number.
11. The second page of the paper starts page numbers in the upper right-hand corner. Example: 2 (There is no p. abbreviation, no period, or anything else except the numeral.)
12. Other pages are numbered consecutively in the same way.
13. Graphs, maps, charts, and so on are put in an Appendix and given a page number. An Appendix, if any, comes at the end of your paper, before the footnote page if you are collecting footnotes at the end of the paper.
14. If you are collecting all your footnotes at the end of the paper, title the first page of footnotes Notes.
15. Bibliography page(s) comes last (no page numbers here either). This section is titled Bibliography. Each entry begins at the left margin and if it continues on to the next line, the next line is indented 8 spaces.
16. Proofread carefully and correct any errors in ink.

PARENTHESIS SYSTEM: MLA STYLE

This system, developed by the Modern Language Association, depends on parentheses inserted into the research paper itself in order to immediately identify sources of borrowed information. More complete information about the sources is given at the end of the paper on a page labeled Works Cited.

We will show you how to use the MLA format first. This format is illustrated in the second version of the sample research paper on weather forecasting. We will also show you a common variation of the parenthesis system which is used in the social sciences. It is called the APA (American Psychological Association) style, and it is illustrated in the sample research paper on hypnosis. Finally, there is a brief example of the variation used in several sciences, known as the number system.

Identifying Quotations

Here is an example, illustrating how an idea, recorded on a note card, could be borrowed and then documented in a research paper.

Note card

```
              sky color

"Evening red and morning gray,
Help the traveler on his way;
Evening gray and morning red
Bring down rain upon his head."

"There is, therefore, a real physical basis for,
and much truth in, the proverbs that declare one
result to follow the red sky of the morning, and
quite another that of the evening."

--dust, condensation, etc.

Humphreys, p. 32
```

Part of a research paper borrowing and documenting this idea (see p. 302)

According to W. J. Humphreys, who quotes this saying in his *Weather Proverbs and Paradoxes*, weatherlore about sky color has "a real physical basis . . . and much truth" (32).

Notice that the exact page number is identified within parentheses (32). At the end of the research paper the student will complete this information with additional details from a bibliography card and will enter it in an alphabetical list according to the author's name.

Bibliography card

```
              Bibliography

Humphreys, W. J.

Weather Proverbs and Paradoxes

Baltimore

Williams and Wilkins Co.

1923
```

Part of the bibliography—Works Cited—detailing this source (see p. 306)

(see p. 306)

Works Cited

Grosswirth, Marvin. "Tired of the Weather Bureau? Try the *Old Farmer's Almanac.*" *Science Digest* 80(September 1976):63–69.

Humphreys, W. J. *Weather Proverbs and Paradoxes.* Baltimore: Williams and Wilkins Co., 1923.

Ross, Irwin. "How to Forecast Your Own Weather." *Mechanix Illustrated* 70(May 1974):16,152–3.

If it were not clear from the context in the research paper itself that (32) referred to Humphreys' book, then the parenthesis would have to include his name as well.

Example: But the basic principle is "the higher the clouds, the finer the weather" (Humphreys 50).

If you are borrowing information from two or more sources by the same author, then the name and page alone would not be enough. In this case, you must add a brief title.

Example: (Humphreys, *Weather Proverbs* 50)
or
(Humphreys, *Fog* 89)

Paraphrased material is also documented

Example: Thompson and O'Brien point out that even the government spends more money on cloud research than on any other meteorological feature (82).

No author

Use a brief title instead of the author's name to identify the source.

Example: These official forecasts are improving ("Weather Forecasts" 46).

Punctuation within the parenthesis

Name of author + space + page number(s)

Example: (Humphreys 50)

If you need to add the title, too, then:

Name of author+ comma + space + title + space + page number(s)

Example: (Humphreys, *Fog* 89)

Your bibliography—Works Cited

A separate page at the end, titled Works Cited, lists complete information about your sources. These sources are identified differently depending on whether they are books or articles, that is, *complete* publications like books or magazines, or *parts* of publications like articles in magazines, or poems or essays in collections. Here is each format: order, spacing, and punctuation. Every entry gets its own line, in alphabetical order according to authors' last names, or to the title if there is no author. If the entry is longer than one line, indent the second line five spaces.

A Book

Author, First name. *Title.* Place of Publication: Publisher, date of publication.

Example: Humphreys, W. J. *Weather Proverbs and Paradoxes.* Baltimore: Williams and Wilkins Co., 1923.

An Article

Author, First name. "Title of Article." *Title of Magazine* volume number (date of publication): page number(s).

Example: Ross, Irwin. "How to Forecast Your Own Weather." *Mechanix Illustrated* 70(May 1974):16,152–3.

TYPING GUIDELINES FOR THE MLA STYLE

See the model research paper (pp. 299–306) for detailed examples. Here are some rules to consider now:

1. Double space throughout.
2. Type on one side only of good, white, unruled paper.
3. Leave one-inch margins on sides, top, and bottom of paper.
4. Indent paragraphs 5 spaces. Indent block quotations 10 spaces.
5. Start with the title page, not numbered.
6. Follow the title page with the unnumbered outline page.
7. The first page of the paper itself begins with the title repeated, and no page number.
8. The second page of the paper starts page numbers in the upper right-hand corner. Example: 2 (There is no p. abbreviation, no period, or anything else except the numeral.)
9. Other pages are numbered consecutively in the same way.
10. Graphs, maps, charts, and so on are put in an Appendix, and given a page number. An Appendix, if any, comes at the end of your paper before the Works Cited page.
11. The bibliography page comes last without a page number. This section is titled Works Cited.
12. Proofread carefully and correct any errors in ink.

APA STYLE

A Common Variation of the Parenthesis System

The parenthesis system developed by the American Psychological Association and used in many of the social sciences, is similar to the MLA style in that both insert information about sources within the text of the paper. Both also use an alphabetized list of references at the end of the paper. The main difference is that the APA style stresses the date of publication by giving it within the text and by listing it right after the author's name in the list of references. In the examples which follow, pay particular attention to the way in which the APA format stresses the date. Notice also that the abbreviation p. or pp. is used for reference to specific page numbers. A detailed explanation of the APA style can be found in the *Publication Manual* of the American Psychological Association, third edition, 1983.

Quotations

Here is an example illustrating how an idea, recorded as a short quotation on a note card, is used, along with information from the appropriate bibliography card, in the text of the sample paper.

Note card

```
trance state - confusing terminology

"many misleading implications have accumulated
during the past 200 years."
Spanos & Barber, p. 506
```

Bibliography card

```
                   Bibliography

Spanos, N.P. and Barber, T.X.
Toward a convergence in hypnosis research
American Psychologist
Volume 29
1974
500-511
```

Excerpt from a sample paper:

For Barber and Spanos (1974) the difference between hypnosis and involved imagining is not great enough to justify the construct of a special trance state, a construct which they think should be abandoned because of the "many misleading implications that have accumulated during the past 200 years" (p. 506).

Here is another way this quoted idea could have been handled; the choice is a stylistic one:

The difference between hypnosis and involved imagining is not great enough to justify the construct of a special trance state, a construct which should be abandoned because of the "many misleading implications that have accumulated during the past 200 years" (Spanos and Barber, 1974, p. 506).

Notice that this short quotation is enclosed within quotation marks. A longer quotation would be set off from the rest of the paper as a free-standing block, with no quotation marks.

Any quotation should be identified by author, year, and page number.

Evans (1968) summarizes the difference between the state versus non-state controversy by noting that

Barber raises the question: Do alternative procedures demonstrably elicit effects which can also be elicited by the induction of hypnosis? In contrast, studies such as those [performed by Orne and his associates] raise a slightly different and more productive problem: provided motivational levels and other characteristics of subjects are kept at a constant level, does the routine induction of hypnosis enhance or alter the behaviour elicited, as compared to an untreated control group? (p. 480)

Paraphrased Material Is Also Documented

Furthermore, psychologists differentiate between fear and anger, although there is no way to distinguish between these states on the basis of psychological effects (Orne, 1967).

Two or More Authors

Always cite both names every time you acknowledge borrowing from a source with two authors:

(Tiger & Fox, 1970)

If the work has more than two authors, cite their surnames completely the first time, and then later cite only the first author's surname, followed by "et al." and the year.

First: (Rubin, Provenzano, & Luria, 1974)
Later: (Rubin et al., 1974)

Abbreviations

You can abbreviate "and" with the symbol "&" but only within parentheses.

References

Sources are listed in alphabetical order, according to the authors' surnames (or the first word of a title if there is no author) on a separate page at the end of your paper. Here are two typical examples.

An Article
Spanos, N. P. and Barber, T. X. (1974). Toward a convergence in hypnosis research. *American Psychologist, 29,* 500–511.

A Book
Edmonston, W. E. (1981). *Hypnosis: modern verification of an old equation.* New York: John Wiley & Sons.

Sequence of Information

Author: All authors of the work, with surnames and initials (not full first name) in inverted order.
Date: Place in parenthesis.
Title: Article, chapter, or book. Quotation marks are not used.
Publication facts: For a journal, give the name, volume number, and inclusive pages. For a book, give the city of publication and publisher's name.

Punctuation

Use periods to separate the four major subdivisions of the entry and put a period at the end of the entry. For a journal article, use commas to separate items within the subdivision. For a book, note that a colon separates the place of publication and the publisher.

Capitalization

The letters of all major words in the name of a journal are capitalized, but only the first word of the title of an article or a book.

Underlining

Underline book and journal titles and journal volume numbers.

Several Sources by the Same Author

If this is the case, list the earliest publication first. Use lower case letters (a, b, c) to distinguish works published in the same year.

Hilgard, E. R. (1973). The domain of hypnosis: with some comments on alternative paradigms. *American Psychologist, 28,* 972–981.
Hilgard, E. R. (1979a). Divided consciousness in hypnosis: the implications of the hidden observer. *Journal of Abnormal Psychology, 84,* 196–208.
Hilgard, E. R. (1979b). Hypnosis and ego development. *American Journal of Clinical Hypnosis, 15,* 211–223.

No Author

Use the title to find the right alphabetical place in the list of sources.

Abbreviations

Here are standard accepted abbreviations:

chap.	chapter
ed.	edition
rev. ed.	revised edition
2nd ed.	second edition
Ed. (Eds.)	Editor(s)
p. (pp.)	page(s)
Vol.	Volume (as in Vol. 1)
vols.	volumes (as in 4 vols.)
No.	number
Pt.	part
Suppl.	Supplement
rpt.	reprinted
trans.	translated by

An Abstract Instead of an Outline

APA style requires you to begin your paper with a page titled Abstract which is placed between the title page and the first page of your paper. You know how to write an abstract (see p. 247). An abstract is your own summary (no longer than 1 page) of your own paper.

NUMBER SYSTEM

A Variation of the Parenthesis System

Some sciences prefer a variation of the parenthesis system which uses a number to refer to the source being cited. Here is an example of a few paragraphs from the beginning of an article in *The American Journal of Maternal/Child Nursing*:

> Since Congress passed the National Sickle-Cell Act of 1972, provision of government funds has made possible many advances in basic research and treatment techniques for sickle-cell disease, a group of syndromes that affects approximately 50,000 Americans of African and Mediterranean descent (1). Yet, to date, there is no well-publicized national organization in the United States to promote the cause of individuals and families with sickle-cell disease. Further, very little up-to-date nursing literature exists to help the nurse answer patients' questions and plan care specific to the childbearing family (2,3).
>
> Sickle-cell disease affects both males and females equally. The most common and best known of the sickle-cell syndromes and the one with the most severe symptoms is sickle-cell anemia. One in 500 black children in the United States has the clinical disease (that is, is homozygous for Hb S, the gene for sickling hemoglobin). Both parents must have the gene for sickling hemoglobin in order for their offspring to be clinically affected.
>
> Between 8 percent and 10 percent of the black population have the sickling trait only (Hb AS), or are heterozygous (3). Those who carry the sickle-cell trait have more than 50 percent normal adult hemoglobin (Hb A), which is enough to compensate for their sickling hemoglobin during almost any circumstances (4).

Richardson, Elizabeth A. W. & Milne, Lynne S., "Sickle Cell Disease & Childbearing," The American Journal of Maternal/Child Nursing, vol. 8, #6, pp. 417-422, Nov./Dec. 1983. Copyright © 1983 American Journal of Nursing Company.

The numbers in parentheses refer to sources on a page of References at the end of the article (see p. 282). As is true with the other variations of the parenthesis system, you can insert the author's name, a specific page reference, or both.

Example: Author's name inserted: (Bolsen, 1)
        Page reference inserted: (1, p. 1543)
        Both: (Bolsen, 1, p. 1543)

There are two ways to number the list of references at the end of your paper. One possibility is to alphabetize the list and number each entry. The number corresponding to the source is then inserted in your paper. A second possibility, which is used in most of the medical journals, is to number each source as you use it. The list of references for the article from the *American*

Journal of Maternal/Child Nursing is shown below. Notice that each entry contains the author's name (inverted), the title of the article (only the first word is capitalized), the name of the journal (abbreviations are used, and the title is italicized or underlined), volume number, and inclusive pages, the date.

REFERENCES

1. BOLSEN, B. Advances continue in sickle cell disease. (news) *JAMA* 247:1540, 1543-1545, Mar. 19, 1982.
2. ANIONWU, E. Sickle cell disease. *Health Visitor* 55:336-341, July 1982.
3. KNEUT, C. Sickle-cell anemia. *Issues Compr.Pediatr.Nurse.* 4:19-27, Dec. 1980.
4. MENTZER, W. C., AND WANG, W. C. Sickle-cell disease: pathophysiology and diagnosis. *Pediatr.Ann.* 9:287-296, Aug. 1980.
5. MILNER, P. F., AND OTHERS. Outcome of pregnancy in sickle cell anemia and sickle cell-hemoglobin C disease. An analysis of 181 pregnancies in 98 patients, and a review of the literature. *Am.J.Obstet.Gynecol.* 138:239-245, Oct. 1, 1980.
6. ALLEYNE, S. I., AND OTHERS. Sexual development and fertility of Jamaican female patients with homozygous sickle cell disease. *Arch.Intern.Med.* 141:1295-1297, Sept. 1981.
7. CHO, Y. W., AND AVIADO, D. M. Clinical pharmacology for pediatricians. Part 2. Antisickling agents, with special reference to new vasoerythroactive drugs. *J.Clin.Pharmacol.* 22:1-13, Jan. 1982.
8. LEY, T. J., AND OTHERS. 5-azacytidine selectively increases gamma-globulin synthesis in a patient with beta+ thalassemia. *N.Engl.J.Med.* 307:1469-1475, Dec. 9, 1982.
9. WHALEY, L. F., AND WONG, DONNA. *Nursing Care of Infants and Children.* St. Louis, C.V. Mosby Co., 1979, p. 1386.
10. MILLER, J. M., JR., AND OTHERS. Management of sickle hemoglobinopathies in pregnant patients. *Am.J.Obstet.Gynecol.* 141:237-241, Oct. 1, 1981.
11. MORRISON, J. C., AND OTHERS. Sickle hemoglobin and the gravid patient: a management controversy. *Clin.Perinatol.* 7:273-284, Sept. 1980.
12. KLEIN, H. G. Transfusion with young erythrocytes (neocytes) in sickle cell anemia. *Am.J.Pediatr.Hematol.Oncol.* 4:162-165, Summer 1982.
13. LUKENS, J. N. Sickle cell disease. *DM* 27:1-56, Feb. 1981.
14. WEBB, J. B. Sickle cell disease in obstetrics. *Practitioner* 226:89-94, Jan. 1982.
15. CHANG, J. C., AND KAN, Y. W. Antenatal diagnosis of sickle cell anemia by direct analysis of the sickle mutation. *Lancet* 2:1127-1129, Nov. 21, 1981.
16. ORKIN, S. H., AND OTHERS. Improved detection of the sickle mutation by DNA analysis: application to prenatal diagnosis. *N.Engl.J.Med.* 307:32-36, July 1, 1982.
17. JONES, J. R., AND OTHERS. Antenatal diagnosis of sickle cell disease: amniotic fluid cell DNA analysis. *Obstet.Gynecol.* 59:484-489, Apr. 1982.
18. SCOTT, R. B. Sickle cell diseases: challenges of the eighties. *Am.J.Pediatr.Hematol.Oncol.* 4:161-165, Summer 1982.
19. PIERCE, CAROLYN. Personal communication. Spring 1983.

WORKSHEET 16

Documentation

Name _____   Date _____

List the sources you have used for your paper, using either the footnote format or the parenthesis format.

The following final checklist is for you to fill in before you hand in your research paper.

FINAL CHECKLIST

—The paper is organized to support my thesis.

—The thesis reflects my insight on the topic I researched.

—The paper is based on the best information available on the topic.

—I used the required number of _____ sources.

—Information from the sources has been integrated to show my understanding of the topic.

—The paper meets the required length of at least _____ words/ pages.

—It has a proper title page.

—It has an outline page that begins with a statement of my thesis or it has an abstract.

—The introduction clearly states my thesis.

—I have used separate paragraphs to develop the ideas in my argument.

—I have put most of the information into my own words.

—Quotation marks have been used around any words, phrases, or sentences that are copied exactly from a source.

—All quotations are documented.

—Paraphrases of facts and opinions from sources are documented.

—Documentation follows the FOOTNOTE or PARENTHESIS (circle one) form.

   1.   This paper is *completely* or *essentially* (circle one) my own work.

2. I wish to acknowledge help from the following people. (Explain who helped you do what: proofreading, typing, finding sources, etc.).

Signed _____

Date _____

11. SAMPLE RESEARCH PAPERS

ILLUSTRATION OF THE FOOTNOTE SYSTEM

Do-It-Yourself Weather Forecasting

by

Len Beech

English 111

Professor Coleman

26 February 1984

Outline

Thesis: In addition to consulting a National Weather Service forecast,
          there are some reasonably accurate ways to find out the weather
          yourself.

 I. National Weather Service predictions are not always available.

    A. They are valuable, especially to farmers who need forecasts.

    B. National Weather Service predictions are getting better, but
       they aren't perfectly accurate.

II. You can make your own instruments.

III. You can consult the Old Farmer's Almanac.

IV. You can consult nature.

    A. The sky reveals weather.

       1. Folklore sayings about sky color are generally accurate.

       2. Clouds are the best "clues."

    B. Wind direction is also significant.

    C. Animals indicate weather patterns.

 V. Biometeorology links weather and human health.

    A. Many healthy people respond to kinds of weather.

    B. Some sick people suffer from weather.

Do-It-Yourself Weather Forecasting

Everyone talks about the weather. Why not? There is always
something to discuss, since "The essence of weather is change."[1] What
changes is wind direction and velocity, barometric pressure, and
moisture content in the air. The National Weather Service's 5,000
employees spend their time and our taxpayers' dollars measuring these
variables and predicting how the weather will change.[2] That information
is very valuable. For instance, Dr. Vernon Suomi, a scientist at the
University of Wisconsin, claims that "a really accurate three-day forecast would result in savings of $86 million just for growers of wheat in
the state of Wisconsin."[3] The rest of us rely on weather predictions,
too. We schedule our own work; that is, we decide whether to hang out
the laundry or mow the lawn, we plan our recreation, and we choose our
clothes, all according to the forecast. These official forecasts are
improving.[4] Today the National Weather Service's 12-to-18 hour predictions are generally 85% accurate, 10% better than the 36-hour ones,[5]
but as we all know, they are not perfect. Furthermore, we do not always
have access to them on TV and radio or in newspapers, especially when we
need them, for example, on a fishing or camping trip. In addition to
consulting a National Weather Service official forecast, there are some

[1]Philip D. Thompson and Robert O'Brien, Weather (New York: Time,
Inc., 1965), p. 16.

[2]"Weather Forecasts: Fair, Gradual Clearing, Rising Accuracy,"
Changing Times 32 (February 1978): 46.

[3]Quoted by Alan Anderson, Jr., "Forecasts for Forecasting:
Cloudy," The New York Times Magazine 10 (29 December 1974): 30.

[4]"Weather Forecasts," p. 46.

[5]Thompson and O'Brien, p. 159.

other reasonably accurate ways to find out the weather yourself.

First, you can buy some of the same instruments the National Weather Service uses and make your own instruments. You can even make your own instruments with a kit that, according to one boating enthusiast who assembled such a kit in 12 hours, includes "everything needed for a wind speed and direction indicator, indoor/outdoor temperature readings and barometer--all mounted when completed in a simulated wood console suitable for wall or desk display."[6]

Second, if you can find a copy, you can buy the Old Farmer's Almanac, which uses a secret 184-year-old formula to forecast long-range weather.[7] If the forecast turns out wrong, you still have the other bits of information and humor in this yearly publication. Third, you can consult nature, starting with the sky. There are many versions of this adage:

> Evening red and morning gray,
> Help the traveler on his way;
> Evening gray and morning red
> Bring down rain upon his head.[8]

According to W.J. Humphreys, who quotes this saying in his Weather Proverbs and Paradoxes, weatherlore about the sky color has "a real physical basis...and much truth."[9] The reasons have to do with the refraction of light by dust and condensation in the air.

The most helpful weather "clues"[10] in the sky are not colors

---

[6]J. Dillon, "Build Your Own Weather Monitor," Motor Boating and Sailing 134 (December 1974): 70.

[7]Martin Grosswirth, "Tired of the Weather Bureau? Try the Old Farmer's Almanac," Science Digest 80 (September 1976): 65.

[8]Quoted by W.J. Humphreys, Weather Proverbs and Paradoxes (Baltimore: Williams and Wilkins Co., 1923), p. 32.

[9]Ibid.

[10]Irwin Ross, "How to Forecast Your Own Weather," Mechanix Illustrated 70 (May 1974): 153.

but clouds. Even the government spends more money on cloud research than on any other meteorological feature.[11]   It makes sense. Of the three main ingredients in weather (heat, wind, and water), only one (water) is visible in the form of clouds,[12]   and from them we can guess wind direction and speed. There are a number of sayings about clouds, like "In the morning mountains/In the evening fountains."[13]   But the basic principle is "the higher the clouds, the finer the weather."[14]

If clouds are "the best aids to forecasting the weather of the immediate future," the "best guide to future weather is the wind direction."[15]   A minimum technique for telling the wind direction is wetting your finger.[16]   If you are feeling out-of-sorts, you may also be registering a bad wind, or "Foehn," carrying positive ions, and causing you to release too much serotonin, an antistress hormone. Albert Krueger, University of California microbiologist and pathologist, calls this wind "the ultimate downer."[17]   If you would prefer not to re-spond to this wind, buy yourself a negative-ion machine to counteract it.

Animals also indicate weather patterns. For example, we can tell temperature by listening to and counting "the number of cricket chirps in 14 seconds and add 40. The result is the temperature in degrees

---

[11]Thompson and O'Brien, p. 82.

[12]Ibid., p. 81.

[13]Quoted by Thompson and O'Brien, p. 82, and Humphreys, p. 53.

[14]Humphreys, p. 50.

[15]Encyclopeaedia Britannica, 1975 ed., s.v. "Weather Lore," by L.P. Smith.

[16]Thompson and O'Brien, p. 57.

[17]Quoted by Claire Gerus, "Wind, Weather and Work," The Financial Post Magazine, December 1979, p. 31.

Farenheit."[18] You would seem to need a stopwatch to do this, in
which case you might as well get a thermometer, although this system
is supposed to be accurate. Birds and bats indicate air pressure. The
higher they fly, the higher the air pressure and the finer the
weather.[19] Rats even respond to sunspots. When sunspots are active,
rats catch more colds.[20]

Of course, to take this last example, rats are not people, and
they may not react the same way. But a whole new science,
"biometeorology," has emerged to link weather and human health."[21] It
makes sense, because we all respond to "microweather,[22] as when we
move out of the sun into the shade. Refining these responses provides
the basis for predicting the weather. "The secret of good forecasting
lies in keeping the senses carefully tuned in to the environment."[23]

Thirty percent of people are especially responsive to weather.
They are "literally human barometers."[24] Claire Gerus, who provides
these statistics, claims that three-quarters of these weather-sensitive
people are women, and explains that women lack male sex hormones that
also function to counter stress and cold.

Apart from healthy people, some sick people respond to the
weather. Some people suffering from arthritis cannot help being painfully tuned into the environment, and they have a built-in system for

[18]M. Franz, "Chirping Crickets, Low-Flying Bats and Croaking
Frogs," Organic Gardening and Farming 23 (November 1976): 121.

[19]Ross, pp. 16, 52.

[20]Gerus, p. 33

[21]Ibid., p. 29.

[22]Thompson and O'Brien, p. 114.

[23]Ross, p. 16.

[24]Gerus, p. 29.

predicting storms, at least according to a two-year study on 30 arthritic

patients at the University of Pennsylvania Medical School:

> ...when researchers simulated approaching storm conditions--
> gradually dropping pressures from 31.5 to 28.5 inches and boosting
> humidity from 25 to 80 percent--the results were astonishing. Eight
> out of 10 patients reported stiffness and swelling in their joints,
> and some reported the symptoms within minutes of the change.[25]

And some people develop migraine headaches when the barometer falls be-

low 29.9, although this painful condition may also be triggered by wind

in the face.[26] Other miscellaneous conditions aggravated by the

weather are myocardial infarcts, glaucoma, asthma, and bleeding

ulcers.[27] According to one study,[28] the number of patients admitted

to hospital coincided with high sunspot activity, and some Eastern

European doctors prefer not to operate before the "Foehn," the bad wind

with the positive ions, because patients are weaker then. It would be

interesting to see if there were any comparable figures for hospital

patients in southern California during the same kind of Santa Ana wind

conditions. Perhaps we will soon have information like this, as biome-

teorology develops and gives us weather reports and travel advice in

terms of our own personal comfort.

In the meantime, we can all compete with the TV "Weatherwatch,"

based on official National Weather Service forecasts. All we need are

some data about atmospheric conditions, which we can record with our own

senses, or a few common insruments, and some interpretive principles,

which we can borrow from the folklore stored in our memories or from the

emerging science of biometeorology. In the words of one optimist, "We

---

25Thompson and O'Brien, p. 112.

26Gerus, p. 31.

27Ibid.

28Ibid., p. 33.

can all be neighborhood weather prophets if only we pay a little attention to what Grandma has been saying for years."[29] That doesn't mean
that Grandma knew what she was talking about or that we will be right,
but the Weather Service is not always right either. If we select our
information and sayings carefully, there is more than an even chance
that our own forecasts will be correct and that we will be able to predict the weather for our own convenience and comfort.

---

[29]Franz, p. 121.

Bibliography

Anderson, Alan, Jr. "Forecast for Forecasting: Cloudy." The New York
    Times Magazine 10 (29 December 1974):10-11, 26-27, 29-31.

Dillon, J. "Build Your Own Weather Monitor." Motor Boating and Sailing
    134 (December 1974):70.

Encarlaepedia Britannica, 1975 ed., s.v. "Weather Lore," by L.P. Smith.

Franz, M. "Chirping Crickets, Low-Flying Bats and Croaking Frogs."
    Organic Gardening and Farming 23 (November 1976):120-122.

Gerus, Claire. "Wind, Weather and Work." The Financial Post Magazine,
    December 1979, pp. 29, 31, 33.

Grosswirth, Marvin. "Tired of the Weather Bureau? Try the Old Farmer's
    Almanac." Science Digest 80 (September 1976):63-69.

Humphreys, W.J. Weather Proverbs and Paradoxes. Baltimore: Williams and
    Wilkins Co., 1923.

Ross, Irwin. "How to Forecast Your Own Weather." Mechanix Illustrated 70
    (May 1974):16, 152-3.

Thompson, Philip D. and Ronert O'Brien. Weather. New York: Time, Inc.,
    1975.

"Weather Forecasts: Fair, Gradual Clearing, Rising Accuracy." Changing
    Times 32 (February 1978):45-47.

ILLUSTRATION OF THE PARENTHESIS SYSTEM (MLA STYLE)

Do-It-Yourself Weather Forecasting

by

Len Beech

English 111

Professor Coleman

26 February 1984

Outline

Thesis: In addition to consulting a National Weather Service forecast, there are some reasonably accurate ways to find out the weather yourself.

I. National Weather Service predictions are not always available.

A. They are valuable, especially to farmers who need forecasts.

B. National Weather Service predictions are getting better, but they aren't perfectly accurate.

II. You can make your own instruments.

III. You can consult the Old Farmer's Almanac.

IV. You can consult nature.

A. The sky reveals weather.

1. Folklore sayings about sky color are generally accurate.

2. Clouds are the best "clues."

B. Wind direction is also significant.

C. Animals indicate weather patterns.

V. Biometeorology links weather and human health.

A. Many healthy people respond to kinds of weather.

B. Some sick people suffer from weather.

Do-It-Yourself Weather Forecasting

Everyone talks about the weather. ~~Why not?~~ There is ~~always~~
something to discuss, since "The essence of weather is change"
(Thompson and O'Brien 16). What changes is wind direction and
velocity, barometric pressure, and moisture content in the air. The
National Weather Service's 5,000 employees spend their time and ~~our~~ the
taxpayers' dollars measuring these variables and predicting how the
weather will change ("Weather Forecasts" 46). That information is ~~very~~
valuable. For instance, Anderson quotes Dr. Vernon Suomi, a scientist
at the University of Wisconsin, who claims that "a really accurate
three-day forecast would result in savings of $86 million just for
growers of wheat in the state of Wisconsin " (30). The rest of us rely
on weather predictions, too. ~~We~~ schedule ~~our~~ own work; that is, ~~we~~
decide whether to hang out the laundry or mow the lawn, ~~we~~ plan our
recreation, and we choose our clothes, all according to the forecast.
These official forecasts are improving ("Weather Forecasts" 46). Today
the National Weather Service's 12-to-18 hour predictions are generally
85% accdurate, 10% better than the 36-hour ones (Thompson and O'Brien
159), but as we all know, they are not perfect. Furthermore, ~~we~~ do not
always have access to them on TV and radio or in newspapers, especially
~~when we~~ need them, for example, on a fishing or camping trip. In addition to consulting a national Weather Service official forecast, there
are some other reasonably accurate ways to find out the weather ~~your-
self.~~

First, ~~you~~ can buy some of the same instruments the National
Weather Service uses and make your own instruments. ~~You~~ can even make
~~your~~ own instruments with a kit that, according to J. Dillon, a boating
enthusiast who assembled such a kit in 12 hours, includes "everything
needed for a wind speed and direction indicator, indoor/outdoor tem-

perature readings and barometer--all mounted when completed in a simulated wood console for wall or desk display" (70).

Second, if ~~you~~ can find a copy, ~~you~~ can buy the Old Farmer's
Almanac, which uses a secret 184-year-old formula to forecast long-range
weather (Grosswirth 65). If the forecast ~~turns out~~ wrong, ~~you~~ still have
the other bits of information and humor in this yearly publication.

Third, ~~you~~ can consult nature, starting with the sky. There are
many versions of this adage:

> Evening red and morning gray,
>
> Help the traveler on his way;
>
> Evening gray and morning red
>
> Bring down rain upon his head.

According to W.J. Humphreys, who quotes this saying in his Weather
Proverbs and Paradoxes, weatherlore about the sky color has "a real physical basis...and much truth" (32). The reasons have to do with the
refraction of light by dust and condensation in the air.

The most helpful weather "clues" (Ross 153) in the sky are not
colors but clouds. Thompson and O'Brien point out that even the government spends more money on cloud research than on any other meteorological feature (82). ~~It makes sense.~~ Of the three main ingredients in
weather (heat, wind, and water), only one (water) is visible in the form
of clouds (81), and from them ~~we~~ can guess wind direction and speed.
There are a number of sayings about clouds, like "In the morning
mountains/In the evening fountains" (Thompson and O'Brien 81, Humphreys
53). ~~But~~ the basic principle is "the higher the clouds, the finer the
weather" (Humphreys 50).

If clouds are "the best aids to forecasting the weather of the
immediate future," Smith claims that the "best guide to future weather
is the wind direction" (706). A minimum technique for telling the wind

direction is wetting your finger (Thompson and O'Brien 57). If you are
feeling out-of-sorts, you may also be registering a bad wind, or
"Foehn," carrying positive ions, and causing you to release too much
serotonin, an antistress hormone. Gerus quotes Albert Krueger,
University of California microbiologist and pathologist, who calls this
wind "the ultimate downer" (31). If you would prefer not to respond to
this wind, buy yourself a negative-ion machine to counteract it.

Animals also indicate weather patterns. For example, we can tell
the temperature by listening to and counting the number of cricket
chirps per second. This formula is quite complicated: "Count the
number of chirps in 14 seconds and add 40. The result is the temperature in degrees Farenheit" (Franz 121). You would seem to need a
stopwatch to do this, in which case you might as well get a thermometer,
although this system is supposed to be accurate. Ross explains how
birds and bats indicate air pressure. The higher they fly, the higher
the air pressure and the finer the weather. Rats even respond to sunspots. When sunspots are active, the rats catch more colds (Gerus 33).

Of course, to take this last example, rats are not people, and
may not react the same way. But a whole new science, "biometeorology,"
has emerged to link weather and human health. According to Gerus, the
World Health Organization even called it "a matter of urgency" (29). It
makes sense, because we all respond to "microweather," as when we move
out of the sun into the shade   (Thompson and O'Brien 114). Refining
these responses provides the basis for predicting the weather. "The
secret of good forecasting lies in keeping the senses carefully tuned in
to the environment" (Ross 16).

Thirty percent of people are especially responsive to weather.
They are "literally human barometers" (29). Claire Gerus, who provides
these statistics, claims that three-quarters of these weather-sensitive

people are women, and explains that women lack male sex hormones that
also function to counter stress and cold.

Apart from healthy people, some sick people respond to the
weather. Some people suffering from arthritis cannot help being painfully tuned into the environment, and they have a built-in system for
predicting storms, at least according to a two-year study on 30 arthritic patients at the University of Pennsylvania Medical School:

> ...when researchers simulated approaching storm conditions--
> gradually dropping pressures from 31.5 to 28.5 inches and
> boosting humidity from 25 to 80 percent--the results were asto-
> nishing. Eight out of 10 patients reported stiffness and
> swelling in their joints, and some reported the symptoms within
> minutes of the change. (Thompson and O'Brien 112)

And some people develop migraine headaches when the barometer falls below 29.9, although this painful condition may also be triggered by wind
in the face. Other miscellaneous conditions aggravated by the
weather are myocardial infarcts, glaucoma, asthma, and bleeding
ulcers (31). She reports that in one study the number of patients
admitted to hospital coincided with high sunspot activity, and some
Eastern European doctors prefer not to operate before the "Foehn," the
bad wind with the positive ions, because patients are weaker then. It
would be interesting to see if there were any comparable figures for
hospital patients in southern California during the same kind of Santa
Ana wind conditions. Perhaps we will soon have information like this,
as biometeorology develops and gives us weather reports and travel
advice in terms of our own personal comfort.

In the meantime, we can all compete with the TV "Weatherwatch,"
based on official National Weather Service forecasts. All we need are
some data about atmospheric conditions, and some interpretive prin-

ciples, which we can borrow from the folklore stored in our memories or from the emerging science of biometeorology. In the words of one optimist, "We can all be neighborhood weather prophets if only we pay a little attention to what Grandma has been saying for years" (Franz 121). That doesn't mean that Grandma knew what she was talking about or that we will be right, but the Weather Service is not always right either. If we select our information and sayings carefully, there is more than an even chance that our own forecasts will be correct and that we will be able to predict the weather for our own convenience and comfort.

WORKS CITED

Anderson, Alan, Jr. "Forecast for Forecasting: Cloudy." The New York
    Times Magazine 10 (29 December 1974):10-11, 26-27, 29-31.

Dillon, J. "Build Your Own Weather Monitor." Motor Boating and Sailing
    134 (December 1974):70.

Franz, M. "Chirping Crickets, Low-Flying Bats and Croaking Frogs."
    Organic Gardening and Farming 23 (November 1976):120-122.

Gerus, Claire. "Wind, Weather and Work." The Financial Post Magazine
    (December 1979): 29, 31, 33.

Grosswirth, Marvin. "Tired of the Weather Bureau? Try the Old Farmer's
    Almanac." Science Digest 80 (September 1976):63-69.

Humphreys, W.J. Weather Proverbs and Paradoxes. Baltimore: Williams and
    Wilkins Co., 1923.

Ross, Irwin. "How to Forecast Your Own Weather." Mechanix Illustrated 70
    (May 1974):16, 152-3.

S/mith/, L.P. "Weather Lore." Encyclopaedia Britannica, 1975.

Thompson, Philip D. and Robert O'Brien. Weather. New York: Time, Inc.,
    1965.

"Weather Forecasts: Fair, Gradual Clearing, Rising Accuracy." Changing
    Times 32 (February 1978):45-47.

ILLUSTRATION OF THE PARENTHESIS SYSTEM (APA STYLE)

Hypnosis: What's in a Name?

by

Sylvia Jefferson

Psychology 240

Dr. Kirsch

15 November 1984

Abstract

An analysis of the research on the essence of hypnosis suggests that the debate between state and non-state theorists is a problem of teminology, stemming from different orientations. Barber's research demonstrates that a special hypnotic state cannot be identified on the basis of physiological changes. Furthermore, he shows that most of the traits associated with the hypnotic state can be produced through a process of involved imagining. Barber is criticized for arguing against a position never espoused by state researchers, for paying insufficient attention to the subjective experience of hypnotism, and for flaws in his research design. Edmonston argues that hypnosis is basically a state of relaxation; however, he is unable to fit alert hypnosis into his model. The debate over terminology has practical implications because hypnosis has long been recognized as a powerful and potentially dangerous procedure.

When Anton Mesmer, the father of modern hypnotism, treated his
patients, they spontaneously fell into fits from which they awoke
cured.   Later practitioners discovered that the hypnotized person was
capable of extraordinary feats: clairvoyance, physical endurance,
supression of pain, age regression, and amnesia. Today the fits are
gone, along with many other claims for dramatic changes. In fact,
recent research leads us to wonder if the term hypnosis is an accurate
label for the various traits that have been associated with it.   In
searching for the essence of hypnosis, researchers may have uncovered
several altered states of consciousness. If so, the current difference of opinion between those who view hypnosis as a special trance
state and those who see it simply as a set of easily manipulated behaviors may be a problem with terminology.

Although the therapeutic use of trance states was common in
many societies before the rise of empirical science, Anton Mesmer was
the first to apply the principles of science to the investigation of
trances (Shor, 1979). Reasoning from Newton's laws of gravity, Mesmer
postulated a magnetic force that affected people, as well as objects.
He tested his theory in 1774 by using magnets to treat some of his
patients. Although he had not anticipated that his patients would
fall into a seizure, he assimilated this behavior into a theory that
illness resulted from an imbalance of fluids. Interested primarily in
a theory of magnetism, Mesmer did not focus his attention on the state
into which his patients fell while the cure was taking place.

Mesmer attracted the attention of the scientific community,
most of it rather skeptical of his theories. A committee, which
included Benjamin Franklin, conducted a study of Mesmer's claims, and
concluded that although the remarkable recoveries seemed authentic,
the cause was not physical (magnetism) but due to "mere imagination."
Interest in the therapeutic use of Mesmer's technique spread despite

the committee's conclusions. As the practice spread, reports on the experience began to change. For instance, the Marquis de Puysegur, writing in 1784, stated that the seizure or crisis was not necessary to the cure. Instead he emphasized the sleeplike trance, the hyper-suggestibility, and subsequent amnesia (Shor, 1979). Gradually the analogy with sleep led James Braid in 1840 to rename the phenomenon "hypnosis," derived from the Greek word meaning sleep. Braid was very careful to limit the use of the term to cases where the patient appeared to be asleep and later could not recall what had happened except during a subsequent induction (Edmonston, 1981). Since Braid's time the essence of hypnosis has continued to interest researchers, but there is still disagreement over this most basic issue.

Traditionally the debate has centered on whether hypnosis is a special trance state or a more ordinary set of behaviors that can be elicited through various means. The most recent assault on the equation between hypnosis and trance has been conducted on two fronts. T.X. Barber and his asssociates have argued that hypnosis is no more exotic than the state of mind we achieve when we allow ourselves to empathize with the actors during a play. They suggest that the term "involved imagining" is a less confusing term than hypnosis. A dif-ferent view is proposed by W.E. Edmonston, who links hypnosis with relaxation and urges that we adopt the term "anesis" to describe this passive, receptive state.

Barber's 1979 article pulls together data that prove that the physical traits associated with the hypnotic state are fairly ordi-nary. For example, the stage hypnotist's feat of suggesting extreme rigidity and thereby turning the participant into a "human plank" is not all that difficult. Many nonhypnotized subjects in an experiment were able to achieve the same degree of body rigidity. Barber also explains away most of the other remarkable physical traits associated in the past with hypnotism: skin blisters, temporary deafness, removal of warts, and supression of pain. Summing up, Barber asserts that no physiological indicators have been found that distinguish the hypnotic state. Certain physiological changes, such as raising the skin temperature, can be achieved not only with hypnosis but with "vividly imagining a sensation" (p. 259).

Barber's personal experience has led him to conclude that the hypnotic state consists primarily of focusing one's attention and suspending negative thoughts. He claims that he has been able to experience all the typical hypnotic behaviors without the benefit of another person to induct him into a trance. In a 1965 experiment he tested the hypothesis that the hypnotic induction was not necessary to produce the cluster of behaviors that are associated with hypnosis. He compared a group of hypnotized subjects with a control group and with a group who had been given task-motivational instructions. All subjects were asked to respond to suggestions ranging from locked hands to amnesia. The success rate on each of the suggestions ranged in the control group from 13% to 48%, in the task-motivational group from 39% to 81%, and in the hypnotized group from 29% to 74%. In other words, suggestibility, which has been considered an essential part of the hypnotic state, can be achieved through directions given to subjects who are fully awake.

In reporting his research, Barber depicted his theory as a revolutionary new paradigm which would be met with hostile criticism from those who had a vested interest in the special-state theory of hypnotism. However, most of the contemporary researchers have used terms like "trance state" very tentatively and have admitted that there is no current theory that satisfactorily explains hypnosis (Orne, 1967). Their goal has been to determine whether there is an essential component of hypnosis that cannot be accounted for in terms of the sociocultural context (Orne, 1959).

Barber's research has focused primarily on the observable behavior of the hypnotic subject, and until recently, has eliminated the inner experience of hypnotism as an area of inquiry. His skepticism about subjective reports stemmed from a series of experiments that he conducted between 1965 and 1969 which demonstrated that a subject's report on his inner experience varied with the definition of the situation, the subject's expectations, and the way in which the questions were presented to the subject (Spanos, 1979). State theorists, on the other hand, have concentrated on the inner experience of hypnosis because efforts to develop objective tests of the hypnotic state proved fruitless (Orne, 1959). Rather than concluding that hypnosis was not a trance state, as Barber did, they turned their attention inward, recognizing that context, expectations, and the wording of questions could affect the outcome of subjective reports (Tellegen, 1970).

Supporters of Barber's theory have tried to dismiss subjective reports as scientifically unacceptable, comparing them to reports of spirit possessions (Spanos, 1970). This comparison, however, ignores the fact that psychologists for years have accepted subjective testimony of depression and anxiety as evidence that those states exist. Furthermore, psychologists differentiate between fear and anger, although there is no way to distinguish between these states on the basis of psychological effects (Orne, 1967).

The keystone of Barber's theory, his comparison of hypnosis with task-motivational instructions, has generated a number of exchanges between researchers. Hilgard and Tart (1966) criticized Barber's design and ran a corrected version of the experiment in which the same subject was tested on different days. However, the validity of their research was questioned by Spanos (1970) who pointed out that a subject's experience with one type of suggestibility could affect performance with another type.

A follow-up on Barber's research was conducted by Edmonston and Robertson (1967) who pretested subjects for suggestibility and then matched a task-motivational group with a hypnotic group. Their results showed that hypnosis produced greater suggestibility than task-motivational instructions. Hilgard (1973) replicated the Barber experiment but corrected the directions to the subjects to encourage honesty in reporting. His results showed that hypnosis produced greater visual hallucinations than did task-motivational instructions. Hilgard concedes, however, that these gains are small and that for some types of suggestion, such as pain reduction, task-motivational instructions may work as well as hypnosis.

For Barber and Spanos (1974) the difference between hypnosis and involved imagining is not great enough to justify the construct of a special trance state, a construct which they think should be abandoned because of the "many misleading implications that have accumulated during the past 200 years" (p. 506). The special-state theorists counter this line of thinking by arguing that hypnosis is not synonymous with suggestibility. Hilgard (1973) summarizes research that shows important differences between forms of suggestibility. Specifically, the work of Hull (1933), Furneaux (1945), and

Stukat (1958) showed a distinction between hypnotizability and forms of social suggestibility, such as conformity and gullibility. Additional research (Burns and Hammer, 1970; Moore, 1964) shows that there is no correlation between social suggestibility and hypnotizability. Hypnotic suggestibility is also distinct from that induced by placebos, according to other research cited by Hilgard.

The search for the essence of hypnosis has led Edmonston (1981) to a different equation. He argues that if we examine the inner experience of hypnosis rather than the uses made of this state, such as increased suggestibility, we will see that relaxation is the essential characteristic. He supports this equation by citing research by Evans (1967) which showed that subjects who were given relaxation instructions exhibited the same traits usually associated with hypnosis. Another study (Coleman, 1977) compared a relaxation group and a hypnotic group against two control groups. On tests of suggestibility the subjects in both the relaxation group and the hypnotic group had higher scores than subjects in the two control groups. Furthermore, the suggestibility scores of the hypnosis group and the relaxation group did not differ from one another. Edmonston also points out that the therapeutic results of hypnosis, meditation, and desensitization therapy rely on the common ingredient of relaxation. In his historical review of the literature of hypnosis, he notes that the link between hypnosis and a sleeplike state goes all the way back to the Egyptians.

The major problem with Edmonston's theory is that it does not account for "alert hypnosis," a state that has been identified by Hilgard. Alert hypnosis produced all the characteristics of hypnosis except the resemblance to sleep. Edmonston suggests that alert hypnosis is a state different from traditional hypnosis. Moreover, he believes that certain traits elicited from only a small number of deeply hypnotizable subjects, such as disassociation, may indicate still another state that is different from traditional hypnosis.

At the moment we are left with at least four possible positions regarding the essence of hypnosis: hypnosis is sufficiently different from our waking consciousness to constitute a special kind of trance state; hypnosis is significantly different from ordinary consciousness because we are more relaxed and therefore more open to suggestions; hypnosis is not sufficiently different from ordinary consciousness to be considered a special trance state; the term hypnosis has been used to refer to a variety of related but not identical experiences. There is the additional complication that the experience of hypnosis may have changed over time as the expectations about it and the setting for the research have shifted.

Both the state and the non-state theorists now seem to agree that many of the traits previously associated with hypnosis can be elicited through other means, such as relaxation and involved imagining. At issue is whether we should use the term hypnosis to refer to that mental state which can be achieved through a variety of procedures or whether the term hypnosis should be reserved for deeper trancelike states. State theorists still cling to the small differences between hypotically induced experiences and those achieved through other means. They are interested in mapping the continuum of consciousness and, therefore, want to distinguish between the experience of being entranced by a play or day-dreaming and that of light hypnosis. The non-state proponents seem to be more interested in behavior and, therefore, want to know whether the same therapeutic

results can be achieved with procedures other than the standard hypnotic induction. State theorists suggest that if the same results can
be achieved, then it is because the procedure has induced a hypnotic
state, even if the instructions did not mention hypnosis (Fromm,
1979).

There are practical implications to this seemingly esoteric
debate. For instance, professional and governmental guidelines
recognize the potential for misuse of hypnosis. The government
requires that special steps be folloed in experiments on hypnosis, and
professional societies prohibit the training of lay people as hypnotists. One potential problem is that a person can sidestep these
guidelines by renaming the process. Likewise, if a client objects to
therapy which involves hypnosis, but agrees to relaxation procedures
that create the same level of suggestibility as hypnosis, this raises
another ethical problem. In light of these clinical problems, it is
important that research continue into the nature of hypnosis.

REFERENCES

Barber, T.X. (1965). Measuring "hypnotic-like" suggestibility with and without "hypnotic induction"; psychometric properties, norms, and variables influencing response to the Barber Suggestibility Scale (BSS). Psychological Reports, 16, 809-844.

Barber, T.X. (1979). Suggested (hypnotic) behavior: The trance paradigm versus an alternative paradigm. In E. Fromm (ed.), Hypnosis: developments in research and new perspectives. Hawthorne, N.Y.: Aldine Publishing Company.

Edmonston, W.E. (1981). Hypnosis: modern verification of an old equation. New York: John Wiley & Sons.

Edmonston, W.E. and Robertson, T.G. (1967). A comparison of the effects of task motivational and hypnotic induction instructions on responsiveness to hypnotic suggestibility scales. American Journal of Clinical Hypnosis, 9, 184-187.

Fromm, E. (1979). The nature of hypnosis and other altered states of consciousness on ego psychological theory. In E. Fromm (ed.), Hypnosis: developments in research and new perspectives. Hawthorne, N.Y.: Aldine Publishing Company.

Hilgard, E.R. (1973). The domain of hypnosis: with some comments on alternative pardigms. American Psychologist, 28, 972-981.

Hilgard, E.R. (1979). Divided consciousness in hypnosis: the implications of the hidden observer. In E. Fromm (ed.), Hypnosis: developments in research and new perspectives. Hawthorne, N.Y.: Aldine Publishing Company.

Hilgard, E.R. and Tart, C.T. (1966). Responsiveness to suggestions following waking and imagining instructions and following induction of hypnosis. Journal of Abnormal Psychology, 71, 196-208.

Orne, M.T. (1959). The nature of hypnosis: artifact and essence. Journal of Abnormal and Social Psychology, 58, 277-299.

Orne, M.T. (1967). What must a satisfactory theory of hypnosis explain? International Journal of Psychiatry, 3, 206-211.

Shor, R.E. (1979). Fundamental problems in hypnosis research as viewed from a historic perspective. In E. Fromm (ed.), Hypnosis: developments in research and new perspectives. Hawthorne, N.Y.: Aldine Publishing Company.

Spanos, N.P. (1970). Barber's reconceptualization of hypnosis: an evaluation of criticisms. Journal of Experimental Research in Personality, 4, 241-258.

Spanos, N.P. and Barber, T.X. (1974). Toward a convergence in hypnosis research. American Psychologist, 29, 500-511.

Tellegen, A. (1970). Some comments on "Barber's reconceptualization of hypnosis." Journal of Experimental Research in Personality, 4, 259-267.

INDEX